BEING
ETHNOGRAPHIC

Raymond Madden

2nd Edition

BEING ETHNOGRAPHIC

A Guide to the Theory and Practice of Ethnography

Los Angeles | London | New Delhi
Singapore | Washington DC | Melbourne

Los Angeles | London | New Delhi
Singapore | Washington DC | Melbourne

SAGE Publications Ltd
1 Oliver's Yard
55 City Road
London EC1Y 1SP

SAGE Publications Inc.
2455 Teller Road
Thousand Oaks, California 91320

SAGE Publications India Pvt Ltd
B 1/I 1 Mohan Cooperative Industrial Area
Mathura Road
New Delhi 110 044

SAGE Publications Asia-Pacific Pte Ltd
3 Church Street
#10-04 Samsung Hub
Singapore 049483

Assistant Editor: Alysha Owen
Production Editor: Shikha Jain
Copyeditor: Christine Bitten
Proofreader: Jill Birch
Indexer: Caroline Eley
Marketing manager: Susheel Gokarakonda
Cover design: Shaun Mercier
Typeset by: C&M Digitals (P) Ltd, Chennai, India
Printed in the UK

© Raymond Madden 2017

This second edition published 2017

First edition published 2010 (reprinted 2013, 2015 (twice), 2017)

Library of Congress Control Number: 2017933467

British Library Cataloguing in Publication data

A catalogue record for this book is available from the British Library

ISBN 978-1-4739-5214-0
ISBN 978-1-4739-5215-7 (pbk)

At SAGE we take sustainability seriously. Most of our products are printed in the UK using FSC papers and boards. When we print overseas we ensure sustainable papers are used as measured by the PREPS grading system. We undertake an annual audit to monitor our sustainability.

CONTENTS

PREFACE TO THE SECOND EDITION

This second edition of *Being Ethnographic* brings the author's considerations up to date with more recent issues in the theory and practice of ethnography. This text has added to its characterisation of ethnography by expanding on the central role of intersubjectivity in both theory and practice (Chapter 1). It has added a section on 'smart pens' in the 'writing down' section of the text (Chapter 6). It has also added a small section on qualitative software, arguing for the ethnographer to make use of such tools only if they fit with their data (Chapter 7). It has added a section on cyberethnography and the lessons in this area for ethnographic practice and thought and has expanded on the ethnographic possibilities and potential shortcomings of involving animals as ethnographic participants (Chapter 8). And finally, each chapter includes top tips and advice on being ethnographic to help with the practicalities of actually doing ethnographic research. This edition keeps all the requisite understandings of ethnographic theory and practice that characterised the first edition to expand from this base to bring an updated and fresher insight into being ethnographic.

ABOUT THE AUTHOR

Raymond Madden is a Senior Lecturer in Anthropology in the Department of Social Enquiry at La Trobe University, Bundoora, Melbourne, Australia. Over the past two decades, he has conducted ethnographic research with Aboriginal Australians from Western Victoria, and more recently, he has undertaken research with people and their greyhounds.

INTRODUCTION

CHAPTER CONTENTS

WHY ETHNOGRAPHY?

Ethnographers are social scientists who undertake research and writing about groups of people by systematically observing and participating (to a greater or lesser degree) in the lives of the people they study. Ethnographers value the idea of 'walking a mile in the shoes' of others and attempt to gain insight by being in the same social space as the subjects of their research. Ethnography has historically been most closely associated with anthropology and qualitative sociology, and has focussed on the indigenous, the exotic, the subaltern, the disadvantaged; in other words, people who stood as some sort of 'other' to the well-educated and well-resourced Westerners who dominated the practice of early ethnography. The later decades of the twentieth century, and into the twenty-first century, have seen ethnography throw off these stereotypical images, and it is now impossible to understand ethnography as the study of the exotic 'other'. Ethnographers study across and within cultures and societies, at home and away. Ethnography is prac-tised by a growing range of social science disciplines and is being used in domains beyond, such as marketing and journalism; ethnography is no longer a jealously guarded 'possession' of anthropology. And, like other social science approaches, ethnography is searching for ways to remain useful and relevant in a rapidly changing world.

Ongoing relevance

In this book I argue for the continuing significance of ethnographic research in our diffuse global world system. Globalisation has involved massive movements of people, information and goods, and has dissolved all sorts of older cultural, social, economic and political barriers. These global flows have triggered renewed localised identifications as humans strive to find their particular place in a rapidly changing world order. Yet much of what we might term 'classical' ethnographic practice is still as purposeful as it was a century ago when Malinowski and Boas used ethnographic research to begin the formation of two key anthropological traditions in Britain and the United States of America. The study of the particulars of everyday human existence is an ongoing task for ethnographers today, and the bulk of this book will be dedicated to a critical overview of the formative theories and practices that have kept ethnography as purposeful as it was 100 years ago. I want to suggest, however, that if ethnography wants to remain relevant into the future it must find ways to understand how contemporary local identities are networked in a global system, and it must strive to understand the place of technology-mediated sociality in today's social and cultural systems. If ethnography's strength has been its ability to appreciate the social and cultural particulars of human existence, it now needs to also appreciate these particulars as part of a global human complex. The current generation of 'digital natives' who socialise in cyberspace and maintain friendships via mobile telephones are an obvious example of the changing landscape of society and culture that ethnographers are confronted with. How an ethnographer studies humans and social settings that do not have face-to-face interactions is a challenge for cyber ethnography that I will revisit at the conclusion of this book.

THE AUTHOR

An aspect of this journey into ethnography will be to understand the role of the ethnographer and how their personal story plays out in the research they undertake. I approach questions about the 'ethnographer as author' with what I call a methodological reflexivity. There is a need to account for the inevitability of the ethnographer's influence on the research process and to manage the tension between objectivity and subjectivity in order to produce better portraits of the human condition. Dealing rigorously with reflexivity is an important aspect of contemporary ethnography. In this vein it is appropriate to say something about the person who brings you this encounter with ethnography.

I am an anthropologist who was trained in a combined anthropology and sociology department. No doubt as a consequence of this I have never made much of the distinction between qualitative sociology and anthropology, and do not propose to alter my lack of enthusiasm for boundary policing in this book. If one looks to methods one can find grounds for distinction between these areas of study, but this is not of primary interest here, as the focus will be on an ethnographic approach that is utilised across these disciplines and beyond. I am primarily interested in exploring why we might want to undertake ethnography, and how we can do it well.

I carried out my doctoral fieldwork in rural western Victoria, Australia. My research was concerned with the relationship between the region's European descendants (predominantly English, Scottish and Irish who initially settled in the area in the 1840s to 1860s) and the local Aboriginal population. The project was a mixture of Aboriginal anthropology and rural sociology and was driven by a theoretical concern with the concept of 'culture'. I wanted to locate this theoretical pursuit in a concrete setting that could problematise 'culture' and lead to a more critical understanding of the uses and abuses of this foundational term in the social sciences (Madden, 1999; 2003). I also had a personal reason for undertaking this research; the region I chose to study was also my natal home. I lived in Western Victoria until I was 20 years old, at which point I left for Melbourne in search of employment and opportunities. My fieldwork was in part an experience of returning to home (see Madden, 1999; for more on 'anthropology at home' also see Jackson, 1987 and Messerschmidt, 1981).

My research into Aboriginal/European relations was partly driven by the fact that my home area's Aboriginal population was almost unknown to me when I lived there; the geographic closeness of the two communities did not lead to a ready dissolution of social boundaries. There were always exceptions to this social segregation, but by and large the region's 'Whitefella' and 'Blackfella' populations had rather constrained and limited social interactions; it was possible to live parallel existences. This deficit in my understanding of the social and cultural profile of my own natal community was a strong motivating factor behind my desire to undertake an ethnographic project in my home, and using this motivation constructively was one of the subjective influences I had to learn to manage. I expected that in undertaking an ethnographic project at home I would find the familiar in my own natal non-indigenous culture, and the unfamiliar in the local Aboriginal community. These presuppositions were challenged by some of my early experiences in the field and this early, naïve, almost bumbling ethnographic endeavour was nevertheless one of the more illuminating phases of my research. Doing ethnography inverted my expectations, challenged my assumptions and forced a critical rethink of ideas I had held to be unproblematic, teaching me valuable lessons in the process. These lessons are a useful starting point in answering the question 'Why ethnography?' My experiences in this research phase will be revisited often in this book as I present examples of my successes and failures in the field.

Subsequent to my doctoral studies, I worked as an applied anthropologist in the 'Native Title' sector in Australia (where Aboriginal land claims are examined and attempts are made to resolve them). The role of anthropologists in this domain is to gather anthropological and historical information on the rights and interests Aboriginal communities may or may not have to tracts of land they claim under the Australian Native Title Act. This work is typically rapid ethnography; it requires a strong understanding of the legal and bureaucratic context behind each case, and is inevitably politically charged, given that local, state and national governments are some of the most important and well-resourced stakeholders in the process. In this setting I came to appreciate the potential and limitations of ethnography done under time pressures and understand how ethnographic perspectives can engage in a useful conversation with other epistemologies or ways of constructing knowledge (for example, legal and/ or bureaucratic approaches). It was interesting to see how useful an ethnographic approach could be in these ultimately legal, bureaucratic and political land claim processes. The lessons I learnt in the rigours of applied ethnographic research will also be revisited from time to time in this text. The examples I draw on will be of relevance to budding ethnographers entering the rapidly expanding world of applied ethnographic research. The experiences I had as an applied anthropologist also act as a corrective; the ethnographic endeavour is not a limitless world of possibility. The fact that applied ethnography is typically produced in political, legal, economic and personal circumstances that constrain the nature of the research is important to note.

I have also taught ethnographic methods and applied anthropology subjects to second and third year university students for a number of years. Of particular interest have been the hundreds of small ethnographic research projects I have supervised and assessed. I remain fascinated by the variety of settings in which students undertake their ethnographic projects; pubs, senior citizen centres, migrant resource centres, sporting clubs, public transport facilities, student associations, political associations, cafés, urban, suburban and rural networks, indeed almost anywhere people gathered into some form of recognisable social group. These semester-long (term) exercises crystallised some of the key moments in the ethnographic endeavour. They taught students about project proposal and design, entering the field and gaining access to participants, the ethical dimensions of ethnographic research, participant observation, interviewing and note taking, analysis and interpretation, and finally, writing up and finding the ethnographic 'story' in their data. They also taught me that certain sorts of experiences and insights crop up time and time again in the early stages of the ethnographer's career, and I hope to pass on some of these lessons in this book.

These student projects constitute a wealth of information on the trials and tribulations of doing ethnography. Almost all of the students had difficulties at one or more stages in their projects, but they had to find ways to resolve them before the submission date (no different to what occurs in the so-called real world of professional ethnographic work). Some students were tempted to do an ethnographic methods subject because they liked the *idea* of ethnography, but then found that the face-to-face negotiations and the everyday politics of ethnographic engagement were something they were not comfortable with; this is a timely reminder that while ethnographers strive to develop natural, easy and trusting relations with participants, doing ethnography is really a rather strange way to be with other people. It is not for everyone. Some students struggled to find their ethnographic story, and wondered what it was that tied their research activities together into a useful insight into their group and the human condition. When these students reached what I call a 'light bulb' moment, when the key theme of their ethnography suddenly shone out of the fog of uncertainty, they too met with that initial realisation I recall from my early studies – 'Now I get it! So that's why we do ethnography!' These teaching and learning experiences will not be referred to directly, but they infiltrate this text and influence the manner in which I present the mix of theories, practical advice, suggestions and questions that appear in each chapter.

In more recent times I have developed a research interest in the social relations that exist between humans and companion animals (or human animals and non-human animals, to use the preferred terminology). Like cyber ethnography, these relationships pose some interesting challenges for classical ethnography. The rise of the companion animal in contemporary society has led to people forming a new kinship with animals based on shared social lives, shared domestic spaces and a growing sense of 'pets' as real members of human families. How do ethnographers tackle this social phenomenon? Are companion animals part of the background field setting, like physical structures or the natural environment, or are they participants with agency and social roles worthy of proper ethnographic consideration? As with the example of cyber ethnography, the human/animal question is one I will return to at the end of this book in order to critically examine the potential and constraints of an ethnographic approach.

The corpus of ethnographies and ethnographic textbooks that have informed and educated me will be a point of reference as we proceed. I do not attempt anything like a comprehensive survey of the current state of ethnographic literature; rather I will be selecting useful sources from the body of work to contrast and compare to my own experiences (and those of my students), extending the discussion beyond my own antipodean experience and on to a global domain of practice and ideas.

Aneurism

In November 2013 I had a severe aneurism which was an initially very debilitating occasion. I had to spend over three months in hospital, take over two years leave from my lecturing and research work and I had to learn to walk again (amongst other things as part of my recovery). This experience has left me with ongoing issues of fatigue and the practice of doing fieldwork is still currently beyond me as I find such encounters too physically taxing. However, I was lucky to even survive such an event, and I have developed an increased appreciation of both the recuperative and conceptual aspects of the mind. I have been reminded, in no uncertain terms, of the important relationship between the doing of, and thinking about, ethnography. Theory and practice must find a productive engagement with each other to produce insights into the human condition. The following text will reiterate this important relationship.

A storied reality

I have a particular way of teaching an appreciation of ethnography, and it reflects a certain bias towards the transformative ability of ethnography when it is presented as a 'storied reality'. An ethnography is ultimately a story that is backed up by reliable qualitative data and the authority that comes from active ethnographic engagement. All ethnographers undertake research in order to write or visually represent human groups or institutions, and so a solid appreciation of ethnography requires an understanding of the power, techniques and poetry of textual and visual representation. I see the act of inscription (including image capture) as a core element of ethnographic practice and I utilise a three-phase approach that I refer to as 'writing down' (notes), 'writing out' (data) and 'writing up' (text), but there's much more to consider besides. The act of inscription needs to be seen as part of a larger narrative, one that has its origin story, iconic characters and characterisations, and an interesting and challenging future. Furthermore, ethnographic inscription is informed by a larger body of practice and theory. The relationship between the way we 'do' ethnography and the way we 'think about' ethnography is one of the key targets of this text.

Doing plus thinking equals being

We are now in an era when anthropological and sociological writing has well and truly articulated with literary theory; reflexivity and subjectivity are now commonplace, indeed expected, in the critical discussion of, and pedagogy related to, ethnography. In this context there are two dominant types of ethnography textbooks produced: (1) those that deal mainly with the 'doing' of ethnography, listing the 'rules' and practical considerations involved in ethnographic research, and (2) those influenced by the reflexive turn, focussing mainly on bringing the personal, subjective experiences of the ethnographer to the reading audience. While this distinction has some logic in terms of differing textual strategies and styles, it also has the tendency to compartmentalise the 'doing of' ethnography and 'thinking about' ethnography into two discrete processes, and to do so in a way that does not reflect the reality of the relationship between practice and theory. In this text I seek to combine general advice and tips for doing ethnography, with reflections on theory and the subjective experience of ethnographic fieldwork to produce a text that articulates 'doing' and 'thinking' into a logical whole; an approach I call 'being ethnographic'. Reflections on ethnography are not just pre- and post-fieldwork musings or intellectual bookends for the 'real' business of doing research. Theory, reflection, musings, quandaries, inspirations and analytic leaps of discovery are all contemporaneous with the practice of doing ethnographic research. A text that seeks to convey the lived reality of ethnographic research should portray the interdependent relationship between doing and thinking which produces the state of 'being ethnographic'.

LAYOUT AND INTENT OF THE BOOK

This book has nine chapters spread over four thematic sections which provide an overall introduction to ethnographic theories, methods and writing. It also seeks to provoke discussion and argument and point to the potential and limitations of an ethnographic approach to understanding the human condition. The book is a critical overview that can form the basis of a graduate course on ethnography. Along the way this book poses questions and makes suggestions for further reading that can complement this text and expand the learning experience. The questions posed at the end of the chapters will also reflect the approach I call 'being ethnographic', and will provide a series of queries that relate to the practical organisation of ethnographic research and the role of the ethnographer, as well as giving the chance to reflect critically on ethnography as a knowledge production system.

The first section of the book (Chapters 1 and 2) deals with the 'Key Concepts and Theoretical Frames' of ethnography. Chapter 1, '"Definitions", Methods and Origins' does not present a hard and fast definition of ethnography because the variability in the human condition and the different approaches of individual ethnographers make a rule-bound approach to defining ethnography impractical. Ethnography is a way of writing about people, a way of being with people, and in combination, a way of theorising about people. As a participant observer an ethnographer is both within and outside of the research process; she or he is both a researcher and a research tool. As such Chapter 1 also discusses embodiment and the role of reflexivity in contemporary ethnography. We then look at ethnographic methodology and discuss the important relationship between the theoretical and practical aspects of ethnography; how ideas and techniques combine to shape a practice. Ethnography also has an origin story which typically begins in social anthropology and moves to urban sociology and then outwards to areas like cultural studies. We examine this narrative and ask the question, 'what has changed over the last century of ethnographic research?' Finally, this chapter looks at the applications of ethnography and the ethical dimensions of ethnographic research, thus setting up a broad overview of the practice upon which the subsequent chapters can build.

Chapter 2, 'Ethnographic Fields: Home and Away', argues that an ethnographic field is an emergent, contingent domain that comes into being when we systematically examine the social relations that bound or characterise a particular time and space. Ethnographers create investigative places they call fields, and we look at some favourite constructions. The key point of this chapter is that fields are more than physical settings; they are interrogative frames that are shaped by the ethnographer. Ethnographers can't take a field setting for granted but have to actively play a part in bringing it to life by asking questions about the relationship of the people to their setting. The theoretical and practical aspects of undertaking ethnographic research in both unfamiliar and familiar settings are then explored, and the growth of multisited and rapid research is examined.

The second section of the book (Chapters 3, 4 and 5) deals with 'Doing Ethnography'. In Chapter 3 ('Talking to People: Negotiations, Conversations and Interviews') we discuss how talking to people is the pivotal first step in 'doing ethnography'. Ethnographic projects live or die on the ability of ethnographers to negotiate with other people. 'Negotiation', therefore, is a useful theme to explore how ethnographers create and plan their projects and how they navigate the initial, often politically charged, process of gaining access to a group of people or field site. We will then investigate the concept of 'conversation' to lay out strategies for building rapport and trust with a participant group and to introduce the informal, unstructured ethnographic interview.

In Chapter 4, 'Being with People: Participation', I ask the question, why does ethnography value the practice of participant observation so highly? Furthermore, why do ethnographers work so hard to make a strange experience familiar? In answering these questions we will explore the idea of cultural and social immersion, step-in-step-out ethnography, and what embodied experience means for ethnographic claims to knowledge. Chapter 4 argues that an approach I call 'close but not too close' best represents the sort of relationships ethnographers should seek in their fieldwork. That is to say ethnographers should value an insider's perspective, but without giving up on the all-important critical outsider's perspective on their field relationships. This chapter will also highlight the ethical dimensions of the relationships that typically exist between ethnographers and their study group members by looking at participant rights, safety and the ethnographer's obligations to their respective disciplinary codes of practice.

In Chapter 5, 'Looking at People: Observations and Images', we turn to questions like, how do ethnographers 'look' at people? What do they 'see' and not 'see'? In this chapter we have the opportunity to examine the ethnographic gaze, and discuss how it is ethnographers turn the everyday act of 'looking' into systematic observation. This chapter provides some guidelines and tips for seeing the physical structures and human behaviours that are relevant to ethnographic investigation. Beyond the observational aspects of the field, Chapter 5 also examines the use of visual media, arguing that photographs and film are important aspects of past and contemporary ethnographic methodology. Visual material is something more than a simple adjunct to an ethnographic text; it is a vital element in ethnographic representation.

The third section of the book (Chapters 6, 7 and 8) focuses on the act of 'Inscription'. In Chapter 6, 'Description: Writing "Down" Fieldnotes', we examine the rich, information-packed notes that form the basis of any successful ethnographic project, and look at how they can become a resource to be mined over many years of subsequent research. But how does an ethnographer find time to record data in the hurly-burly of participation? What strategies do ethnographers use to sort out what it is they should and should not be writing down? Chapter 6 explores standard note-taking techniques such as jottings, journals and diary entries. It also examines the role of sketching, mapping and image capture as aspects of note taking. We will discuss some of the formal do's and don'ts of note taking (with respect to reactivity, confidentiality, security of data and ethics) and outline ways in which the coding and analysis of ethnographic fieldnotes can begin in these early data gathering stages. Finally, Chapter 6 offers some advice on particular issues of note taking as they relate to applied ethnographic settings and suggests that good ethnographers need to be able to adjust their note-taking strategies to suit particular contexts.

In Chapter 7, 'Analysis to Interpretation: Writing "Out" Data', we turn to the issue of what to do with all this data once we have gathered it. Here we look at the important role organising primary and secondary data plays in analysis and interpretation. It is typically stated that data are 'crunched' or in some sense reduced and compressed to form a frame on which to hang ethnographic interpretations and conclusions. To my mind, this metaphor of reduction misreads what we do with data. While data analysis and interpretation may in some sense reduce the quantity of the data, it should also 'value add' to the emerging story. This is what I mean when I say we write 'out' data. This writing out involves thematically coding and indexing to make sense of the piles of notes, sketches, maps and pictures that have been gathered. We discuss how ethnographers articulate their primary data with existing secondary ethnographic, archival and historical data of relevance to their study group or site. Chapter 7 suggests that ethnographic analysis is not so much a matter of sifting through data to find the meaning already in it, but one of actively making meaning from our data. It is argued that making meaning from data needs to be understood with the same sensitivity towards reflexivity and positionality that we ascribe to field experience and interpretation. By doing this the ethnographer can move surely through the stages of organising, analysing and then interpreting their data.

By Chapter 8, 'Interpretation to Story: Writing "Up" Ethnography' we are examining the issue of producing a good ethnography. Anthropology's engagement with literary theory from the 1980s onward has created increased interest in text, tropes, poetics and persuasion in social science writing. How do ethnographers write 'up' in order to remain true to the ethnographic reality they seek to convey, while nevertheless making the ethnography a 'good read'? In Chapter 8 I will suggest that good writing is arguably the most important aspect of ethnographic interpretation. By looking at the conventions that have characterised ethnographic writing in the past and by engaging with the more recent literary turn, this chapter argues that an approach I call a 'storied reality' captures the best of the objective and subjective elements of ethnographic writing. Chapter 8 also examines structure in ethnographic stories, and looks at the question of style in ethnographic writing.

Finally, in the fourth section, 'Expanding Ethnography' we will recap our portrait of ethnography so far before looking to the future. Chapter 9, 'Conclusion: Ethnographic Horizons' finishes the text by exploring the realm of cyber ethnography and human/animal sociality. We look at these issues in order to discuss the future of ethnography in a world that is creating new forms of sociality. By positioning cyber ethnography as a challenge to the 'face-to-face, natural setting' approach characteristic of ethnography over the last century an opportunity is created to critically analyse the strengths and weaknesses of the approaches outlined so far. As technology continues apace to mediate ever more intimately today's socialisation patterns, as we literally hook ourselves up to more and more 'machines', how can ethnography deal with disembodied socialisation? Following this we will spend some time on the idea of ethnography as applied to the human animal/non-human animal relationship (anthrozoology) and discuss how the new kinship between humans and their animal companions can be understood in ethnographic terms. As such, in Chapter 9 we will critically re-evaluate and conclude on the strengths and weaknesses of an ethnographic approach. I will finish by arguing that a critical yet welcoming approach to cyber ethnography and ethnography beyond the human should be an integral aspect of our contemporary ethnographic toolkit.

This book structure therefore contains the typical pedagogical elements you would expect in a textbook about the theory and practice of ethnography, but it is presented as a series of characterisations as opposed to a recipe with set rules. The infinite variability of the human subject and the fact ethnographers with their passions, intellectual interests, biases and ideologies are themselves part of this infinitely variable human condition means that every project is different and that every ethnographer will bring something different to their projects. This suggests to me that, basic concepts aside, learning about ethnography from a book is not really a process of assimilating definitions and rules. Rather, this process should be a long and critical conversation around, about and towards the object of our understanding, in the knowledge that we will never reach a final and definitive level of comprehension. More usefully, once basic practical matters are grasped, we should strive for a relational understanding of who we are as ethnographers, and how this relates to the ethnography of others. All of this preparation, of course, is designed to encourage and guide the budding ethnographer as they take on ethnographic projects of their own, be it class exercises, postgraduate research or applied work.

With this in mind I will be accompanying the reader through this text as a narrator. As we move through the various stages I have outlined in ethnographic practice, I will recall the successes and failures I experienced at these points; it's just as important for budding ethnographers to get a sense of what can go wrong as it is to understand what might work. Therefore this book presents itself as more than a textbook (although it is indeed that) but also as a critical conversation on being ethnographic based on the original research experiences of the author and how these compare with the broad canon of ethnographies and ethnographic textbooks dedicated to theory and methods; this book is part practice manual and part critical reflection on practice. I hope you enjoy the journey.

PART ONE

KEY CONCEPTS AND THEORETICAL FRAMES

ONE
'DEFINITIONS', METHODS AND APPLICATIONS

CHAPTER CONTENTS

CHARACTERISING ETHNOGRAPHY

A quick perusal of texts dedicated to ethnographic methods will turn up a large variety of 'definitions' of the practice. As mentioned in the introduction, ethnography is not the sort of endeavour that readily submits to a neat and bounded definition – the humans that do ethnography and the humans that are the subject of ethnographic research are too complicated and 'messy' to allow ethnography to be understood in neat and simple terms. Ethnography as we know it today has its origins in British social anthropology, American cultural anthropology and the qualitative sociology of the Chicago School (O'Reilly, 2009: 3). This shared ancestral heritage allows us to identify some common aspects of ethnographic practice and some mutually valued characteristics to find a basis for what we can agree is good ethnographic practice. This book provides an introduction to the practice and the production of ethnography, and how these aspects overlap in all sorts of ways, but it will begin by focussing on the practical side of the ethnographic endeavour, namely, what characterises the 'doing' of ethnography and what intellectual and theoretical forces have shaped this practice.

Writing about people

The term 'ethnography' comes from Greek and broadly means 'writing about people', but has a narrower meaning of writing about particular groups of people, that is to say ethnically, culturally or socially defined groups. An ethnographic text is an interpretive and explanatory story about a group of people and their sociality, culture and behaviours, but it is not a fictional account; it is a narrative based on systematically gathered and analysed data. A great deal of practical work and planning goes into producing ethnographic texts and rendering them as reliable as possible. As such, ethnography is not just an act of writing; ethnography is a practice (framed by a methodology) *and* the textual product of that practice. It is the doing of social research and the final product that comes from writing up that research.

Being with people

Ethnography is a qualitative social science practice that seeks to understand human groups (or societies, or cultures, or institutions) by having the researcher in the same social space as the participants in the study. Ethnography is typically face-to-face, direct research. It is a practice which values the idea that to know other humans the ethnographer must do as others do, live with others, eat, work and experience the same daily patterns as others. This approach is called participant observation, and it has been a fundamental aspect of ethnographic research over the last century. In some cases, definitions of ethnography simply equate it with participant observation. We will be working up a much broader understanding of ethnography than this singular methodological definition, but participant observation remains at the core of all reasonable understandings of ethnography. Intimate contact with participants raises issues of obligation, reciprocity, trust and the formation of friendships. And these human relationships impose serious responsibilities on ethnographers. Rapport building is crucial to the ethnographic process and it can take some time to establish – one can't afford to rush things, be too pushy and risk being alienated by one's participant group; it is a 'gradual building up of trust' (O'Reilly, 2009: 175).

Ethnographers study people in typical circumstances, where people interact with each other in routine or even ritualised ways, but in ways that are typical of that situation. The ethnographer does not usually seek to distort or manage the natural setting of their research, or ask people to do things they normally wouldn't do in any given circumstance. Therefore, a key distinction between ethnography and laboratory or clinic based methods is that ethnographers cannot control, and do not want to control, what happens in their field situation. Unlike laboratory based experiments where the total environment is controlled (at least as far as a set of known variables), ethnographers are both observers and participants in an open experimental field (LeCompte and Schensul, 1999a: 2).

Ethnography was once seen as a long-term commitment where researchers sometimes lived with communities for years, with a 12–18 month stay typical. These ethnographies were often attempts to holistically describe the socio-cultural life of a particular community, group or institution (O'Reilly, 2009: 99). Evans-Pritchard's *The Nuer*, for example, dedicated chapters to the large sociological categories of primary production, ecology, time and space, the political system, the lineage system, and the age set system in compiling his holistic ethnographic account of a Nilotic people (1940). Nowadays, while long-term, single-site projects are still undertaken, many ethnographic projects are conducted over much shorter periods of time and may be multisited and/or focus on a particular aspect or element of a society or culture. Funding constraints, and time pressures in universities that have curtailed the length of doctoral and masters research, mean it is no longer always possible to spend the amount of time living in communities that was once typical. The admirable goal of holistic description that was once part and parcel of ethnography is not always attainable, nor is it desirable in some cases. Nevertheless, what both long-term and short-term ethnography share is that these studies seek to build theories of culture and society, theories of human behaviour and attitudes, and to appreciate what it means to be human in particular social and cultural contexts.

Theorising about people

Ethnography is not description for description's sake, it is description and analysis coming together to answer questions and build theories, which in turn can respond to future ethnographic issues and generate future ethnographic theories. This theory generating characteristic of ethnography is important, and there are two perspectives to consider in the way ethnographers build their theories of the human condition.

Ethnographers attempt to marry narrow and broad approaches to theory building by combining inductive and deductive perspectives. Inductive theory building can be described as 'bottom up' theory based on the observations and interactions ethnographers have in the field and the hypothesising this encounter creates. It is particular theorising. Deductive theory can be described as 'top down', or general, or grand theory, that is to say, the theories that ethnographers acquire in educational institutions and against which they test the particular theories they generate from fieldwork (after LeCompte and Schensul, 1999a: 8).

The task for ethnographers is to tell their explanatory stories in such a way as to find a middle road between the inductive and the deductive, between particular, bottom-up theory and general, top-down theory. This process is called recursive or grounded analysis, and it is undertaken in order to find an explanatory framework between the particular and the general. However, the recursive or grounding process is not an 'end of project' task; ethnographic research constantly 'moves back and forwards between inductive analysis to deductive analysis' (LeCompte and Schensul, 1999a: 15). These processes happen simultaneously; ethnographers are always inductively hypothesising from their specific situations outwards, while at the same time applying more general deductive processes to their particular ethnographic situation (see Glaser and Strauss [1967] and O'Reilly [2009] for more discussion of grounded theory).

Theory is a term that causes a lot of needless anxiety in the social sciences, but theory can simply be seen as a thinking tool we use in our attempts to explain human behaviour. Theory in the social sciences isn't necessarily definitive or certain in the way we have 'theory-as-law' in the natural sciences (for example, Boyle's Law of Gases or Newton's Law of Gravity). Theory should not be treated as a rule to which we find people to tightly conform; it is a guide to help us understand why humans do and think the things they do.

■■■ TOP TIP 1.1 ■■■

Theory is our tool to master; it should not master us. Use it to guide and improve your understanding of your research subject, but make sure to keep your eyes open to exceptions and circumstances that might not fit neatly into your original theory.

Ethnographers should use theory to improve understandings, to solve problems, to build more complex stories and to generate new questions. With this in mind, one of the reasons we seek to mesh inductive and deductive theory is not just to find stability or conformity between theoretical levels, but to find challenges, exceptions and problems from our inductive, bottom-up standpoint that cause us to reconsider and refine our deductive, top-down perspectives. This critical and transformative relationship of the ethnographic particular to general bodies of anthropological, sociological and other social science knowledge remains one of the most persuasive arguments for the ongoing importance of ethnographic research. In other words, practice is good for theory, and *vice versa*.

The ethnographer's body

Ethnographers have enthusiastically engaged with embodiment as an issue, indeed there has been something of a 'somatic turn' in ethnography (Monaghan, 2006: 238). As LeCompte and Schensul say, the participant observer is the primary 'tool' of ethnography (1999a: 1). The ethnographer's body, and the sensations it records, are part of the ethnographic script. We use our eyes and ears in systematic, targeted observations, and of course we use our hands to record our perceptions during fieldwork and during writing up and reflection; as Coffey says, 'fieldwork is necessarily an embodied activity' (1999: 59). We build up embodied knowledge by training our bodies to do things our participants do; we attempt to acquire another's 'habitus' and we train our bodies to fit into the field (Coffey, 1999: 65). But we also bring a 'habitus', which is to say, a generative embodied history (Bourdieu, 1990), to bear on our fieldwork. One of the challenges for the ethnographer's body is to find some resolution between their and the 'other's' somatic way of being in the world (there will be more on this issue in Chapter 4).

Participant observation might sound like an oxymoron (how does one observe while participating?), but it isn't – participant observation is a whole of body experience that has us observing with our eyes as we participate, but we also 'observe' with all our senses. Touch, smell, taste, sound and sight come together to form the framework for memories, jottings and consolidated notes that form the evidentiary basis of ethnographic writing. Good ethnographers will use their whole body as an organic recording device. The challenge for ethnography is to adequately record these senses as data and then to be able to stand back from the bodily experience and analyse, interpret and draw conclusions from these ethnographic experiences.

Insider and outsider

Another key characteristic of ethnography is that it attempts to find a relationship between 'emic' and 'etic' understandings of human behaviour. An emic perspective is one which reflects the insiders' or research participants' point of view, whereas an etic perspective is one which echoes the outsiders' or researchers' point of view (the terms etic and emic are taken from the linguistic terms phonemic and phonetic). This positionality in some ways resonates with attempts to marry inductive and deductive theories, yet it is not a neat analogy. Finding a relationship between emic and etic perspectives is not simply a matter of balance, but rather these two ways of seeing are synthesised to explain particular human phenomena against a broader canvas. Many characterisations of ethnography will stress the emic or insider perspective over the etic, and see fieldwork as a narrow endeavour that seeks the 'folk' or 'native' or 'insider' point of view. However characterising ethnography as fieldwork designed to elicit an emic point of view is but part of the story; there's more to consider. The act of cultural translation, be it across perceived cultural gaps or some other communication divide, relies on the ethnographer never losing sight of their own etic perspective and the driving questions that brought them to the field in the first place. Proper ethnographic reflexivity requires that we must not forget that we will always maintain some sense of the 'outsider' despite the fact we may be or become very familiar with the people we choose to study. Thorough, resolved ethnographic accounts make sense of both the emic and the etic of their given situations. Reflexivity has a central role to play in this resolution process.

REFLEXIVITY

The terms reflexive, reflexivity, and reflexiveness have been used in a variety of disciplines to describe the capacity of language and thought – of any system of signification – to turn or bend back upon itself, to become an object to itself, and to refer to itself. Whether we are discussing things grammatical or cognitive, what is meant is a reflex action or process linking self and other, subject and object. (Babcock, 1980: 2)

The idea of the ethnographer being the central research tool raises questions about the 'scientific' or objectivity claims that ethnographer's might like to make of their research, and also raises the issue of subjectivity being a component of the ethnographic research and writing experience. Claims to 'scientific' validity in ethnography are made on the basis of the rigour with which ethnographic methods are framed and assessed, but if the ethnographer is both a method (tool) and methodological assessor, we need to assess validity in ethnography with an eye on the ethnographer's influence on the research process. Let's, therefore, turn to the theme of methodological reflexivity and look at the role of the ethnographer.

I began my doctoral research in my home town with the assumption that a reflexive element would be evident in my ethnography because I was working in such a familiar social and geographical landscape to which I had already formed all sorts of subjective attachments. Subjectivity and reflexivity are not the same thing, but the subjective nature of my engagement led me to reflect a lot on my role and gave rise to a strong reflexive element in my research. However, the subjective and reflexive elements were in the end not a problem to be overcome; rather they were a productive force I had to learn to confront. It has been said that 'when anthropologists talk about reflexivity, either they do not know what they are talking about or they are talking about something other than what they seem to be talking about' (Watson, 1987: 29). There is more than a grain of truth to this statement. So often one will see reflexivity being treated as a marginal note in ethnographic writing; it is an issue that is paid lip service without being more properly discussed in terms of how it informs particular projects (a notable exception is Hammersley and Atkinson, 2007). Watson argues that 'reflexivity is a pervasive and ineluctable feature of all accounts; it is not something to be remedied; it is not a *special* problem of anthropology at home' (1987: 30). I concur with this point of view and given in this text I am suggesting that reflexivity is central to ethnographic research, I should expand on how I see reflexivity working in ethnography. I argue that if we embrace the methodologically productive aspects of reflexivity then we can go beyond 'merely managing' reflexivity to a proper engagement with it. As an act of engagement let's critically discuss George Marcus's analysis of ethnographic reflectivity.

In *Ethnography Through Thick and Thin* (1998), Marcus identifies four forms of reflexivity operating in the social sciences: (1) the 'basic' or 'null' form, (2) 'sociological reflexivity', (3) 'anthropological reflexivity' and (4) 'feminist reflexivity'. Marcus writes:

The null form of reflexivity is the self critique, the personal quest, playing on the subjective, the experimental, and the idea of empathy. (1998: 193)

When I first entertained the idea of a reflexive element in my ethnography, this 'null form' was pretty much the model I had in mind. Yet I soon discovered that this approach in itself is not methodological, rather it is more aligned to post-fieldwork musing and 'navel gazing'. Marcus goes on to say that while we should take this form seriously the most likely outcome from such a reflexive approach is an 'introspective voice' that doesn't 'challenge the paradigm of ethnographic research' (1998: 193). I see a more important problem here; a 'null form' of reflexivity does not tell us anything about the people who are the subjects of the research.

The second form of reflexivity Marcus describes is Bourdieu's 'sociological reflexivity', which is:

> ... tied to the commitment to sustain objectivity, the distance and abstraction of theoretical discourse, and empiricism as distinct historical contributions of sociology (and a related social theory) as a discipline. With such a commitment, ethnography retains its identity as a method and reflexivity becomes valuable only in methodological terms as a research tool. (1998: 194)

Marcus is critical of this approach to reflexivity, and suggests it has a 'very restricted function' and little potential to 'alter the forms taken by past sociological (and ethnographic) practice' (1998: 195–6). I, however, see a lot to commend in Bourdieu's construction: most obviously it is an understanding of reflexivity that stresses its methodological value and the potential for such an approach to dissolve the putatively oppositional relationship between the subjective and the objective, the emic and the etic, the inductive and the deductive. Bourdieu's reflexivity conjures up the potential for reflectivity to help create a resolved ethnographic account (see Bourdieu and Wacquant, 1992, and also Whyte, 1993: 280–3).

The next two forms Marcus deals with are 'anthropological reflexivity' and 'feminist reflexivity', which are both characterised as dedicated to understanding the politics of 'positionality'. Anthropological and feminist reflexivity, argues Marcus, allow us to see that any one representation of an 'other' is just that; only one way of seeing things. This attitude comes from the idea that truth is partial, not absolute. Through anthropological reflexivity we are able to 'forgo nostalgic ideas of discovery' and appreciate 'the complex ways that diverse representations have constituted anthropology's subject matter' (1998: 197). Feminist reflexivity argues for partial truths that help to more faithfully represent the real world than totalising representations, and as such create a reflexive form of objectivity (echoing, curiously, Bourdieu's sociological reflexivity). The distinction Marcus draws between anthropological and feminist reflexivity amounts to an acknowledgement of, and engagement with, different positionalities. However, what Marcus is talking about in relation to both anthropological and feminist reflexivity might usefully be described as 'personal–political reflexivity'.

In my case, a critical appreciation of positionality is a tool with which to check my ethnographic baggage for presumption and prejudice; to remind myself I bring just one perspective to ethnography and that perspective is informed by my own upbringing, education and history. Ethnographers, just like the groups they study, come with histories and socialisation, and the influence of these elements in ethnographic research needs to be properly understood. So, putting to one side the null form of introspective reflexivity, this leaves us with a bipartite construction: a methodologically focussed sociological reflexivity and a personal–political reflexivity that has developed from anthropology and feminism. These two forms are not stand-alone entities however; their influence overlaps, with each waxing and waning dependent on the context and the nature of the interaction. In my own work I engage in reflections on the subjective and objective elements of my methodological approach, I reflect on the politics of location and on the influence my social and historical identity has on the creation of the text, and I do all these things simultaneously. Such reflexivity is simply an essential part of managing the influence of 'me' on the research and representations of 'them'.

■■■ **TOP TIP 1.2** ■■

Don't save reflection until the end of your project – continually reflecting on your research topic, question and methodology will give you a better chance of spotting influences external factors and possible biases may have on the way you conduct and present your research.

The overall point I want to make about reflexivity in ethnography is that despite the strict meaning of the term, reflexivity is not really about 'you, the ethnographer'; it's still about 'them, the participants'. The point of getting to know 'you, the ethnographer' better, getting to know the way you influence your research, is to create a more reliable portrait, argument or theory about 'them, the participants'. Subjectivity is therefore not a problem for a putatively objective ethnography if it is dealt with rigorously. Turning one's gaze away from the obvious influence of subjectivity in ethnography is simply ignoring the elephant in the corner. With this in mind, one can see why I am attracted to a reflexivity that enhances the methodological strength of a project (in the fashion of Bourdieu) and one that interrogates the influence of the subjectivity and positionality of the author on the creation of the text (in the fashion of anthropology and feminism). What this amounts to is an acknowledgement that reflexivity is not for the marginalia of ethnography. Acknowledging the fact that the ethnographer is the primary tool of research and an active participant in the ethnographic field also means that properly confronting the influence of the ethnographer on research and representation is an unavoidable precondition of a reliable ethnographic account.

INTERSUBJECTIVITY

The ability of ethnography to deliver a storied reality relies in large part on the communicative trust developed between ethnographers and their participants and interlocutors; it lies in the quality of the intersubjective exchange. Communicative intersubjective 'trust' is both the paragon quality one wants in ethnographic social exchange (Eipper, 1996) and the most ill-defined and difficult to ascertain. So much ethnographic authority is underpinned by the hope that ethnographers have understood the people they work with in their terms and can faithfully re-present and interpret that worldview. The anxious importance of this trust game is brought into sharp relief by the horror felt for ethnographic fraud (for example see de Mille [2000, 2001] on Carlos Castaneda). Michael Jackson in his *Minima Ethnographica* (1998) discusses the intersubjective turn in anthropology, and puts forward a relational view of the self and subjectivity. The self, subjectivity and identity are, he suggests, 'mutually arising', a product of a Bakhtinian dialogue (1998: 6–7). This is not to 'intend any erasure of the notion of self as an intentional agent' (1998: 6), rather to stress that 'human consciousness is never isomorphic with the things on which it fastens, the objects it makes its own, and the selves which it constructs' (1998: 6). Self thus inexorably fastens onto the other, and the subject onto the intersubject, but this is by no means a seamless and unambiguous coherence. Indeed, Jackson has catalogued seven types of intersubjective ambiguity, noting that 'intersubjectivity is steeped in paradox and ambiguity' (Jackson, 1998: 8) (see also Madden, 2014).

To paraphrase Jackson, firstly 'intersubjectivity is the site of constructive, deconstructive and reconstructive interaction – it moves continually between positive and negative poles'. Secondly, 'being is never limited to human being … intersubjectivity includes persons, ancestors, spirits, collective representations and material things'. Thirdly, 'drawing on Hegel's master/slave dialectic, no matter how great the social inequality self and other are beholden on each for mutual recognition'. Fourthly, 'while the elementary structure of intersubjectivity may be dyadic, it is usually mediated by something outside itself, e.g. a shared idea, a common goal'. In the fifth instance, 'intersubjectivity is shaped by habitual taken-for-granted dispositions as much as it is shaped by conscious intentions and worldviews'. Sixth, 'intersubjectivity reflects the instability of human consciousness – oscillating from the retracted secure self, through fulfilment in being with another, to being overwhelmed by another'. And finally seventh, 'drawing on Merleau-Ponty, there is the problem of knowledge – how can I speak of an "I" other than my own, how can empathy, transference, or analogy bridge the gap between me and you?' (after Jackson, 1998: 8–10; see also Madden, 2014).

This set of propositions adequately reflects the complicated exchanges that characterise the intersubjective moment and in this series of points are nested some essentials; intersubjectivity is not a stable condition (because 'selves' are not stable), it is not limited to humans (Irvine, 2004a, 2007; Taylor, N., 2007), it requires an act of (sometimes asymmetrical) recognition, it infers an object or external reference beyond the intersubjective, it is mediated by agency and habitus (Bourdieu, 1977), it covers the spectrum from 'buffered' to 'porous' selves (Taylor, C., 2007: 37–41), it anxiously interrogates the knowledge gap between 'I' and 'You', and it is ultimately a very tricky business. Therefore, in addition to paying attention to systems and art, the success of ethnography lies in overcoming, to a sufficient extent, the pitfalls, the indeterminacies and ambiguities of intersubjectivity to produce faithful accounts of interlocutors and research participants (however familiar or exotic those subjects might be) (Madden, 2014).

Social science and validity

The influence of subjectivity on ethnography and the lack of control over field settings are the sorts of conditions that are mentioned when some people make the claim that ethnography is not 'scientific' or 'reliable'. This sort of charge unsettles a lot of ethnographers and also points to a certain anxiety that has dogged ethnography and qualitative social science research more broadly – how do we make claims to validity in relation to ethnographic research? The concerns of positivists or 'quantasaurs' about the validity of qualitative ethnographic data are not concerns this text shares to any great extent (after Crang and Cook, 2007). It doesn't really matter if we have a view of ethnography as more or less 'scientific' or more or less 'artful'. Again, most reasonable understandings of ethnography tend to emphasise some combination of science and humanities in the genealogy of the ethnographic endeavour (see Brewer, 2000: 1, 27–38). The expanding appeal of ethnography to a range of social science disciplines beyond anthropology and sociology, and the manner in which these disciplines have taken up ethnography, have only reinforced this view of ethnography. What ethnography needs to work towards is: (1) validity, reliability and veracity built upon the construction of thoughtful and appropriate methodologies; (2) the systematic gathering of data; (3) the systematic interrogation of that data; and (4) the thoughtful, indeed artful, presentation of the material as an ethnographic story. If all these steps are followed then ethnography need not worry itself with narrow 'scientific' assessments of validity. What is needed is a more broadly 'social scientific' assessment of the validity of ethnographic research, one that pays attention to the fact the social sciences are in fact a child of the natural sciences *and* humanities (this intellectual genealogy is discussed in further detail when we look at ethnographic methodologies later in this chapter, see Figure 1.1).

The issue of validity in ethnography can be further reduced to a simple set of propositions: (1) an ethnography which is not informed by scientific principles (like systematic data collection, analysis and presentation) is not good ethnography, it's more like fiction; and (2) an ethnography that is not informed by the art of prose writing, argument, rhetoric, persuasion and narrative, is not ethnography, it's just data. So, we do require a systematised and disciplined approach to produce good eth-nography, to validate the application of our ethnographic methods, to substantiate the interpretation of our ethnographic data and the representation of ethnographic situations. But this prescriptive framework still leaves much room for the inventive, the imaginative and the experimental; all things that have the potential to make doing and reading ethnography something fundamentally educational and trans-formative. There is no need for conflict between science and art, between fact and story. A brief discussion of the relationship between methods and methodologies will help fortify this point.

METHODS

What are methods?

Firstly, a method is just a tool. These tools (participant observation, interviewing, recording, surveying, etc.) will be discussed in turn as we work through this text.

Let's step back a bit by looking at the broad field of the social sciences. As Brewer notes, the social sciences is an inheritor of the older philosophical and intellectual traditions that study human beings and the natural world, and it modelled itself in some ways on both the humanities and the natural science traditions, taking aspects from both to construct the meta-discipline of the social sciences and the pendant disciplines of anthropology, sociology, cultural studies and so on (2000: 1). Brewer suggests one can see this inheritance as a case of the social sciences taking meth-ods from the natural sciences and a subject matter (humans) from the humanities, and while things are clearly more complicated than this, it's a very useful point to consider when we try to understand the anxiety about validity and science in eth-nography. Methods:

... are merely technical rules which lay down the procedures for how reliable and objective knowledge can be obtained. ... Thus, they lay down the procedures for constructing a hypothesis (methods of research enquiry), for designing a questionnaire, conducting an interview, or doing participant observation (methods of data collection), or for working out some statistical formulae etc. (methods of data analysis). (Brewer, 2000: 2)

Importantly, Brewer highlights that methods are not just a matter of data collection; they are also tools that get employed in research planning, analysis and interpreta-tion. We should add to this that the manner in which we treat text and acquit our writing also has methodological implications; style, voice and character in writing can impact upon the reception of ethnographic accounts. *Writing is a method* and therefore an element of a thorough discussion on methodology.

What is a methodology?

Firstly, a methodology is simply a justification of the use of a particular set of methods (a toolkit). Methods are what tools you use; a methodology is an explanation of why you use those tools.

This distinction between methods and methodology is straightforward, but nevertheless, one can read countless methodology sections from ethnographies and find they basically list the tools the ethnographer used to gather the data, and not much more. So an ethnographer may report that they spent 12 months in a particular village, were engaged in participant observation for the entirety of their stay, but also conducted 50 informal interviews, took a household census, took hundreds of photographs and gathered genealogical information from all the households in their field site. The proper methodological dimensions of such an ethnographic account should also discuss *why* the data gathering (and analysis and interpretation) was undertaken in this manner. In other words what are the philosophical and intellectual foundations of this particular ethnographic practice? What is the value of being in this place for 12 months? Is there something about the cycle of life in this setting that requires the ethnographer to commit to a 12 month stay in order to properly comprehend the life of this village? Why do informal interviews in this setting? What is it about the local cultural and social mores that make informal approaches to data gathering more successful than, say, formal questionnaires?

There is a tendency in the qualitative social sciences for ethnography and participant observation to be put forward as an unqualified good. But rigorous methodological discussion should challenge this presumptive good, for while we ethnographers will form intense attachment to the idea that we have the best of ways to know fellow humans (what could be a more powerful way to know others than actively being in their social lives?), ethnography, nevertheless, is not for every human situation and is not beyond critique (Hammersley, 1992). An important part of getting beyond ethnography's anxiety about validity is for ethnographers to outline clearly why they did what they did when they did it; a case of 'data transparency'.

━━ TOP TIP 1.3 ━━━

Show your work! Once you have determined an appropriate and ethical methodology, taking the time to outline it clearly will help eliminate concerns that your methods aren't valid.

Again, a serious acknowledgement of the role of the ethnographer (not just reflexivity for the sake of it) gives methodological fortification to a project and puts debates about objectivism and subjectivism in their proper place, that is to say, they are not opposing elements that need to conquer each other; they are partners in any good ethnographic account. An ethnographer being transparent about the way they acquire data, and their reasons for dealing with data in the way they have, can only add to the task of forming a credible ethnographic story.

Figure 1.1 schematically represents the ethnographic endeavour from the genesis of its ideas (intellectual and philosophical ancestors) through its divisions and disciplines (which will have their own clusters of theories and important intellectual antecedents), to the way we do ethnography, and then to the manner in which we write up or represent the product of our practice; from thought to practice and back to thought again. It is on this journey that ethnographers deal with their role in the process, and the manner in which they go about their work. A sound methodology is one way to help make the journey unfold in such a way as to produce a 'social-scientifically' valid outcome.

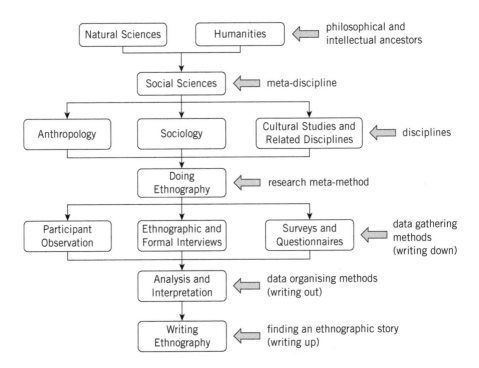

Figure 1.1 Ethnography – from thought to practice to thought

PRACTICAL AND CONCEPTUAL ORIGINS

Imagine yourself suddenly set down surrounded by all your gear, alone on a tropical beach close to a native village, while the launch or dingy which has brought you sails away out of sight. (Malinowski, 1961[1922]: 4)

Talk of intellectual inheritance behoves us to turn to the people and concepts that created ethnography as we know it today. Ethnography did not emerge in an instant or from the activities of just one person; it was a way of studying humans that was emerging in several contexts in Europe and the United States in the early years of the twentieth century. Ethnography as we know it today developed at a time when there was a shift from a monolithic view of culture and civilisation to the idea of cultural pluralism, and social and cultural relativity. Cultural relativist approaches recognise that distinct groups of humans have their own worldviews and cultural logic, and it is the ethnographer's job to penetrate and understand these particular worldviews. In line with this, in the early 1900s American cultural anthropology began to promulgate ideas of cultural pluralism and cultural relativity. This focus on relativist culture has come to dominate ethnography in an unparalleled way. Yet, culture and cross-cultural understanding is by no means a simple matter:

Culture is one of the two or three most complicated words in the English language. This is partly so because of its intricate historical development, in several European languages, but mainly because it has now come to be used for important concepts in several distinct intellectual disciplines and in several distinct and incompatible systems of thought. (Williams, 1988: 87)

Writing on the emergence of the culture concept in anthropology, Friedman also mentions that the 'concept of culture has a long and confusing history':

In ... early anthropology it was associated with the entire repertoire of a 'people', usually very closely associated, that is, [with] a 'people's' defining characteristics. This included everything from technology to religion. In other words culture was simply what was distinctive about others. (1994: 67)

This 'differential culture' model was lodged as a central concept in American anthropology by Franz Boas and in this process the concept of culture was transformed from a monolithic idea that was synonymous with 'high culture' or 'civilisation' to a plural concept related to 'tradition' (Kahn, 1989; 1991). That is, American cultural anthropology set up the conceptual frame which suggests that the important thing about cultures is what separates and distinguishes them, and not what they share.

Boas propagated this pluralistic concept of culture as a 'counterweight to "race"', as another way to explain human variation and discrete human divisions without recourse to the odious imaginings of nineteenth-century evolutionism (Kahn, 1989; 1991). In this regard, it was a welcome and well-intentioned paradigm shift. However, it would be unfair to characterise Boas and his heirs as naïvely representing cultures as discrete, separable wholes. They in fact spoke often of cultures borrowing elements from each other (Sahlins, 1999). The point is, nevertheless, that Boas and his intellectual heirs did not intend to critically engage the 'space' of cultural overlap. Being cultural relativists, they were really concerned with the spaces containing difference (Stocking, 1968: 199–200; 1974: 17). Here we can see one of the generative factors that created the discrete ethnographic 'field' that was a characteristic of much early twentieth-century ethnography.

Early twentieth-century British social anthropology, while ostensibly concerned with the social and not the cultural, nevertheless also had the examination of difference as its reason for being (Friedman, 1994: 68–9). Holistic studies of the differing social, economic, political and cosmological aspects of discrete societies were a feature of the emerging structural–functionalist British ethnography which believed that to understand a society you needed to unlock its underlying and unique features. Thus, in both the American and British traditions, radical alterity was the fetish and the focus; this difference was situated in 'other' cultures and societies. The fundamental concept here is *essentialism* in the sense that each culture was defined as possessing a discrete essence (Friedman, 1994: 73).

Malinowski

If the British structural–functionalist tradition of this time saw discrete social structures with their own behavioural and structural logics as the primary target of ethnographic study, then Bronislaw Malinowski is undoubtedly the key figure in this tradition. Malinowski is consistently referred to as the 'grandfather' of ethnography, and sections of his *Argonauts of the Western Pacific* (1961[1922]) are often cited in ethnography textbooks as foundational moments in the practice (see O'Reilly, 2005: 8–18, for example). It is worth us having a quick look at this material in order to make two points about the influence of Malinowski and to understand why he looms large in the ethnographic pantheon.

The first thing we can say about Malinowski is that he was systematic in laying out his preferred methods for collecting ethnographic data, and the philosophy behind his approach, such that sections of *Argonauts* have become a baseline ethnographic manifesto or charter for how and why we should conduct our ethnographic research. Malinowski knew that a methodology section was more than list of 'tools' used; it was an argument for the use of those tools. The second point to examine in relation to Malinowski is that ethnography has been a remarkably durable and consistent way of studying humans for nearly a century. This methodological durability from Malinowski's time to now is noteworthy.

The overall purpose of *Argonauts* was to explain the fabled 'Kula Ring', a trade and social network that united islands in the Trobriand Archipelago of eastern Papua New Guinea. In the system described by Malinowski, shell necklaces were traded in a clockwise direction across the archipelago, while shell armbands were traded in an anti-clockwise direction. This trade, or more properly, ceremonial exchange (the shell items did not have a use-value outside this exchange) reinforced social ties and marked status and authority across the dispersed island group. However, the section of *Argonauts* that concerns us here is the introduction, 'The subject, method and scope of this inquiry' (1961[1922]: 1–25). Malinowski begins the introduction by reinforcing the scientific nature of his enquiry. He writes:

Before proceeding to the account of the Kula, it would be well to give a description of the methods used in the collecting of the ethnographic material. The results of scientific research in any branch of learning ought to be presented in a manner absolutely candid and above board. (1961[1922]: 2)

This is a call for 'data transparency', so that the reader can judge the ethnographic evidence on its merits, and is typical of this time period where the desire to be firmly scientific in doing ethnography was pervasive. In addition to the 'candid' presentation of data, Malinowski goes on to make the following point about the necessity to know the role of the ethnographer:

It would be easy to quote works of high repute … in which wholesale generalisations are laid down before us, and we are not informed at all by what actual experiences the writers have reached their conclusion. No special chapter or paragraph is devoted to describing to us the conditions under which observations were made and information collected. I consider only such ethnographic sources are of unquestionable scientific value, in which we can clearly draw a line between, on the one hand, the results of direct observation and of native statements and interpretations, and on the other, the inferences of the author, based on his common sense and psychological insight. (1961[1922]: 3)

Here we have an early recognition of the importance of gaining both emic (insider) and etic (outsider) perspectives in ethnography, long before these terms were to become fashionable. Like the relativists of early American cultural anthropology, Malinowski is interested in the worldviews of discrete human groups and how these are to be translated by 'scientific' ethnographers. The translation of this ethnographic material means systematically gathering it in the 'tribal' realm and taking it off to the 'scribal' realm for expert translation. Malinowski rightly identifies this as a tricky business:

In ethnography, the distance is often enormous between the brute material of information – as it is presented to the student in his own observations, in native statement, in the kaleidoscope of tribal life – and the final authoritative presentation of the results. The ethnographer has to traverse this distance in the laborious years between the moment when he sets foot upon a native beach, and makes his first attempts to get in touch with the natives, and the time he writes down the final version of his results. (1961[1922]: 3–4)

But perhaps sitting above all the concerns about science, data, the role of the ethnographer and insider and outsider perspectives, is the concern from Malinowski that ethnographers find appropriate fields to ply their trade. As I have already said, in ethnography's early days this field was constructed around the notion of difference such that geographic isolation from western influences, cultural 'purity' and exoticism were seen as characteristic of 'good conditions of work':

Indeed, in my first piece of Ethnographic research ... it was not until I was alone in the district that I began to make some headway; and, at any rate, I found out where lay the secret of effective field-work. What is then this ethnographer's magic, by which he is able to evoke the real spirit of the natives, the true picture of tribal life? As usual success can only be obtained by a patient and systematic application of a number of rules of common sense and well known scientific principles and not by the discovery of some marvellous short-cut leading to the desired result without effort or trouble. The principles of method can be grouped under three main headings; first of all, naturally, the student must possess real scientific aims, and know the values and criteria of modern ethnography. Secondly, he ought to put himself in good conditions of work, that is, in the main, to live without other white men, right among the natives. Finally, he has to apply a number of special methods of collecting, manipulating and fixing his evidence. (Malinowski, 1961[1922]: 6)

While, in this evermore connected and diffuse global world system ethnographers no longer fetishise isolation, 'purity' and exoticism with the zeal of earlier ethnographers, and talk of scientific aims is somewhat tempered by scepticism about the 'truth' claims of science, this list of attributes laid out by Malinowski has strong continuities with today's practice. Disciplined scientific aims, undertaking ethnography in situ with the participants and applying appropriate methods to the gathering, analysis and interpretation of ethnographic data are still core values of ethnography today. The more things change the more they stay the same.

To reiterate, this particular origin story of ethnography shows us that, methodologically speaking, in terms of the way we practise ethnography, very little has changed in the last 100 years. Of course, theoretical and epistemological paradigms have risen and fallen, intellectual currents have come and gone, the influence of universities and other research centres producing and defining ethnography has waxed and waned, and yet ethnography retains its value to social scientists through the very strengths that Malinowski identified way back in his Trobriand days (O'Reilly, 2009: 143). Being with people (or more precisely, being ethnographic with people), in their time and space, in all their strangeness and in their mundane and quotidian flow, is still one of the most valued ways to build a qualitative understanding of the particulars and generalities of the human condition.

This is rather remarkable, given that 'theory' in the social sciences does not emulate the 'test of proof' definition of natural science theories, and that social science theories have come and gone with regularity for the last 100 years. One could be excused for expecting that ethnographic methodology would also have changed frequently. While ethnography is not a solution to understanding all human conditions, there still remains a strong adherence to the belief that we gain valuable insights and knowledge from being with others. While this doesn't necessarily sound critical and scientific, it is *sensible*. We all know that a close and deep experience with some 'other' (regardless of their relative strangeness or familiarity) can be a transforming experience. The 'other' can take the tourist to the extremes of romanticism or ethnocentrism, the 'other' can jade the journalist or appal the international business traveller, and with the right critical tools at our disposal, the 'other' can teach the systematic ethnographer in a way that is hard to match. This is not to say that ethnography is *better* than other social science approaches to constructing knowledge, but the durability of Malinowski's broad approach to ethnographic work suggests that ethnography has created knowledge in a manner that generations of ethnographers see as sufficiently important and reliable to persevere with. Indeed Malinowski might be rather surprised to see that ethnography has not only continued in a form he would recognise, but that it has expanded its application well beyond the anthropological domain.

APPLICATIONS AND ETHICS

Ethnography is employed in countless social and cultural contexts, and is only limited in its application by the desire to understand relationships between humans in particular social and cultural settings. However, ethnographic research is often directed towards solving very particular social problems faced by a community or group of people or institution – this is 'applied ethnographic research' (applied anthropology or applied sociology). Applied ethnographic research is concerned with understanding sociocultural problems and using these understandings to bring about positive change in communities, institutions or groups. It is by its very nature interventionist, and as such raises questions about a basic ethnographic ethics dictum, 'first, do no harm'. I will not pursue an examination of applied ethnographic domains in this book, but I do want to raise the point that the things that make ethnography valuable to the social scientist are the very same aspects that can render it as a negative experience for the participants in ethnographic research. It's worth noting that the value ethnographers place on systematically gathering detailed and extensive qualitative data can leave ethnography open to the charge of 'spying'. Indeed, ethnography has been used to gather military and other intelligence on populations and this has happened right from the outset of ethnographic research (see Price, 2000; Kürti et al., 2005). Ethnographic information about humans can be interesting and educative, but also sensitive and potentially dangerous; there is a constant need for ethnographers to manage the ethics of gathering and representing ethnographic information (see Murphy and Dingwall in Atkinson et al., 2007: 339–51).

Ethics – everywhere, every time

At every phase of ethnographic research there is an ethical backdrop. In designing research, ethnographers need to make ethical decisions about its structure, in conducting research ethnographers will make ethical decision after ethical decision as they negotiate the field situation, and as they analyse and write up their data ethnographers will make ethical decisions about what material to include or exclude, and about the evolving issues of privacy and confidentiality that arise in the writing process. Even after ethnographers have departed the field they will have ethical issues to consider about the nature of their departure and ongoing association with their participant group. Ethnographers never really leave a long-term field experience – they probably haven't done their job as a participant observer if they are able to completely sever ties after 12 months or more of living with a group of people. The pervasiveness of ethical issues in ethnographic research means that at all stages ethnographers need to be aware of the range of possible consequences of their actions. This issue is perhaps at its most pointed in the act of participant observation, when ethnographers are with participants in their everyday lives, and as such we will devote more to this issue in Chapter 4. While ethnographers can only act in the present, making decisions on the basis of what is going on around them, they must also have an eye on the past and the future in relation to their involvement. The use of ethnography for questionable purposes has a long history. We need to critically examine this history in order to minimise the potential for it to happen in the future.

SUMMARY

Ethnography is a direct, qualitative social science research practice that involves ethnographers doing fieldwork with human groups, societies or cultures, experiencing the daily ebb and flow of life of a participant group. Ethnography is also a form of non-fiction writing that is based on systematically gathered data from fieldwork and other relevant secondary sources. From the combination of research and writing ethnographers build theories about the human condition.

By undertaking participant observation ethnographers are both guiding research and a tool of the research. Ethnography is a whole of body experience. Because of this, it is important for ethnographers to be reflexive; to understand and manage their influence on the research process. A methodologically reflexive ethnography allows for the dissolution of the putative opposition between subjectivity and objectivity, and can help to resolve the apparent contradiction of participant observation.

Ethnographers employ methods in the manner of tools, yet need to be able to explain why they prefer one particular toolkit over another. A strong philosophical and intellectual justification of one's methods defines a good ethnographic methodology.

Ethnography has well and truly 'escaped' from anthropology and qualitative sociology, and is finding favour in many areas, and yet there is remarkable methodological continuity in ethnography from the time of Malinowski and Boas to the present day.

Ethnography doesn't have an ethical element – ethnography is an ethical commitment from the very outset, and through all phases of ethnographic research and writing. All ethnographers must deal with the responsibilities and obligations that go with forming close human contacts and contracts.

QUESTIONS

Ethnography has been characterised in a reasonably straightforward manner in this chapter in line with the idea that such a complicated subject matter (the human condition) and the variety of histories and experiences individual ethnographers bring to their research will mean that any rule-bound definition of ethnography is unlikely to reflect the diverse reality of practice. Nevertheless, we can still talk of core values in the ethnographic approach. What attributes do you think are essential to ethnography? Is it necessary to do participant observation to be a 'proper' ethnographer?

Isn't it a common-sense proposition that being with people is the best way to understand them? Why do we need to devote effort to building up a justificatory methodology every time we do ethnographic research?

What has reflexivity got to do with improving the validity of ethnographic research? Isn't the acknowledgement that there is a subjective element in ethnography tantamount to saying ethnography is more of an art than it is a science?

What is Bronislaw Malinowski's ethnographic legacy? Why is he seen as the grandfather of ethnographic research? What are the key contributions of Franz Boas to the way we construct ethnographic research?

What do you understand intersubjectivity to mean? What about it is considered central to ethnographic research?

How do national anthropological and sociological associations (such as the American Anthropological Association or the United Kingdom's Association of Social Anthropologists) deal with the tension between universal human rights and cultural relativism?

SUGGESTED READINGS

Bernard's *Research Methods in Anthropology: Qualitative and Quantitative Methods* (2006) and LeCompte et al.'s *Essential Ethnographic Methods: Observations, Interviews and Questionnaires* (1999) provide in-depth characterisations of ethnography and ethnographic methods that will assist in your own understanding of ethnography. Brewer's *Ethnography* (2000, especially Chapter 2) provides a useful expansion on our discussion of the methodological and intellectual heritage that informs ethnography and will aid this debate. *The Handbook of Ethnography* (Atkinson et al., 2007) and *The Sage Handbook of Fieldwork* (Hobbs and Wright, 2006) both provide an informative selection of articles on ethnography and fieldwork. See Marcus's *Ethnography Through Thick and Thin* (1998, Chapter 8) for an expanded discussion of reflexivity. O'Reilly's *Ethnographic Methods* (2005) and Stocking's *The Shaping of American Anthropology* (1974) are useful in addressing the question related to Malinowski and Boas. O'Reilly's *Key Concepts in Ethnography* (2009) provides a series of short, no-nonsense entries on most of the main issues in ethnography. For those of a more sociological persuasion, Alan Bryman's *Ethnography* (2001) is worth a read. To understand more about conducting ethical long-term, participant observation ethnographies, David Calvey's *Covert Research: The Art, Politics and Ethics of Undercover Fieldwork* (2017) gives insight into executing fair and valid covert research. Visit the internet pages of some national anthropological and sociological associations and examine their ethics charters or statements. There are also a range of online journals dedicated to ethnography (such as *Ethnography* or the *Journal of Contemporary Ethnography*, both SAGE) that can provide a wealth of resources. For an introduction to why ethnography is being put in the foreground and why it is socially important, see either Adams (2013) *Markets of Sorrow, Labors of Faith: New Orleans in the Wake of Katrina* or www.bbc.co.uk/programmes/articles/16mlCRBL D67XtL4hlMMHdF7/ethnography-what-is-it-and-why-do-we-need-it.

BEING ETHNOGRAPHIC

It is significant that the histories of human and natural sciences have combined to form the social sciences. Knowing your past can help you to move forward!

TWO

ETHNOGRAPHIC FIELDS: HOME AND AWAY

CHAPTER CONTENTS

MAKING PLACE: WHAT IS AN ETHNOGRAPHIC FIELD?

The relationship between humans and places is complex and multi-layered. Humans are place-makers and places make humans. If we consider that spaces are places not yet imbued with human meaning then humans turn geographical spaces into places by residing in them, building on them, extracting from them, mapping, naming, thinking about and owning them. There are myriad of ways humans connect to place: people form territorial, legal, economic, spiritual, emotional and even consubstantial connections to places. In some cases (for example, a place called 'home') people may form all of the above attachments. In other places (for example, a place called 'work') a narrower range of associations, or indeed negative associations, can be formed with place. Many human stories are framed by the theme of connection, or lack of connection, to place. From the struggles of indigenous groups to maintain their traditional lands in the face of rapidly encroaching development to the themes of lost places that one finds in the stories of refugees, forcibly torn from their homelands by war, politics or pestilence; indeed it's difficult to image a human story that hasn't been framed in some way by reference to a place. There is something essential about the relationship of humans to place, there is a constant 'dialogue' between humans and the places they inhabit, and this is not only true for indigenous peoples whose deeply religious and animated connection to land is a salient feature of many ethnographic accounts, but it is true of humans generally. From remote, to rural, to urban settings, people are in a lifelong reproductive and reflexive dialogue, a dialectic, with their surrounds. The variety and complexity of the attachment of humans to places gives the ethnographic field tantalising quality.

To restate an obvious point, ethnographers are humans too (despite the fact that many classic ethnographic accounts have the ethnographer as some sort of disembodied, spectral presence floating between the lines of the text). Therefore, ethnographers are place-makers. However, ethnography turns someone's everyday place into another very particular sort of place, but it's not something we can 'take for granted' (Stein, 2006: 59). Ethnographers create a thing called a 'field'. It's an old ethnographic cliché that there are pre-existing ethnographic fields out there awaiting discovery, all one has to do is walk into them (I recall an anthropologist telling me that he knew of a valley in Papua New Guinea that had 'at least ten PhD sites just waiting to be taken up!'). This myth of the ethnographic site as some sort of virginal land ripe for discovery was and perhaps continues to be a powerful trope. But it's also an anachronistic vision that is a vestige of the early 'science-as-discovery' attitude that was influential in anthropology. Ethnographic fields *do not exist* beyond the imaginings of the ethnographer. One of the first commitments one makes as an ethnographer is to make a field; we must engage in this particular and disciplined form of place-making we call fieldwork.

▬ TOP TIP 2.1 ▬▬▬▬▬▬▬▬▬▬▬▬▬▬▬▬▬▬▬▬▬▬▬▬▬▬▬▬▬

Set your scene! Before you conduct any fieldwork, make sure you clearly define the boundaries of your field of study.

The construction of an ethnographic field allows for an investigation of the socialisation or enculturation of a particular space. This is not to suggest that socialised spaces do not exist beyond the imaginings and activities of ethnographers (a Hopi village was a Hopi village long before an ethnographer entered it, and will continue to be a Hopi village long after the ethnographer goes home); rather ethnographic fields are created as a consequence of particular research projects.

An apparent contradiction is looming here. One of the characteristics of ethnography put forward in Chapter 1 was that ethnographers do not seek to overtly manage or control their field setting, and this is indeed true. But isn't the act of the construction of a field the ultimate act of control over an experimental site? Well, no. Constructing an ethnographic field is not an attempt to control the behaviour of a human group or institution in a particular setting. Constructing a field site is an attempt to put boundaries around an ethnographer's enquiries into a human group or institution. Constructing a field site (or sites) is about controlling the thought processes of the ethnographer, not the behaviours or thoughts of the participant group. An ethnographic field has as part of its makeup an embedded question (or series of questions) that impel the ethnographer towards resolution. An ethnographic field, therefore, helps to set up a problem or series of problems to investigate. In this way an ethnographic field attempts to marry the interrogative or investigative inclination of the ethnographer to the place that has been made by a group of people. An ethnographic field provides an interrogative boundary to map on to a geographical and/or social and/or emotional landscape that is inhabited by a participant group. So, an ethnographic field is not equivalent to a simple geographic or social space, nor is it a simple mental construct of the ethnographer, but it does require both these elements. It is the synthesis of concrete space and investigative space that defines the ethnographic field and gives it its reason for being – it exists to describe, to interrogate, to question, to problematise, to theorise and to attempt to solve questions about the human condition.

SOME FAVOURITE FIELDS

An ethnographic field is therefore 'good to think', and over the years the character of ethnographic fields have shifted and changed, reflecting contemporary theoretical and intellectual currents, following the trends of what has been ethnographically 'good to think' over time. In the early days of ethnography one of the best things to think about was the *radical alterity* or stark difference of so-called 'primitive' people. And these 'primitive' people just so happened to live in 'exotic' places.

The exotic and anthropology

Recall from Chapter 1, the extract from *Argonauts* that has Malinowski alone on the beach:

Imagine yourself suddenly set down surrounded by all your gear, alone on a tropical beach close to a native village, while the launch or dingy which has brought you sails away out of sight. (1961[1922]: 4)

Malinowski's Trobriand Islands is the *quintessential* exotic field. Confident he could remove himself to a place beyond the deleterious influence of western civilisation, confident he could encapsulate a whole society within his project, and utterly authoritative in his ability to translate the social and cultural exotica he encountered, Malinowski gave anthropology and the social sciences more broadly a strong vision of the ethnographic field. If one revisits the quotes from Malinowski's *Argonauts* that were presented in Chapter 1, one can see that in addition to providing a methodological template for the conduct of 'proper' fieldwork, Malinowski presents a fundamental template for the construction of a 'proper' ethnographic field. It is part mental construct, part geographic fact. The intellectual framework for this construction was the emerging structural-functionalism of British social anthropology, an approach to understanding humans that saw societies as mechanistic wholes, with each element in the society functioning in a dependent relationship with all other elements to sustain an entire structure. Therefore the material conditions to best explore this approach were supposedly isolated groups of people living outside the influence of the larger world. All the better if one could find a remote island surrounded by a large ocean to reinforce the image of separation.

With the gift of hindsight we can now look back at this foundational version of the ethnographic field and see that in reality it was interpenetrated with myriad forms of influence from 'outside' and far from the isolated entity that is conjured up in work like Malinowski's. Yet at the time the idea of isolatable, socially and geographically discrete human groups which ethnographers could interrogate in order to answer questions about the general human condition, was pervasive and persuasive. Of course Malinowski's diaries, published after his death in 1967, tell of another form of exotica and cross-cultural being. Grumpiness, despondency, racism, sexual fantasy and vitriol pour off the pages of this account. This latter 'contribution' to ethnography has placed Malinowski in an interesting position. Firstly he is seen as the grandfather of fieldwork and the architect of that most powerful ethnographic trope – the exotic and primitive field. But his diaries threw up another sort of field altogether, and their publication presaged the era of reflexivity, the crisis in representation and the impossibility of separating the ethnographer, as a person, from their account of other people. We'll have more to say about reflexivity later, for the moment let's keep track of the classic ethnographic field by looking at the key textual device to establish the image of the ethnographic field; the arrival scene.

In Raymond Firth's *We, the Tikopia* (1963[1936]), one of ethnography's classic arrival scenes is laid out in the first two paragraphs of the text proper. Firth introduced the reader to his field site thus:

> In the cool of the early morning, just before the sunrise, the bow of the *Southern Cross* headed towards the eastern horizon, on which a tiny dark blue outline was faintly visible. Slowly it grew into a rugged mountain mass, standing up sheer from the ocean; then as we approached within a few miles it revealed around its base a narrow of low, flat land, thick with vegetation. The sullen grey day with its lowering clouds strengthened my grim impression of a solitary peak, wild and stormy, upthrust in waste of waters.

> In an hour or so we were close inshore, and could see canoes coming round from the south, outside the reef, on which the tide was low. The outrigger-fitted craft drew near, the men in them bare to the waste, girdled with bark-cloth, large fans stuck in the back of their belts, tortoise shell rings or rolls in the ear lobes and nose, bearded and with long hair flowing loosely over their shoulders. Some plied the rough heavy paddles, some had finely plaited pandanus-leaf mats resting on the thwarts beside them, some had large clubs or spears in their hands. The ship anchored on a short cable in the open bay of the coral reef. Almost before the chain was down the natives began to scramble aboard, coming over the side by any means that offered, shouting fiercely to each other and to us in a tongue of which not a word was understood by the Mota-speaking folk of the mission vessel. I wondered how such turbulent human material could ever be induced to submit to scientific study. (1963[1936]: 1)

This romantic arrival scene has all the hallmarks of the classic ethnographic field; isolated, rugged, with radically different and 'turbulent human material'. The map of Tikopia Island, presented on the facing page of the 1936 edition, further reinforces the isolated character of the site and allows for the idea of a discrete social whole to be established as an important element of this particular field site, indeed, Firth tells us it is 'rarely visited by Europeans and with no white residents' (1963[1936]: 3). Firth gives some fairly intricate detail on the appearance of the Tikopia, successfully setting them apart from himself by reference to their garb (bark-cloth), accoutrements (ear and nose piercings) and 'long flowing' hair styles. This is not to say that the difference encountered in this case wasn't real, or was simply a textual product, no doubt Firth's encounter with the Tikopia was indeed marked by real differences, but the presentation of these cultural chasms in the scene-setting of ethnographic accounts became a clichéd device that helped to bound the ethnographic field (particularly in anthropology) as a site that asked questions about difference in priority to exploring issues of similarity. Isolation and a stark difference in appearance were also used successfully in Napoleon Chagnon's *Yanomamo: The Fierce People*:

The Yanomamo Indians live in southern Venezuela and the adjacent portions of northern Brazil ... Many of the villages have not yet been contacted by outsiders, and nobody knows for sure how many uncontacted villages there are, or how many people live in them ... they are one of the largest unacculturated tribes left in all of South America. (1977: 1)

Upon his entry to a Yanomami village, Chagnon wrote:

My heart began to pound as we approached the village and heard the buzz of activity within the circular compound. ... The entrance to the village was covered over with brush and dry palm leaves. We pushed them aside to expose the low opening to the village. The excitement of meeting my first Indians was almost unbearable as I duck-waddled through the low passage in the village clearing.

I looked up and gasped when I saw a dozen burly, naked, filthy, hideous men staring at us down the shafts of their drawn arrows! Immense wads of green tobacco were stuck between their lower teeth and lips making them look more hideous, and strands of dark green slime dripped or hung from their noses. ... My next discovery was that there were a dozen or so vicious, underfed dogs snapping at my legs, circling me as if I was going to be their next meal. I just stood there holding my notebook, helpless and pathetic. Then the stench of the decaying vegetation and filth struck me and I almost got sick. I was horrified. (1977: 5)

Here we have the ethnographer as an intrepid, heroic character, setting up a field that is fraught with culture shock and danger, in order to triumph over these obstacles and to deliver a vital portrait despite the difficulties. The ethnographic field thus encapsulated not only difference, but tricky, difficult difference and this enabled the ethnographer to demonstrate their expertise in matters cross-cultural by eventually overcoming the turbulent human material to reach an understanding of their study group they could then translate to a wider audience. This particular construction of the ethnographic field in anthropology therefore gave preference to questions of difference and demonstrated expertise from the ethnographer based on their capability to deal with said difference. The ethnographic field is therefore involved in shaping the questions that are pursued and also the style, rhetoric and form of the presentation of the ethnographic account.

These representations of stark cross-cultural differences were not only the preserve of anthropologists, as early qualitative sociology in its ethnographic pursuits also worked up highly delineated fields that were bounded by difference. These constructions are interesting against the anthropological material, as the classic sociological ethnographic fields were encapsulated in large cities that were multicultural and pluralistic. Chicago was the prime example being 'one of the most complete social laboratories in the world' (Hutchinson, 2007), where 'social life could be studied first-hand' (O'Reilly, 2009: 29).

The city and sociology

The history of the Chicago School demonstrates that anthropology did not have ethnography to itself, even in its early days. The Chicago School, especially in the first three decades of the twentieth century, established an influential model for urban ethnographic studies, and one of the most influential figures was the sociologist Robert Park. The relationship between the exotic anthropological ethnographic field and the urban sociological field can be seen in this assessment of Park's influence:

Park formulated a new theoretical model based upon his observation that the city was more than a geographic phenomenon; the basic concepts of human ecology were borrowed from the natural sciences. Competition and segregation led to formation of *natural areas*, each with a separate and distinct *moral order*. The city was 'a mosaic of little worlds that touch but do not interpenetrate'. (Hutchinson, 2007)

Here too, the idea of discrete, isolatable social groups was important in the construction of field sites dedicated to issues like gangs (Thrasher, 1927), ghettos (Wirth, 1928), urban segregation, affluence and slums (Zorbaugh, 1929), African-American families (Frazier, 1932), urban night life and dance clubs (Cressey, 1932) and many other sociologically discrete units that made up the metropolis of Chicago in the early twentieth century. However, the pressing fact that the Chicago School was keenly focussed on the issue of social change (Abbott, 2008) meant that the idea of a socially discrete field site was always going to be problematised in these urban settings where supposedly discrete social domains were always touching upon each other, diffusing into each other and influencing each other.

Perhaps in the example of the ethnographic studies from the sociologists of the Chicago School we see aspects of both the continuum of the discrete ethnographic field (the ghetto, the gang, the ethnic enclave and urban segregation) and the beginnings of the dissolution of the idea of a geographically discrete and knowable ethnographic field. Along similar lines, anthropology was focussing more on social change and undergoing the same process of dissolution of the strict geographic sense of the ethnographic field; a by-product of the eclipsing of structural-functionalism as the dominant theoretical force in favour of more evolutionary approaches like cultural materialism and a more overt engagement with the study of historical forces.

More and more this impressed upon ethnographers the previously understated element of the ethnographic field, that is to say, a field is as much a mental construct of the ethnographer, shaped by their intellectual interests, as it is a concrete place bounded by coral atolls, or jungle, or vast desert, or dangerous city streets or other classic bordering devices.

■ TOP TIP 2.2 ■

Having trouble deciding what your field should be? Begin with a personal inventory – what kind of person are you? What types of conditions and situations do you like, and which do you dislike? What amount of time and resources are at your disposal? Take the practicalities into account, not just your interests.

The growth of ethnographic projects undertaken in 'western' contexts, or more narrowly, the growth in ethnographic projects done at 'home' in the natal communities of ethnographers has continued this geographic boundary dissolution apace, but it hasn't in any way lessened the desire of the ethnographer to mark off some form of field or interrogative-cum-social-cum-geographic reason for asking the questions and participating in the manner they do.

In the following section I want to lay out the way in which I wrestled with the idea of the ethnographic field being also my home-town area, albeit a home-town area that had pockets of unfamiliarity in the form of the local Aboriginal Community (see Madden, 1999 for more detail on this early fieldwork experience). I present this examination of ethnography at home because the familiarity of home has a way of disarming one's sense of being ethnographic; it's difficult at times to maintain an ethnographic perspective in a familiar setting. This sometimes problematic domain can therefore tell us something about the underlying nature of the ethnographic field.

ETHNOGRAPHY AT HOME

'Home' is one of those commonplace terms that is uncritically bandied about, not just in the social sciences, but in all facets of life. It is a term used in the expectation that people will know exactly what one is talking about – it has a taken-for-granted quality. Its uncritical application in the social sciences mirrors the use of terms such as 'community' and 'society', that is to say, they are supposedly neither contentious nor lexically problematic. However, like community and society, home is a term that is typically used inconsistently, or rather, is broadly interpreted, even in anthropology.

In an ASA collection titled *Anthropology at Home* (Jackson, 1987), 14 anthropologists detail what the concept of home means to them with regard to their ethnographic experiences and theoretical approaches, and a great diversity of representations are put forward. Containing, as it does, such a range of people, situations and experiences, this volume is a most useful text with which to approach a critical understanding of the concept of home in anthropology. There is, for example, an English anthropologist working with gypsies and her ethnography undertaken in Britain is said to be at home (Okely, 1987: 55–74). Here we have home, broadly, as a nation state, and more specifically as a series of familiar counties. A Dane who undertakes ethnography in various parts of Scandinavia considers the region to be some sort of home (Hastrup, 1987: 94–108). Home in this setting is a culture and/or macro-language bloc. An Indian Jew, who moves to Israel to live and undertake fieldwork, considers the field, and Israel, her 'new' home (Weil, 1987: 196–212). Here we have ethnography as adoption agency: the field becomes home. And so on. There is much variance in the conceptualisation of 'home'.

I hadn't imagined home could be such a big place. I always thought of it as a small 'homely', or *gemeinschaftlich* environment. My concept of home is more personalised and intimate than the bulk of the authors from the above mentioned ASA publication. From my perspective, *Home is familiar*. I know it very well, it is a geographical region within which streets, highways, back roads, houses, sheds and other buildings, as well as landscape, are known. *Home is parochial*. It is a place that elicits an uncritical attachment. *Home is discrete*. I know where it starts and ends, in both a geographical and social sense. I have it mapped out in my mind. *Home is habitual*. Old habits of speech, manners, attitudes and moods come back to me when I go home. One could say that my personality changes when I go home, or conversely, that I just become myself again. *Home is permanent*. After more than half my life living outside my home regions in the city of Melbourne, I still go 'down home to the country'. *Home is birth*. It is where I spent my childhood, and also my youth. As such, it has shaped my adult personality. *Home is death*. It is where family members and relations are buried. From the hilltop house I grew up in I could look out one window and see the house my father and grandfather were born in, and look out another window and see the cemetery where they, and most of my relatives, lie buried today. And finally, *Home is ambivalence*. Home is a place I felt the need to leave, and to which I need to return. The more time I spend in the city, the more home tends toward the euphemistic, becomes romanticised and somewhat sanitised in my mind; a bucolic idyll, a Steinbeckian world of simple values, of struggle and hope. It is a problematic, yet attractive domain.

My recipe for home is therefore a mixture of geographical, emotional, social and cultural components, which are brought together under the rubric of familiarity. It is also an obviously personal and subjective definition, such is the idiosyncratic nature of 'home' that no two people will be likely to define it in the same way. These personal characteristics are meant to convey the smallness of scale and the familiarity of the place. However, it's not enough to say that my everyday working definition of home equates to the home-town ethnographic field. As I have already indicated, part of my desire to study in my home area stemmed from the fact that pockets of this putatively familiar region were unknown to me. Thus I actually conceptualised my home town ethnographic field as a social and geographical space with a series of large question marks hovering over it. My concept of home as an ethnographic field had a major impact on how I conceived of my project, and how I went about my ethnography; it is more than just a place – my home, in an ethnographic sense, is an interrogative space that is mapped onto a geographic locale.

Interrogating home

The questions I ultimately pursued in my PhD research centred around the role of 'culture' in Aboriginal/non-Aboriginal relations and are in some way driven by the fact that my home area's Aboriginal population was almost unknown to me when I lived there. I therefore expected that in undertaking an ethnographic project at home I would find the familiar in my own non-indigenous culture, and the unfamiliar in the local Aboriginal community. These presuppositions were challenged by some of my early experiences in the field.

The Aboriginal community that lives in my home area is based both in Warrnambool and at Framlingham, an old Aboriginal station site 20 kilometres to the north of this town (to which the inhabitants now have title). There is also a closely related community about one hour's drive west at Portland and Heywood, who are descendants of the Lake Condah Mission community (south-west Victoria). While these people were known to me as a group when I lived in the area, I did not have any prolonged contact with individual Aboriginal people – only a passing acquaintance with a few youths I went to secondary school with. On the whole, I could not say I knew any local Aboriginal people personally. My return to work in the area was thus a process of revisiting the familiar, in the form of locale, and the so-called 'dominant' culture; and encountering the personally unknown, in the form of Aboriginality. However, the thing that surprised me the most about my initial encounters, the thing I had not prepared myself for, was the degree to which I found familiarity in the local Aboriginal sphere (my expectations betray a naïveté that, looking back, seems almost humorous).

Before I went into the field I had many classic anthropological (or what I would call 'textbook') inspired expectations regarding my early encounters – expectations that were shot through with images and experiences I had appropriated reading famous ethnographers' tales from the field. Many 'classic' questions pressed upon me.

Was I going to make a horrible faux pas and offend somebody with my ignorance? Was I going to be appropriated? Was I going to be shunned? Was I going to feel isolated and lonely? While I did not really expect my initial encounters to mirror the famous ones I had read of, I did, however, expect that I would be in 'ethnographic' situations. That is to say, I expected that I could identify my encounters with reference to the ethnographic canon.

━━ **TOP TIP 2.3** ━━

Worried about unconscious bias creeping into your ethnography? Try making a list of your preconceived expectations so that you can acknowledge and address any possible sources of bias while also maintaining scientific standards to remain as impartial as possible.

───

But my initial meeting with the heads of the local Aboriginal co-operative could not have been further from the folkloric version of entering the field that I had constructed in my imagination. There was no romantic glide into the lives of the study group à la Firth and the Tikopia (1963[1936]: 1–2); and no grumpy 'Nuerosis' like that experienced by Evans-Pritchard (1969[1940]: 12–13). I simply drove my car home, as I had done countless times before. My initial experiences were nothing if not familiar and, in a strange way, comfortable. The first meeting went so well as to be somewhat disappointing – it struck me as being un-ethnographic. Instead of stumbling along trying desperately to fit in I was sitting back in a comfortable office with a cup of tea, having a nice chat.

I was meeting the Director, Cultural Officer, and Manager of the local Aboriginal co-operative, and for the first few minutes they all treated me civilly, but nonetheless, as a city person, indeed a university person. They had obviously had plenty of experience in dealing with students, academics and bureaucrats who had an interest in their affairs. There was a polite distance to their initial exchanges: they were helpful without giving too much away. But when I explained that I grew up locally, but had been living in Melbourne, the dynamics of the meeting changed. All of a sudden questions flowed freely.

'What was your last name again?' I told them and mentioned my parents' names and two of the elder men said in unison,

'I played football against your father!'

The third man looked at me long and hard, and asked, 'Are you Pat's brother?'

'Yes I am', I replied.

'I thought so!' He exclaimed, 'Gee, you look a lot like him. I used to work at the cheese factory with your brother'. This brief bit of biographical exchange was enough for these local aboriginal men to work out they were talking to a descendant of the Irish agricultural community to the west of the town. They now knew me as a 'spud-picker' and were happy to treat with me on that basis.

From the very outset, the familiarity of strangers emerged as an issue in my research. After meeting these three men, and gaining the feeling that I was passing some sort of tacit acceptance test, they called in one of their work co-ordinators. He was introduced to me and told that I was a researcher from a university. Upon hearing this he took an officious and somewhat distanced approach towards me, treating all that was said with caution and gravity. His companions, sensing his somewhat defensive attitude, quickly explained to him that I was originally a 'spud-picker from just out the road'. A look of relief came over his face and he said, 'Fuck! I thought you were someone important!'

Needless to say, we all had a good laugh at my expense. Clearly there had been a shift at the meeting: from distanced introduction to warmer interaction. In no time at all I had been socially positioned and I was known, if not personally to these people, at least in terms of *where* and *who* I came from (cf. Abu-Lughod, 1999: 110). This meant that the men present at the meeting had some sense of how to engage me: that is to say, they could relax in the knowledge that I was neither a city person, nor an over-educated person, even though I came to them as just that. The important thing for them was that I had grown up in their area, and as such I was in some way cognate with them. As I said earlier, all this had struck me as being nothing out of the ordinary, and certainly nothing ethnographic. While I was correct in assessing it as an ordinary occurrence, I was mistaken to assume that this process was not yet part of my 'real' fieldwork. Indeed, what had just occurred, that is to say, the process of socially knowing people, was probably as important to the ongoing viability of my fieldwork as any other event.

Working out where people were from, who someone's parents, cousins or uncles are, and so on, is a process that my own family and friends 'down home' in the country engage in. It is also undertaken with great interest by local Aboriginal people. The fact that this process was so familiar to me meant that when I initially engaged with Aboriginal people on the subject I failed to consider it part of my fieldwork. And perhaps, more importantly, I failed to consider the possibility that a familiar process could, in fact, be both European and Aboriginal in terms of its cultural origin. In this event we have a hint of how the concept of home problematises the concept of the ethnographic field. My somewhat naïve and blinkered expectations about the nature of fieldwork were subsumed under the familiarity and habits of homely interaction. Initially I found it difficult to be an ethnographer in this situation.

While belonging to the same geographical area as these Aboriginal people had helped me make a connection and created a friendly atmosphere, it also raised new imponderables – both for them and me. They wondered aloud what on earth an ex-spud picker was doing with a university education. And what was a local non-Aboriginal doing with an interest in Aboriginality, and social research? For me, the questions I now had to deal with were to do with issues of familiar/unfamiliar overlap. The fact that I never came across these people in all the time I lived there, and that I knew little about how they coped from day to day, in what it is fair to say is a rather discriminatory town, meant that the easy-going nature of our exchange did not in any way give me a feeling for the less obvious aspects of their lives. The familiar and the unfamiliar were both present at this meeting, yet without contradiction and without a sense of schism. I obviously needed a more sophisticated way of coming to terms with this complex, contingent situation. Outsider/insider, emic/etic, subjective/objective – these old standards of anthropological positioning were less than useful in this context as they caused me, incorrectly, to feel I was two people, or in two places at once. Not surprisingly, this familiar/unfamiliar overlap was also present when I met and talked to local non-Aboriginal people.

With local Whites, once the conversation got beyond the point of explaining that anthropology has nothing to do with ants, dinosaurs, ancient civilisations or digging, I had to explain what it was I actually did ('But what do you *do*?' they'd insist). Once I mentioned my research involved living Aboriginal people, the interaction generally altered markedly. Some changed the subject quickly, others dropped the subject, dropped the conversation and made excuses to be somewhere else. Some became incredulous, and couldn't resist the chance to express their surprise. I noticed two general types of response. One was disdainful and dismissive, the other was characterised by a patronising fascination. The dismissive can be typified by a response I got from an old school mate: 'Why would you want to have anything to do with those [insert offensive expletive]?' Some attached a fraternal concern to their disparagement: 'Why would you want to do that? You want to be careful you don't get bashed up'.

Both responses relied on the assumption that I had lost my common sense in the city. When I tried to explain myself with phrases such as 'intellectual pursuit' or 'stimulating and interesting', I again met expressions of disdain. I found myself explaining my ongoing education as a necessary step on the way to becoming a 'teacher'. As this is a job recognised as worthy, most were satisfied with that, leaving me alone to wander off and puzzle over how much I had changed since moving to Melbourne (further evidence for them that the city was okay to visit, but you wouldn't want to live there). Sometimes they tried to get through to the 'old' me again by telling me a deprecatory joke about Aboriginal people. When I did not laugh, they finally gave up on me.

Of course, political correctness recalcitrants met in local hotels were not the total-ity of my interactions with local Whites. As stated above, I also met 'liberal' minded people, who, while inevitably confusing socio-cultural anthropology with archaeol-ogy ('So do you go out on digs?'), were nevertheless curious about my research. They asked questions about Aboriginal people such as: 'What are they really like?' Or: 'Is it true that they actually [insert stereotype]?' There was usually also a hint of concern for my well-being, for example, in a confidential aside such as: 'I think you're very brave for doing what you're doing'.

Both positions – the disdainful disparager and the patronisingly interested – were characterised by distance and ignorance. These characteristics permeated most, but not all, of my interactions with the non-Aboriginal community. It is here that my time away from this rural milieu is brought into focus, and can be appreciated for its influence on my research. My time in the city pursuing my education aspirations, replete as they are with urban middle class mores, meant that some facets of my natal community had become strangely unfamiliar. I realised that in my time away from the country my emotional, political and ethical sensibilities had changed markedly. This ongoing estrangement was a source of tension in my fieldwork and highlights the sensation I have that the whole project is being undertaken in a domain where the familiar/unfamiliar overlap in myriad and unexpected ways.

A tale of two homes

About six months into my fieldwork, I was approached by the then Chairperson of the local Aboriginal co-operative and asked if I would assist him in producing the story of his time growing up on the local Aboriginal station (what he called a 'Mission'). He wanted me to hold a tape recorder, ask the occasional question to keep the stories running, and give him assistance with computer skills. We began the process with him taking me out to the mission and showing me all the places he would be referring to in our dialogues. He was keen to implant a strong map of the area in my mind. The process was a curious one for me because I knew the countryside surrounding the old mission site but had not been onto this Aboriginal land before. It was an unfamiliar locale in a familiar landscape. After this, we visited other sites of significance in the area – middens, graves and favourite food-gathering spots. We then settled into a rou-tine of meeting at his place for informal tape-recorded sessions, where he would relate to me his formative experiences growing up on the mission (see Lowe, 2002). It was during this process of extended dialogue that the feeling of familiar/unfamiliar over-lap surfaced again as a dominant issue (just as it had in my initial meetings with the local Aboriginal co-operative directors). This man was familiar to me in an avuncular manner, but he was a Koori (the local Aboriginal term for themselves), one of a group I'd never had any interaction with in my time growing up in the area. And for him,

I was easy to get along with but nevertheless a local non-Aboriginal, a descendant of the local 'redneckery'. These tensions were tacitly negotiated in our interactions, never interfering with the process, rather giving us cause for the occasional reflection on issues of similarity and difference.

When this man took me out to show me sites of significance to him, they often turned out to be significant to me, yet for different reasons. A case in point was the Aboriginal shell deposits or 'middens' in the sand dunes of the local coastline. These sites, which indicate thousands of years of aboriginal food gathering, are immensely important to the local aboriginal community; they are a tangible manifestation of a deep-time connection to an area where their status as 'original owners' is often challenged by others. Local non-Aborigines were sometimes destructive of these sites and ignorant of their status in Aboriginal life. Yet these dunes with their middens are the same dunes I rambled about as a child. For me, this area has a lot of emotional warmth and parochialism attached to it. Many memories and emotions are stirred up when I visit such a place. I went there again with this particular Aboriginal elder. He stood me on the edge of the midden and told me of the poisoned opposition he encountered in his battles to get the site preserved. He talked of massacres that occurred within sight of where we stand. He told me of 'Sunday shoots' perpetrated by White men on horseback. He told me how certain middens can make him 'see' into the past, where he visualises the 'old Blackfellas', as he calls them, fossicking for shellfish, sitting around fires with the smoke hanging over the dunes. I stood there in awe and allowed myself a politically incorrect moment of envy for his primordiality. It was fascinating to have such a familiar place described to me in such a new and unfamiliar way. My home is his country: it is the same place producing different narratives and differing ideas about relating to land.

I assumed that my initial fieldwork experiences and my interactions with hitherto unknown indigenous people from my home town would be dominated by the influence of unfamiliarity and discomfiture, when in fact I discovered not long into the fieldwork that the experience was shot through with feelings of familiarity. In representing the above situation, I made somewhat of a straw man out of an anachronistic, 'classical' model of anthropology; an anthropology that found its raison d'être in the unfamiliar and the exotic. By emphasising my own naïveté and bewilderment at the expense of an authoritative arrival scene I also made a straw man of myself. This caricature-driven approach was employed to emphasise something that I sense anthropology has known about itself but has been reticent to admit, namely, that anthropology ought to muster the same enthusiasm for representing and translating the familiar as it does for the representation of the exotic. I suggested that the idiosyncratic domain of the home-town field, coupled with a reflexive approach to fieldwork, was instrumental in making this point salient. So while I still maintain a sense of home based on the mixture of geographical, emotional, social and cultural characteristics, this real world is rendered rather different when interrogated against a series of concerns that relate to humans and culture and race and history. My social home is a comfortable place; my ethnographic home is an unresolved problem.

MULTISITED AND UN-SITED ETHNOGRAPHY

So far our discussion of the ethnographic field has focussed on singular sites, and how it is that ethnographers map their own intellectual concerns on to these individuated sites. In the current conditions of globalisation and post-modernity the idea of neat bounded sites for the investigation of the human condition has been thoroughly overthrown. That is not to say that such sites no longer exist, but that rather they are no longer a precondition of a 'good' or 'proper' ethnographic project. The concept of multisited ethnography has grown in importance during this time. As ethnographers seek to understand the human condition as it manifests in a global world system, then a range of sites for comparative and contrastive purposes is seen by some to be part and parcel of the ethnographic field in late modernity (see Falzon, 2009). Moreover, this diffuse world-system approach to the field has raised the spectre of an 'un-sited' ethnographic field, where the generalised, non-localised human condition within the ebb and flow of the global world system is the focus (Marcus, 1998). At the risk of being dismissive of the concepts of multisitedness or 'un-sitedness' (Cook et al., 2009), these field constructions don't really challenge the idea of the singular ethnographic field because the notion of a field that is not solely reliant on geographic space, but rather informed by interrogative boundaries, is able to encompass the singular, multisited and un-sited ethnographic field. Interrogative boundaries are not troubled by geographic or social plurality, nor are they challenged by mobility in ethnography (c.f. O'Reilly, 2009: 144–9). There is no real difference or special significance required in the consideration of multisited ethnography; it's not the paradigm shift it is sometimes represented to be (Marcus, 1998), as long as we define ethnographic fields as part geographical, part social, part mental construct (as I feel we should). The conceptualisation of the interrogative boundary, that is to say, the questions which impel the ethnographer, overarch geographic considerations and tie diffuse, loose, separate, mobile or distant places together into a single ethnographic field of enquiry.

SUMMARY

The relationship between humans and places is complex, with each shaping and forming the other. Through a variety of relationships humans imbue places with meaning. Ethnographers also instil places with meaning, but do so in very particular ways. Ethnography turns someone's everyday place into a thing called a 'field'.

An ethnographic field is not equivalent to a simple geographic or social space, nor is it a mental construct of the ethnographer, but it does require both these elements. An ethnographic field provides an interrogative boundary to map on to a geographical and/or social and/or emotional landscape that is inhabited by a participant group.

An ethnographic field has an embedded question (or series of questions) that impels the ethnographer towards resolution. An ethnographic field, therefore, helps to set up a problem or series of problems to investigate.

Historically, anthropology formed out of an attachment to the remote, exotic field and sociology pioneered ethnographic fieldwork in the city, but these distinctions largely collapsed in the late twentieth century and choice of field site no longer operates as a basis to distinguish anthropology from sociology. Likewise the idea of one discrete singular field has collapsed in the face of multisited ethnography, although this hasn't altered the manner in which overarching questions unite separate geographic spaces into a unitary interrogative field.

A case study based on my home-town fieldwork demonstrated that a field is not always what you expect it to be, and that any place, exotic or familiar, can be constructed as ethnographic. From the most mundane and the most extraordinary, when looked at with the ethnographer's investigative gaze, places come into their own as ethnographic fields.

QUESTIONS

Humans form diverse and interesting attachment to places; they reside in, work in, worship, and extract resources from places. Discuss some of the varied ways humans around the world make meaning of places and the ways ethnographers have described them.

What advantages and disadvantages do ethnographers encounter by conducting ethnographic research in the homes and workplaces of other humans? Are there aspects of the human condition that ethnographic fieldwork cannot properly investigate?

Ethnographic fields are found in all sorts of everyday and unusual places, but what role does the ethnographer play in constructing an ethnographic field? How do ethnographers place boundaries on their research fields?

What are the key differences and similarities in the way anthropologists and sociologists have undertaken fieldwork? Discuss with reference to their origin and history up to the present day.

What are some of the special characteristics of doing ethnographic fieldwork in familiar places? Does ethnography at home involve a different set of problems than that encountered by other ethnographers? If so, what are they?

SUGGESTED READINGS

Read the opening chapters of Malinowski's *Argonauts of the Western Pacific* (1961[1922]), Firth's *We the Tikopia* (1963[1936]) or Chagnon's *Yanomamo: The Fierce People* (1977) for some classic scene setting in the anthropological field. For a classic sociological view on the field, look at the Chicago School's work from the late 1920s and the early 1930s, for example, Thrasher, *The Gang* (1927), Wirth, *The Ghetto* (1928) or Cressey, *The Taxi-Dance Hall* (1932). Jackson's (1987) *Anthropology at Home* provides a collection of articles that interrogate the familiar ethnographic field, and *The Sage Handbook of Fieldwork* (Hobbs and Wright, 2006) has a number of chapters that usefully interrogate the concept of the field, and 'Selecting a field site' from Michael Angrosino's *Doing Ethnographic and Observational Research* (2007) will help hone the selection of a field. Students may also want to look at *Ethnographic Fieldwork: An Anthropological Reader* (Robben and Sluka, 2012). Chapter 3 of *The SAGE Handbook of Qualitative Data Analysis* (Flick, 2014), 'Analytic inspiration in ethnographic fieldwork', discusses the empirical grounding of ethnographic methods. Students might also find the article entitled 'Accessing, waiting, plunging in, wondering, and writing: Retrospective sense-making of fieldwork' (Magolda, 2010) helpful. Marcus's *Ethnography Through Thick and Thin* (1998) provides material on multisited ethnography and reflexivity in ethnography (among other issues); however the theme of multisitedness is taken further by the discussion in Falzon's *Multi-sited Ethnography* (2009). Students may also find solace and encouragement in Sarah Foxen's account of her recent ethnography experience ('What they don't tell you about ethnographic fieldwork', 2015). For more information about space and place, see Tuan's *Space and Place* (1977).

BEING ETHNOGRAPHIC

Every social situation can be an ethnographic situation. Ethnography is everywhere social relations exist; from the most exciting to the most, apparently, mundane. You can be ethnographic anywhere that a social interaction occurs!

PART TWO

DOING ETHNOGRAPHY

THREE

TALKING TO PEOPLE: NEGOTIATIONS, CONVERSATIONS AND INTERVIEWS

CHAPTER CONTENTS

NEGOTIATION

Talking to people is the crucial first ethnographic task. The opening conversations and communications one has in setting up ethnographic projects are typically forms of negotiation and pleading. Negotiation plays an integral part in securing funding, access to field sites, explaining and setting the parameters of research, committing to time frames and potential outcomes, and reaching agreement on the time and effort required from one's potential participants to acquit a project. An ethnographer needs to be able to explain their sometimes obtuse intellectual motivations to a lay audience with the aim of having a project proceed. There are important social, historical and cultural politics at play in these initial contacts. What is the relationship of the ethnographer's natal society to that of the participants? For example, how do international politics affect an American seeking access to do fieldwork in an Iranian village? How does the gender of the ethnographer affect the ability to conduct initial negotiations? For example, a woman seeking permission to undertake ethnographic research in strongly patriarchal settings where such decisions were made exclusively between men may encounter barriers because of gender. What are the apprehensions the participant group may have about the role of ethnographers? For example, have ethnographers previously gathered information for outside agencies, such as the military, or for organisations whose aims were seen by the participants as inimical to their ways of life? Does this community have a history of negative associations with ethnography and the social sciences? The list of potential problems around the politics of doing fieldwork is extensive. Furthermore, the list continues to grow as the world is a place where mass communications and mass movements are bringing together groups of humans who may never have met or heard of each other before, and in encounters there is a growing awareness of the sometimes tricky politics of the knowledge acquisition that occurs in ethnography. Above all ethnographers need to be able to negotiate the ethical dimensions of their research and answer participant questions about the value of the research to the participants (which may or may not be the same value the ethnographer places upon the research).

There is no way to engage in ethnography and avoid these political issues; indeed it is not advisable in some case to even try to minimise the impact of these forms of political action, as they may be part and parcel of the real-world, everyday setting that one wishes to encounter by doing ethnography. In such cases it is best not to try and micro-manage these issues, but to let them unfold as part of the ethnographic experience. The politics of ethnography is therefore not a problem to be overcome; it is a social fact to be negotiated. In order to equip oneself for this fact of negotiation, one must pay attention to the currency of negotiation – language.

Language

Ethnographers work in diverse settings that have a range of language and communication issues. Classic anthropological ethnography was typically done across salient language boundaries, and one of the key attributes for ethnographers in these times was to be conversant in the language of the tribe, community, culture, subculture or society they were studying. This is often only mentioned in passing in classic anthropological accounts, spoken of as a matter-of-fact element in the development of the ethnographer, such as 'I spent the first four months in the field gaining some proficiency in the language'. However, language acquisition is a daunting and ongoing task and anthropologists who study across language boundaries may be able to get their projects rolling after acquiring a basic proficiency in the language, but they will also work at refining their understanding of the language spoken around them for the duration of their research.

TOP TIP 3.1

Don't give up! If you're having trouble understanding a dialect you need to know proficiently for your ethnography to be successful, study local television programmes or performances in that language to see how body language and gestures might also communicate participant behaviour. Informants or translators can also be of great help.

Of course ethnography is also done within language areas, but language may still be an issue at the level of dialect, slang, argot or even idiolect (a language that is particular to an individual). In culturally heterogeneous and predominantly English speaking countries like the United States of America, Great Britain, Ireland, Canada, Australia and New Zealand one can find indigenous or pre-colonial languages (for example Gaeilge, Maori, Yolngu Matha, Cree or Inuktitut); regional forms of English that are marked off by vocabulary and accent (for example, Cockney versus Scouse, New Yorker versus Texan, and the rapid, migrant-influenced English of metropolitan Australia versus the slower, drawn out, nasal English of rural Australia); and dialects or idioms that are associated with socio-economic groups or age cohorts (teenager versus parent language, upper-class versus working-class language). Indeed, one can typically associate linguistic markers with most forms of social grouping or division; ethnicity, race, class, educational status, age, gender, indigenous, migrant, and so on. In all these contexts, across all these linguistic markers, be they salient or subtle, the use or misuse of language or dialect can aid or impede the attempts of the ethnographer to make headway in initial negotiations. Indeed, over time, difficulties with language can severely affect the ethnographer's attempts to find a workable level of acceptance and tolerance from their participants, such that the fieldwork can be reduced to a period of 'standing on the outside looking in'.

To speak or not to speak

It is perhaps a truism that when languages, dialects or idioms meet where the differences are comparatively slight, the boundaries are patrolled and marked with particular zeal and rigour. Take the average parent–child relationship for example. Here we have a pairing that typically grew up speaking the same tongue, in the same household, yet we can all picture the scorn and derision teenagers have for bumbling parents in their attempts to engage with teenagers via outmoded or ill-fitting vocabulary that mark the parent off as 'old-fashioned' – 'Dad! We don't say "cool" anymore!' (This type of scene has of course passed into cinematic cliché.) This example offers a corrective to the advice that it is essential to know the language of the participant group. While it is essential to know the language, it's not always advisable to use it. There are many cases where participant groups welcome the ethnographer's attempt to engage with them in their own tongue, often taking care to gently correct and encourage the ethnographer in the correct use of the language. Yet, as with the parent–child relationship, one cannot expect to gain acceptance by using a language that simply doesn't belong to you. Ethnographers of teenagers will, of course, make a study of the age-cohort idioms, but will know not to overdo their use of it. The ethnographer can too easily appear to be a 'try-hard', someone who is desperate to fit in, if they talk in a manner radically different to the way in which they are expected to by the participant group. The politics of language difference and overlap can be prepared for by researching any existing literature on language of the participant group one intends to work with; however, such material is not always available and simple trial and error is often what ethnographers have to engage in as they wrestle with the issue of language in their early fieldwork phase. In my fieldwork with an English speaking Aboriginal community (Madden, 1999), I had to quickly work out the do's and don'ts of local language convention, and I was not always successful.

Aboriginal English

Aboriginal English is a recognised yet varied idiom that stands apart from the dominant Australian English. In some parts of Australia, particularly the remote north, Aboriginal English is closer to a 'Creole' or 'Pidgin' language that is only loosely associated with general Australian English. In other areas of the country, particularly the more closely settled areas, Aboriginal English has much more in common with general Australian English, while still marking itself off in tangible ways such as vocabulary and style (see Eades, 1991: 97–115). Yet when participants in my research spoke, while I recognised it as being Aboriginal English first and foremost, I was surprised by some of the idiomatic similarities that it contained in relation to the rural Australian idiom that I grew up speaking (after only a short period back home I still cannot help speaking in this manner – a habit that is all too evident to my urban friends who often sarcastically remark, 'Been in the country, have we?' when I return from fieldtrips).

This degree of overlap threw up a tantalising, yet tricky avenue of communication for me that I sought to utilise in my early fieldwork experiences.

The similarities I encountered between the local Aboriginal English and my own speech idioms often lay in the vagaries of oral aesthetics. The local Aboriginal idiom was not a difficult speech pattern for me to comprehend; I did not have to listen too closely, or constantly ask people to repeat what they said, and I could reply in kind, without fear of misunderstanding. I knew when to enter a dialogue and when not to interrupt, when to exhibit surprise or be blasé, when to laugh and, importantly, when not to laugh. Indirect questioning, a well-documented feature of Aboriginal English, is also prevalent in rural non-Aboriginal communities. A cautious approach to giving individual opinions, another documented facet of Aboriginal English (see Eades, 1991: 104–8), also characterises my home-town milieu. The main differences centred on accent and content: Aboriginal English being peppered with Aboriginal words, and in my case, a predilection for turns of phrase that harkens to the ongoing influence of Irish ancestry on my community's speech patterns. What I'm suggesting here is that because of some of the similarities between the two idioms, I find myself slipping back into home-town speech patterns when I converse with Aboriginal people. Such anthropological dialogues have a sense of the familiar about them. There is not the chasm between cultures requiring an expert translator (the anthropologist) I had expected. Further to this, the image of the Aboriginal storyteller has many similarities to that of the Irish–Australian storyteller, that figure who amused, terrified and enthralled me as a child. When my informant sits down by a river bank and tells me stories of *murrups* (ghosts or spirits), eel spearing, land rights or football, a part of me is transported back to my childhood, and I enter into the familiar realm of the avuncular raconteur. Even though the subject matter may be new and exotic, the interaction is anything but strange.

Yet this partial similarity, this idiomatic overlap, was also a tricky space to negotiate. While I had quickly acquired some local Aboriginal vocabulary and had a sense of relative comfort with the speech patterns that were replete with these new terms, I found myself overusing the argot, being too keen too early to 'fit in' linguistically, and ironically marking myself off as an outsider because of my enthusiasm to talk just like my participants. In this case, developing cross-cultural ease was not really a function of language competence, but more a function of familiarity and rapport, both of which took time to build. I learned from trial and error to slowly work up my Aboriginal English exchanges, to slowly build Aboriginal vocabulary into my conversations, in such a way as I didn't appear to be a 'try-hard'.

In the same manner, classificatory or fictive kinship terms (where kin are grouped together under labels like 'uncle', 'aunty', 'brother', 'cousin' outside the categories of an English genealogical system) were a feature of the local Aboriginal speech patterns, and relative social closeness was marked, for example, by referring to another community member as a 'brother' or 'bro' (close), or a 'cousin' or 'cuz' (less close). In attempts to find an easy and comfortable conversational relationship in my early fieldwork I wondered whether I should employ such terms in my own speech. I sensed that this was a tricky business, and fortunately, I did not rush into these sorts of exchanges, for I saw people (both indigenous and non-indigenous) inappropriately refer to others with classificatory or fictive kin terms only to be rebutted. This social overreach was met with phrases such as, 'you're not my Bro, you'd be lucky if I call you Cuz'! Therefore these kin terms were not always set in stone, and were sometimes fluid markers of shifting degrees of social closeness and distance, a living measure of contingent sociality that a novice ethnographer had little hope of being able to quickly find their place in without being 'put back in their place'. It took me almost five years into my relationship with my main informant before I stopped referring to him by his first name, and became comfortable calling him 'Uncle'. This evolution in our relationship betrays an overly cautious approach on my part, but the point is, one doesn't want to rush these things and risk being sent back to the starting line. This discussion of language and the brief exploration of some language issues in my research highlights the point that language is political and has attendant sensitivities regardless of whether the language in the field is a matter of stark language difference, dialect differences, the argot of subcultures or age cohorts, or idiomatic subtleties. Home or away, language proficiency, in the linguistic *and* political sense, is a key attribute in the ethnographic toolkit.

CONVERSATION

Negotiation and the language we use to establish relationships are matters of immediate and ongoing importance in ethnographic work. After the setbacks and successes of the introductory phase of fieldwork the ethnographer may have learned the art of getting people to talk, but has also to learn how to *keep* people talking. The theme of conversation suitably encapsulates this phase of ethnographic exchange.

The act of human conversation is typically represented as a natural behaviour, an easy-going outcome of proper socialisation, indeed 'social life is heavily dependent (in most contexts) on conversation and talk' (O'Reilly, 2009: 125). While we all know fellow humans who are 'difficult to talk to' or who are shy to the point of finding conversation anything but easy and natural, conversing is seen as an everyday act that is an important part of normal human interactions. We could characterise a good conversation as one that will exchange information, fill in time, entertain, enthral and be of everyday relevance, without being burdensome or causing obligations or responsibilities to be created. Non-binding, everyday conversation is 'good to think'.

Ethnographers are always trying to fit in during their fieldwork, and gaining enough language proficiency to cultivate natural interactions and to keep participants at ease is vital to keeping people talking. But just as ethnography causes us to be in unusual relations and to construct places in unusual ways, it also draws us into unusual conversations. The usual character of ethnographic conversations lies in the tension between the 'naturalness' of good conversation and the 'instrumentality' embedded in the ethnographic endeavour.

▬ TOP TIP 3.2 ▬

Having trouble getting participants to engage with you? If the conversation feels forced, try connecting your research to a higher goal – many people are more likely to participate willingly and freely in an activity if they believe their time and effort will help achieve a greater good.

Instrumental conversation

Ethnographic fieldwork leads to all sorts of obligatory, reciprocal and asymmetrical relations. In my fieldwork I became involved in a reciprocal exchange whereby while I was doing my research I also assisted one of my key participants to compile his autobiography (Lowe, 2002). This exchange was enormously important to my fieldwork as it led to a highly personal insight into the life of an Australian Aboriginal family, an insight that proved to be instrumental in shaping the character of my PhD thesis. My participant's autobiography started out as a personal record – he was worried his memory was failing him and he wanted to create a written account of what it was like growing up on the local Aboriginal reserve in the 1950s and 1960s in order to educate his grandchildren. He was initially wary of tape recorders and computers, and could not get comfortable dictating the story or typing it up himself. He needed an interlocutor to create the performance of storytelling that his style of recollection demanded. After a few months of watching me bumble around the field, gradually making some headway in fitting in, he took me under his wing and asked me if I would engage him in his life story as if it were a conversation, prompt him, ask questions and generally keep the narrative flowing. Of course, I jumped at the opportunity.

I was put in charge of recording the story telling sessions, I was then to transcribe the tapes and bring them back to my participant in order for him to make his editorial changes. We drove around the region, we walked across fields and through the bush, and we sat in his home, with me shadowing him with the recorder and microphone. My naïve and genuinely interested questions were perfect probes for him to work off and expand the detail of his story and to give it both an informative and explanatory character. The conversations often took the form of a social history lesson for me (and other subsequent readers). After a couple of sessions I impressed upon him that I thought that the stories were good enough to warrant publication. He thought briefly about that proposition, and agreed he would like to take the stories to a larger audience. I suspect he had always harboured desires to be a published storyteller, and the least encouragement was all he needed to explore that desire. So we went ahead from that point and recorded his reminiscences with an autobiography in mind. But I also had my scholarly ethnographic instrumentalities in mind, of which, I might add, he was well aware. We talked openly about the fact we were both getting something from this exchange, and that it was good that we had found a way to make our individual instrumentalities complementary. Furthermore, the overt acknowledgement of the instrumentality involved meant we could in effect put that behind us and free ourselves up for a more easy-going form of conversation. Consequently, the recording sessions were times we would both look forward to with interest.

The initial part of each recording session was targeted: we wanted to get through a series of set stories that he had in mind for the manuscript. It was after a period of doing this that we would inevitably wander off the track and the interaction became less of a recording session, and more of a general conversation. By the end of these sessions we were usually well off the topic of his specific Aboriginal experience, discussing instead football or whatever was on television (which was always on in the background when we spoke at his house). In effect instrumentalist interaction inexorably slipped into 'chatting'; talk without overt instrumentality. The intersubjective space went from one mediated by a mutual instrumentality, to a more comfortable space characterised by lack of forethought. At least that was the apparent character of the drift from instrumentalist to conversationalist. Looking back however, I realise I learned as much, if not more, about Aboriginal life in my home-town after we had turned off the tape recorder and the interview process had ceased being directed by the task of recording the autobiography. This wasn't simply a matter of reactivity to the recorder diminishing as an influence on the exchange, but rather that from the ethnographer's point of view all conversation from the most general everyday chatting to formalised interviewing is highly instrumental in character.

One never really stops being an ethnographer regardless of how comfortable and 'natural' one feels in a conversational space. The recorder that resides in the body of the ethnographer is always 'on'. The ethnographer needs to be aware of this, as typically the participants one works with never forget that you are a 'recorder' regardless of how comfortable they become in your presence. Instrumental conversation is not something the ethnographer should seek to bury under the cloak of natural and easy-going relations, nor should it dominate an interaction. However, being overly instrumentalist, that is to say, giving off a sense of being greedy for information, of taking without giving, is not well received; a grab and run approach to gathering ethnographic data will have you shown to the door in very quick time.

TOP TIP 3.3

To avoid being overly instrumentalist in an ethnographic conversation, treat the informant as someone who is there to impact wisdom, not confirm your hypotheses. Instead of approaching the conversation with specific information goals in mind, treat it like an informational interview – what sort of research topics might you want to think about?

The ethnographer requires some balance that acknowledges the ethnographer's task of information gathering with the conventions of everyday human conversations (which are not meant to be overly burdensome). So much for conversation; there are however verbal ethnographic exchanges which because of the way they are set up allow a much more instrumentalist or extractive approach to information gathering while minimising the risk of appearing rude or too 'data hungry'. So, if you want to ask a lot of nosy questions, set up an ethnographic interview.

INTERVIEWING

Interviewing as a means of establishing knowledge is utterly pervasive. One can find interviews in many forms of television shows like news reports, current affairs, 'chat' shows and biography shows. Interviews are used in courtrooms and police stations, for oral history collection, and in many other places and for other purposes besides. Interviewing is also a cornerstone ethnographic method and social science researchers are increasingly using ethnographic interviews (Heyl, 2007: 369). The ethnographic interview is prized because it supposedly gets to uncover valid and truthful statements as a consequence of the face-to-face and interrogative nature of the exchange. That's a claim we take with a grain of salt, but nevertheless interviewing does remain one of the most important ways of knowing others, for both ethnographers and many other types of data collectors.

Interview styles in the social sciences range across a spectrum from less to more formal (Bernard, 2002: 204–6). The most informal ethnographic interviews equate to the unstructured conversational exchanges referred to in the previous section. More structured interviews might have a series of key questions or topics that an ethnographer wants to pursue with a participant in the course of a conversational exchange, and fully structured interviews are basically face-to-face questionnaires or surveys where a range of participants are asked the exact same set of questions for purposes of easy comparison and analysis. Ethnographers can use all these interview forms, in some cases employing the range of interview techniques in the one project, beginning with the more informal approach early in the project and moving towards more and more formal questioning as the project proceeds and the participants become more used to the ethnographer questioning them. However, in this text we are going to concentrate on the informal and less structured end of the interview spectrum as these forms of interviewing dominate ethnographic practice. As a convenience we will refer to these less structured interviews as 'ethnographic interviews' (after Spradley, 1979). The engine of a good ethnographic interview is the question, but just as with negotiation and conversation, questions in ethnographic research can be a tricky business.

Questions

Take this example from Evans-Pritchard's *The Nuer*:

Questions about customs were blocked by a technique I can commend to natives who are inconvenienced by the curiosity of ethnologists. The following specimen of Nuer methods is the commencement of a conversation on the Nyanding river, on a subject which admits of some obscurity but, with willingness to co-operate, can soon be elucidated....

I: Who are you?

Cuol: A man.

I: What is your name?

Cuol: Do you want to know my name?

I: Yes.

Cuol: You want to know my name?

I: Yes, you have come to visit me in my tent and I would like to know who you are.

Cuol: All right. I am Cuol. What is your name?

I: My name is Pritchard.

Cuol: What is your father's name?

I: My father's name is also Pritchard.

Cuol: No, that cannot be true. You cannot have the same name as your father.

I: It is the name of my lineage. What is the name of your lineage?

Cuol: Do you want to know the name of my lineage?

I: Yes.

Cuol: What will you do with it if I tell you? Will you take it to your country?

I: I don't want to do anything with it. I just want to know it since I am living at your camp.

Cuol: Oh well, we are Lou.

I: I did not ask you the name of your tribe. I know that. I am asking you the name of your lineage.

Cuol: Why do you want to know the name of my lineage?

I: I don't want to know it.

Cuol: Then why do you ask me for it? Give me some tobacco.

I defy the most patient ethnologist to make headway against this kind of opposition. One is just driven crazy by it. Indeed, after a few weeks of associating solely with Nuer one displays, if the pun be allowed, the most evident symptoms of 'Nuerosis'. (1940: 12–13)

Every time I read this passage I can't help but admire the skilful deflections and counter questions of Cuol as he bats away question after question from Evans-Pritchard. I also hope I never run into anybody like him when I'm trying to conduct an ethnographic interview. Cuol, by counter-questioning Evans-Pritchard, by obfuscating, by demonstrating concern about the ultimate use of the information, by hesitatingly providing answers about his personal and social identity, and by demanding some form of 'payment' or reciprocity, has encapsulated many of the special problems of the ethnographic interview in one short pithy exchange. As I said above in relation to the preference for indirect questioning in the communities in which I have done ethnographic fieldwork, direct questions can be considered rude and discomforting in many social settings, and ethnographers need to understand that an ethnographic interview is not as simple as asking a series of direct questions and getting unproblematic answers. An ethnographic interview is a complicated exchange that while obviously instrumental in character, still relies on many conversational norms and patterns to help it to flow and be productive.

The formation of ethnographic questions is therefore something ethnographers have to consider closely. In order to keep informal or semi-structured ethnographic

interviews flowing one must avoid ambiguity in questions while giving the participant enough conversational space to explore the answer as an act of conversation.
With this in mind ethnographic interviews tend to use open-ended rather than closed
questions. One does not want to provide a participant with the possibility of only a
yes/no answer or a more/less option, as is the case with closed questions. As LeCompte
and colleagues write:

An open-ended question leaves the response open to the discretion of the interviewee
and is not bounded by alternatives provided by the interviewer or constraints on
length of the response.

The apparent looseness of the open-ended interview is deceptive; a good
ethnographer does extensive preparation for such data collection and has developed a
set of general questions to guide the interview prior to beginning. (1999: 121, 135)

So open-ended questions are ways to subtly steer an interview, they allow for expan-
sions and clarification. But they also raise the possibility of getting sidetracked, and
this must be managed in the course of the interview by the ethnographer.

▬ TOP TIP 3.4 ▬

To keep your interview on track without enforcing too much structure, make a checklist
of values that you want to qualify or topics you want to bring up with each informant so
that you can steer the conversation back to these subjects. Don't be too quick to pull
the conversation back though – sometimes pauses, lags and tangents can be opportunities for expanding or elaborating provocative statements.

However, one doesn't always want to be too hasty in steering an interview or individual response, as often the apparently peripheral information that accompanies long
responses to open-ended questions turns out to be relevant in the larger scheme of
things, and can provoke useful follow-up questions. The degree of control the ethnographer exerts over the response to questions is an ethnographic common-sense
judgement that is made on a case-by-case basis, my personal preference being to let
participants 'ramble' somewhat as I usually find they return themselves to the task at
hand, but in the process leave you with interesting additional information.

One also needs to be clear about the distinction between a direct and indirect
question. An indirect question is a less interrogative or demanding form of a direct
question. In the manners and norms of western societies, indirect questions are seen

as being more 'polite' (but of course, politeness is a cultural and plastic concept and will vary from society to society). Let's look at one of Evans-Pritchard's questions to Cuol as an example. Evans-Pritchard asks Cuol, 'what is your name?' This is a direct question. To render this question indirect one could formulate it as, 'I was wondering if you could tell me your name, please?' The second version is simply a more polite and less demanding form of question. However in some cultures and societies, this simple transformation to a polite form of question would not lessen the interrogative quality enough to put the participant at ease. In some situations one must find ways to ask questions that appear as statements or vague opinions, and therefore don't place a direct obligation to form an opinion on the participant. For example one might say/ask, 'your neighbours seem like nice people'. While technically mildly opinionated, this is a statement that will provoke a response, such as, 'They're OK, a bit noisy, but we get along fine most of the time'. Contrast this form of statement-as-question to the direct question, 'do you like your neighbours?' This direct question may be unproblematic in a situation of a positive neighbourly relationship, but where someone doesn't like their neighbours, and also is reticent to express negative opinions (the 'if you can't say anything nice, just don't say anything' rule), then that sort of direct question could be burdensome.

Another question formation issue to be aware of is double-barrelled questions. A double-barrelled question is one that has two or more questions rolled unwittingly into one. While it may seem an easy task to simply ask one question at a time, we can make mistakes on the basis of our ignorance of the way participants group things together, categorise or typologise. For example, take the question, 'is the consumption of drugs and alcohol prevalent in your community?' In societies where the consumption of drugs (illicit) and alcohol (licit) are said to belong in different categories of behaviour, that question is double-barrelled and requires separate questions for drugs and alcohol. However, in a different society that sees alcohol and drug consumption as equally illicit forms of behaviour then the above question may not be apprehended as a tricky double-barrelled poser (of course the sensitivities that may be attached to topics like illicit drugs and alcohol mean that there are other issues in this question to consider, but they lie outside of the realm of question formation, and relate to question content).

Finally, leading or loaded questions are a trap for ethnographers also. A leading question gives an indication to the participant that the ethnographer would like them to respond in a particular way. They are often identified by additional phrases or tags that hang off the question, such as, 'Don't you think? Wouldn't you say? Isn't that right?' The trap here is that these are some of the sorts of phrases that people might use in order to take the directness out of a question, but in ethnographic situations it is very common for participants to want to help the ethnographer they have formed a rapport with, and 'helping' can often translate into 'agreeing with' without really considering the question. To invert this problem of leading, loaded questions can unwittingly entrap the participant, or leave them in a situation where they simply do not want to answer the question at all for fear of incriminating themselves. An example of an interrogative form of entrapment is a question like, 'have you stopped taking drugs yet?' A person that has never taken drugs can't provide an answer and has to go to the trouble of explaining the problem inherent in the question. This stopping and explaining does not encourage a good conversational flow in an ethnographic interview. For someone who has taken or continues to take drugs (assuming shame or opprobrium attaches itself to this behaviour), the question becomes one of incrimination regardless of the way in which it is answered. While this is a rather stark case of interrogative entrapment, there are subtle ways in which requiring a response from someone can incriminate, shame or embarrass.

The overall point to consider in relation to ethnographic questions is that question formation is not a simple act; there are many pitfalls in relation to manners and cross-cultural norms with questions that mean that poor questioning can bring an ethnographic interview to a dead stop. There are innumerable sensitivities that may be attendant on particular ethnographic projects, certain 'no-go' areas of overt enquiry that mean the content of the question will vary enormously from project to project. And while we can list obvious ways in which questions can be problematic (direct, double-barrelled, loaded, leading), it is not possible to give a template or list of a series of good ethnographic questions for general use, other than to say don't make these mistakes. Each project having different ethnographers, with different participant groups, with different cross-cultural or inter-social issues, and different aims and guiding questions, means that in each case ethnographers have to use the rapport, knowledge and sensitivity they develop with their participant group to make ethnographic common-sense decisions about question formation. The ever present practice of trial and error will influence how we build up successful strategies for enquiry. Having done that the ethnographer can then set off and undertake ethnographic interviews with a much better chance of doing so successfully (see Werner and Schoepfle, 1987 for more on question formation).

The ethnographic interview

James P. Spradley, in his classic text *The Ethnographic Interview* (1979), has broken down interviewing into a series of elements that demonstrate the conversational structure of the 'speech event' that is a good ethnographic interview. While Spradley's text is now nearly 40 years old his analysis of the ethnographic interview is still worth some reiteration especially regarding the manner in which Spradley dissects the structure of an ethnographic interview. Spradley suggests an ethnographic interview can have the following twelve speech events (some of which he further breaks down into smaller units):

1 greetings
2 giving ethnographic explanations
3 asking ethnographic questions
4 asymmetrical turn taking
5 expressing interest
6 expressing cultural ignorance
7 repeating
8 restating informant's terms
9 incorporating informant's terms
10 creating hypothetical situations
11 asking friendly questions
12 taking leave. (Spradley, 1979: 67)

While most of these 12 steps are self-explanatory, a few are worth some expansion. Spradley argues that 'giving ethnographic explanations' is an ongoing task in ethnographic interviews whereby the ethnographer has to explain and reiterate the nature of the project, the type of questions to be asked, the way in which answers are being recorded, and the nature of the interview process itself. One needs to be able to accomplish this in a manner that makes sense to the interviewee.

To ask 'ethnographic questions' is to interrogate in a manner that draws out descriptive ('how do you...?'), structural ('what's the relationship between ...?') and comparative ('what's the difference between...?') responses from an interviewee. A good ethnographic interview will give the ethnographer insight into how a participant sees the world in analytical, typological and relational ways, and such information helps to create an insight into the participant's worldview (*Weltangschauung*).

'Asymmetrical turn taking' refers to the idea that the ethnographer should be doing most of the questioning, while the interviewee should do most of the talking. Of course in a conversational ethnographic interview, interviewees will ask questions and interviewers will tell stories, but the balance should weigh heavily towards the interviewee doing most of the talking. 'Expressing cultural ignorance' is used to get the interviewee to 'educate' the interviewer about what they do. Using expressions like, 'I never knew that!', or, 'I didn't realise that you were so ...' are ways to keep information flowing as a form of corrective knowledge, as interviewees are typically very keen to clarify misunderstandings or ignorance about themselves, their culture or social group.

'Repeating', 'restating informant's terms' and 'incorporating informant's terms' are ways in which the ethnographer begins to refine questions and then incorporate the terms or language of the interviewee in order for the interview to be conducted in more familiar speech terrain for the interviewee, and to demonstrate that the ethnographer is learning to see things from the point of view of the interviewee. Such demonstrations are important in building rapport throughout the interview process. As a test of the ethnographer's acquisition of interviewee terminology, the formation of a hypothetical question is a good way to begin the process of abstracting out from the present situation to build knowledge about other possible situations. Again, success with hypothetical questions will depend upon the level of language acquisition and the level of abstraction appropriate to the particular subject of the hypothetical question.

While Spradley's 12 speech events amount to a comprehensive wish list of elements in an ethnographic interview, successful ethnographic interviews may not incorporate all of these speech acts, and certainly need not have these conversations unfold in this precise order, as Spradley's analysis of one of his own interviews shows (1979: 61–6). Nevertheless, of the overall structure of informality and friendliness upon starting and explaining purpose (steps 1–2), working slowly and sensitively through to information gathering and checking (steps 3–10), and finally to informally and friendly leaving (steps 11–12), are the crucial larger structural forms at work in an ethnographic interview. You need to get interviewees to be as comfortable as possible (one can't expect everybody to be absolutely at ease) in order to get the required information and leave them in such a way that they will not be averse to speaking to you again in the future. With at least these three larger elements of friendly introductions and explanations, sensitive information gathering and friendly leave taking, an ethnographic interview has a good chance of being successful (see also Heyl, 2007).

SUMMARY

Ethnographers do a lot of talking throughout their projects but in the first instance they must negotiate with their participants. Successful negotiation in ethnography relies on both political and linguistic skill, but it is not a matter of simply having the 'gift of the gab'. Rather, it is a matter of being able to explain one's research project in lay language and in a way that properly discloses one's intentions and engenders a sufficient level of trust to gain the permission of the participant group for the research to go ahead.

Language acquisition, be it across salient language barriers, or at the level of dialect, argot or slang, is both an immediate and ongoing task for ethnographers. Just as importantly, certain circumstances will dictate that it is or isn't appropriate to demonstrate one's linguistic ability. At certain times in ethnography, it's best not to try too hard to fit in.

All cultures have right and wrong ways of negotiating and exchanging information. Asking questions is not always a straightforward matter, and successful ethnography will require the ethnographer to appreciate the do's and don'ts of negotiating and questioning.

Ethnographers try as much as possible to replicate appropriate local forms of conversation in participant groups, but ethnographic conversation has a particular instrumentality. While one doesn't want the spectre of instrumentality to interfere in an ethnographic conversation, it must also be acknowledged that ethnographic conversations are very deliberate means of gathering information. It's best to have these understandings out in the open.

The ethnographer is a form of recording device that must always be 'on'. At the least likely points in a conversation, ethnographers may learn new and valuable things. To get to this point sometimes requires ethnographers to relax their sense of control over an exchange and 'go with the flow'. But cultivating a sense of naturalness also involves understanding the right way to ask questions and solicit information in one's ethnographic setting. There are many traps in question posing that can inhibit the conversation between an ethnographer and their participants.

Interviewing is a pervasive form of information gathering in most societies. Ethnographers use interviewing and do so on a scale from less to more formal. The informal end of the spectrum, what Spradley calls the 'ethnographic interview', is a key form of verbal exchange in ethnography. Learning how to structure these interviews so that they are experienced as polite or comfortable exchanges on the part of the participants, and learning how to pose questions within this comfortable structure, are fundamental skills that ethnographers need to develop.

QUESTIONS

What are some of the contemporary political issues surrounding the practice of ethnography that shape the initial negotiations undertaken when setting up ethnographic projects? Are there some topics or sites that are too politically sensitive for an ethnographic approach?

Ethnographers undertake research in settings that have stark linguistic issues and in settings where participants may speak the same language as the ethnographer. Does speaking the same language as your participants make ethnographic fieldwork easier? What range of language issues confront ethnographers working in cross-cultural situations?

Why is it that much ethnographic interviewing is of the more informal type? How do the conventions of everyday conversation relate to the ethnographic interview? Discuss in relation to Spradley (1979).

Is it not the case that the conventions of everyday conversation (naturalness, not being burdensome) and the instrumentality of ethnographic information-seeking are incompatible? Therefore, isn't ethnographic conversation (like participant observation) a contradiction in terms? Discuss.

What can't we learn about others from talking to them? What are the limitations of a conversational approach to gathering ethnographic data?

SUGGESTED READINGS

Glesne and Peshkin's *Becoming Qualitative Researchers: An Introduction* (1992) discusses rapport and subjectivity and O'Reilly's *Ethnographic Methods* (2005) has two chapters dedicated to interviewing and asking questions. Spradley's *The Ethnographic Interview* (1979) is relatively old now, but it's still worth a read for its breakdown of the key ethnographic speech events. Bernard's *Research Methods in Anthropology: Qualitative and Quantitative Methods* (2002) also provides some good material in Chapters 9, 10 and 11 on informal and formal interviewing techniques. Heyl's chapter on 'Ethnographic interviewing' in Atkinson et al.'s *Handbook of Ethnography* (2007) is also useful. Chapter 6 ('How to gain research participation') of Jensen and Laurie's *Doing Real Research* (2016) also provides valuable advice on gaining participant trust and encouraging engagement. Also, a guide to the ethnographic interview is available online at www.ccs.neu.edu/course/is4800sp12/resources/EthInterview.pdf. Quick ethnographic interviewing tips for university students can be found at David Jordan's University of California San Diego website (http://pages.ucsd.edu/~dkjordan/resources/InterviewingTips.html). For more information about other types of reviewing, see Adriansen (2012).

BEING ETHNOGRAPHIC

Ethnographic conversation has to have a natural feel to it, but one can't forget that it is instrumental in that it seeks data; but do such data harvesting politely! Being ethnographic means being a respectful and polite researcher.

FOUR

BEING WITH PEOPLE: PARTICIPATION

CHAPTER CONTENTS

Ethnographic participation (whereby the ethnographer joins in with the normal activities and routines of the participant group) is one of the more distinctive characteristics of being an ethnographic researcher. Participation is central to 'being ethnographic'. Of course, talking with people (the focus of the previous chapter), being with people (this chapter), and observing people (discussed in the next chapter) are not divisible ethnographic actions. Ethnographers talk, participate and observe simultaneously; the sum total of all these actions creates participant observation in its broadest sense. Nevertheless, for analytical purposes we can look usefully at participation as an element of ethnographic theory and methodology, in the way we have just done with the subject of talking to people. In this chapter we will explore the idea of cultural and social immersion, what embodied experience means for ethnographic claims to knowledge, and look at some examples of ethnographers being with people that reinforce the key ideas presented in this chapter. Being with people in their everyday lives, through all their trials and tribulations, gives a great deal of experience to ethnographers, but it also enmeshes them into responsibilities and obligations to their participants. Exploring the theme of 'being with people' is therefore a suitable point at which to revisit the ethical dimensions of ethnographic fieldwork.

IMMERSION ETHNOGRAPHY

So far we have come to the understanding that an ethnographic field is a particular sort of investigative domain that is mapped onto existing social and geographical domains. Additionally we understand that ethnographic 'talking' (negotiation, conversation and interviewing) are particular instrumentalist forms of speech dedicated to the task of investigating issues of relevance to the ethnographic field. It will come as no surprise then when I say that 'being with people' in ethnographic research is not simply a matter of 'being' in an ordinary sense; it is not some form of unstructured 'hanging out' with people. While the aim of being with people is to approximate as closely as possible the 'feel' or sensibility of everyday sociality between the ethnographer and the participants, ethnographic 'hanging out' is also saturated with instrumentality. It is a deliberate form of association that is targeted at gathering information germane to the research project in question. This is not to say it is not fun, comfortable, or interesting to 'be with people' in ethnographic research. Nothing could be further from the truth, and ethnographic participation very often doesn't feel like hard-graft, data-gathering 'work' at all. But there is no point denying the instrumentality of successful ethnographic participation; it is targeted, favours certain forms of participation over others and is bounded by the question(s) which drive the research. The reasons for this are both clear and obtuse. Ethnographic projects obviously have timeframes and intellectual boundaries, so ethnographers will take these issues on board in determining where and when to be with participants; one cannot be everywhere and do everything, particularly in the increasingly common rapid fieldwork of contemporary ethnography. Regardless of whether or not ethnographers admit this in their accounts, they will typically form a hierarchy of socially and culturally potent sites at which they prefer to be with people (note that these sites may not be the busiest or most socially intense, for example, an ethnographer interested in themes of ennui or boredom may find quiet, less than busy social settings more 'potent'). The more obtuse explanation of the instrumentality of being with people comes with an examination of social or cultural immersion.

What ethnographers really mean when they say they were deeply and fully immersed in a society or culture is that they got close to 'being at one' with the sociality of their participant group (sometimes, very close). Ethnographers who go all the way into social and cultural immersion (going 'native' as it was termed in early anthropology) tend not to remain as ethnographers and therefore are 'lost'. I suspect this happens more than is recognised, and in and of itself, such a commitment is not problematic as long as the attendant ethical implications are understood in each specific context (ethnographers typically enter fields in positions of relative power to those of the participants).

Ethnographic fieldwork can be highly transformative and revelatory; some ethnographers accidentally find out who they really want to 'be' in their encounters with 'others', and sometimes the person they want to be is not the ethnographer, but a member of the group. While that is a choice for ethnographers to make, 'going native' is not ethnography. The ethnographic manner of being with people is to find a way to get close, but not so close one can't step back again. One attempts to experience, to a very high order, what it feels like to be a member of a particular human group. One acculturates and socialises to the point of being comfortable with representing the ethnographic context, but one doesn't give over totally to the cultural and social immersion. Many accounts of ethnographic fieldwork make much of the claim of total social and cultural immersion, but such accounts are contradictory. If you are reading a good ethnographic account, then the ethnographer must have had the wherewithal to avoid total immersion to return from the field to write up the account. Thus, this is a more obtuse, somewhat elided instrumentality and strategy of being ethnographic. One doesn't simply hang out in some aimless socio-cultural immersion exercise; one has questions and motivations for getting very close to one participant group, but one will never answer those questions if one gets too close. Being with people in an ethnographic context is therefore a partial immersion, albeit, a sufficiently deep and transformative plunge to give the ethnographer a more than adequate simulacrum of what it's like to 'walk a mile in their shoes'. It is from this perspective of 'close, but not too close' that ethnographers attempt to build reliable portraits of the human groups they work with. Being close allows for the ethnographic authority of 'being there' to be parlayed into the text (the emic perspective), while remaining 'not too close' allows for the authority of the critical expert to be present in the text (the etic perspective). The 'correct' form of being, that which finds a balance between closeness and distance, is required to give a reliable and critical account and to produce a more rounded form of ethnographic authority.

STEP-IN-STEP-OUT ETHNOGRAPHY

The discussion of social and cultural immersion has so far been based on the presumption of long-term or co-residential ethnographic research, where the ethnographer lives within the group they are studying, however tightly or loosely one wants to define the relevant human group. But ethnographic research today is just as likely to be short-term and/or not co-resident, particularly as ethnographers engage in more multisited fieldwork, or engage subjects that are closer to their own natal society (as with a lot of ethnographic sociology). We could call this 'step-in-step-out' ethnography; however, some ethnographers, especially anthropologists, may see the idea of stepping in and out of ethnographic contexts as inimical to 'proper' ethnography, which they prefer to define by long-term engagements. In some situations, where ethnographers work in a familiar setting, they may spend only portions of days 'in the field' and return to their homes at the day's end to write up notes and debrief.

■■■ TOP TIP 4.1 ■■■

No matter how long you plan to immerse yourself in the field, make sure you allow adequate time for debriefing your findings. You run the risk of forgetting or missing key experiences if you try to rush the process or save it all for the conclusion of your fieldwork.

Yet even with short-term or step-in-step-out ethnography, the strategies and instrumentalities of being with people are essentially the same. The ethnographer wants to get as close to the participants as they can in the time given, and yet maintain their critical ethnographic position.

In my fieldwork in Australian Aboriginal communities I was mostly engaged in some hybrid form of immersion and step-in-step-out ethnography. As the field site was my home-town area I had already undergone a process of absolute immersion into this domain, yet in order to render it an ethnographic field (as I said in Chapter 2) I had to refigure this familiar field in a way that caused the familiar to become unfamiliar. In addition, while undertaking my research I spent longer and shorter periods of time involved in actual fieldwork. For the most part I was spending two weeks out of every month 'back home' doing fieldwork, and the other two weeks in Melbourne, working on other non-fieldwork aspects of my research. During the times I was in the field there was a curious tension about the status of my 'ethnographic being' at any given point in the day. My main interest was being with local Aboriginal families, in particular one family that I had formed a strong connection with and who were becoming the centre of my research project. Yet I was also very interested in the larger social context, the more familiar domain of my home-town area, and how local Aboriginals and Whitefellas negotiated their part parallel, part intertwined existences. On reflection I can see that all aspects of this research were 'in the field' and that regardless of the fact that I had finished research with local Aboriginal people for the day, and had returned to my sister's house (where we would discuss the day's events and she would act as one window onto the larger community's views on local Aboriginal issues), I had never really 'clocked off' from work. Every bit of information, every scrap of detail about the interactions between local Aboriginals and Whitefellas was consumed and stored by me, no matter where and when it came up. While this had been my home in the straightforward sense of the word, it was now an interrogative space that made me 'be' ethnographic for the entirety of the time I was there, regardless of whether I was with Aboriginal people or in my natal community.

Close, but not too close

Nevertheless, during this time I was nagged by the thought that sitting around chatting with friends and family in my home town wasn't part of my proper fieldwork, and I sought to escape the more familiar domain and embed myself more closely in the lives of the Aboriginal family I was closest to. This family had a caravan in their back yard that their son used when he was in town. At the beginning of my research time he was away, and their other grown-up children had moved out and married, so just the husband and wife were living in the family house. I asked if I could use the caravan as the base for my regular fieldwork visits, thinking that this would be a great way to get into their everyday routine. They gave their permission, but were somewhat bemused. Why would I want to stay in a cramped caravan in their back yard, when I had perfectly good, indeed familiar, accommodation at a number of siblings' houses nearby? Coming from a culture that valorised extended family socialisation and obligations, they thought it odd that I could come home and not be staying with my family. But I decided to overlook their bemusement and began a stint of staying in the caravan. However, this strategy did not bring me closer to this family; it became obvious after only a few days that while they were more than comfortable with me being with them in their work and recreation hours, visiting important places and meeting other Aboriginal families, they were not going to be comfortable with me as a house guest. They wanted to 'clock off' from my fieldwork at the end of the day.

In this little anecdote we have an interesting corrective to the views I have put forward about being ethnographic so far. It's not always the choice of the ethnographer as to how they wish to be in the field; it's not a mere matter of ethnographic strategy and perception as to which approaches to fieldwork will work best for your given project. Being ethnographic is a negotiated state of being that requires one to have some intersubjective understandings with the very people who drove your ethnographic interest in the first place. While these negotiations are not always symmetrical, with both ethnographers and participants at various times being in relatively strong positions of power, they still require negotiation to enable the sort of rapport and trusting instrumental relationships that characterise good ethnography to be developed and maintained. And so it was that I learned a lesson about getting closer to a family in my fieldwork. I would eventually get closer if I gave them space, if they could get a daily break from being in my ethnographic world. With hindsight I looked back at times when I wasn't embedded in the distinctively Aboriginal domain of my home-town area and found that the concerns I had about not being 'fully on the job' at all times in the field were misguided.

■■■ TOP TIP 4.2 ■■■

Focus on closeness, not obtaining closure, from your informants. Sometimes the participants, not the ethnographer, have to guide and shape the borders and limits of the field in which they both exist.

Therefore 'being ethnographic' in this situation was a matter of moving with the flow of people's lives in as normal and everyday a manner as possible (my living in the caravan was not seen as everyday) and receiving all of the sensations, interactions and conversations, from the most mundane and familiar, to the new and unfamiliar, as ethnographic. If my ethnographic field is a familiar space with a series of large question marks hanging over it, then my ethnographic being is a curious and questioning perspective that one inhabits akin to a method actor inhabiting a role (in the field one is never out of character). To some ethnographers, this last statement will seem duplicitous because it may suggest that an ethnographer is one sort of person in the field and another outside of it, a plastic and malleable being that isn't 'true' to themselves. Personally, I don't have a problem with this characterisation of the ethnographer, and see nothing tricky or faithless about the differences of being ethnographic against just being oneself in one's 'downtime'. It may be that some ethnographers are so enamoured with the ethnographic state of being that they never leave it regardless of their personal circumstance; however I find being ethnographic both exhilarating and exhausting, and find it impossible not to 'clock off' at regular intervals.

EMBODIMENT AND THE ETHNOGRAPHER

So far this discussion of being in the ethnographic field has treated the issue at a relatively abstract level, focussing on the intellectual dimensions of immersion in the field and the relationship between one's sense of self and one's ethnographic self, that curious, inquisitive being who places time, space, sociality and culture into an interrogative matrix. But what of the 'ethnographer's body'? How does the subjective experience of being in the field write itself onto the ethnographer's body and into ethnography more broadly? In Chapter 1 it was suggested that the ethnographer's body is part of the ethnographic toolkit, an organic recording device that channels and filters observations, sensations, experiences and emotions into the ethnographic account (after LeCompte and Schensul, 1999a). The favoured way of making the most of oneself as a tool of ethnography is to do as others do, to have the same or similar subjective bodily experiences of being in a particular ethnographic place and time. This sounds like the simplest of propositions; if you want to know what it feels like to spear eels, go out with your Aboriginal participants and just try it. If you want to know what caribou tastes like just ask your Sami hosts to feed you some. If you want to know what it is like socialising with urban youth in underprivileged settings, just go and hang out on the street corner with them and feel the noise, heat, cold, camaraderie or danger of their urban scene. Sounds easy, doesn't it?

Being with people in an embodied sense has the same potentiality and limitations we have been discussing in relation to acts of conversation and developing a sense of being ethnographic. First and foremost, the ethnographer's body needs to acquire some competence relevant to the participants they are working with (or at least enough competence to warrant interest in further 'bodily tutelage' from your research participants). This is not to suggest one need be physically skilful, athletic or strong (or though in some cases it can mean just that). Rather I refer here to learning what might be loosely called some basic body language. There are matters of comportment, deportment, physical attitude, stance, physical distance, purity and danger and gender to consider; all these factors can come into play in the ethnographer's body as they seek to be comfortable with, and comforting to, the people around them. The early days of acquiring bodily competence can be humiliating and/or humorous, but are always steeped in learning. One needs to understand how the participants' bodies operate in certain contexts. How is comfort or discomfort written onto their bodies? How can the ethnographer approximate these bodily postures in order to ease participants or communicate their own discomfort in a culturally accessible manner? How does one use one's hand in communication? Is it rude to point, or put your palms out towards your participants, or to touch people? How is embodiment gendered and what rules or norms for bodily communication does this place on men and women in your participant group? There are so many questions about body competence, it is impossible to list them all, but some examples will help to illuminate the issue.

'Don't look them in the eyes'

I was once undertaking some ethnographic research for a native title application (an Aboriginal land claim process), and was being driven by an Aboriginal community liaison officer to meet some of the senior and influential women involved in this native title claim. The liaison officer and I had worked in the field together on many occasions and had developed a friendly, joking relationship that typically involved him tricking me in ways he found hilarious and I found funny once the embarrassment had worn off. On this occasion I was asking him about the people we were to meet (they were his close relatives, so he knew their personalities very well), and I was asking him if there was anything particular I needed to be careful about, any political sensitivities or no-go areas that I should be aware of when speaking with them. He told me there was nothing to worry about, with one exception – 'Whatever you do don't look these women in the eye', he said, 'they are very *grippy*' (inclined to grab and berate you).

At the time I was still a relatively inexperienced ethnographer and I was trying hard to make a good first impression with these important women. I swallowed this piece of 'body language' advice 'hook, line and sinker'. I couldn't see the bemused expression on the faces of the women as I demurely entered the meeting because I was determined not to commit the mistake of looking them in the eye, but my liaison officer laughing uproariously soon alerted me to the fact I had been tricked again. The women, far from avoiding eye contact, were as direct and deliberate a group of communicators as one could meet, and the fact I had fallen for such a misleading representation of them caused them and the liaison officer much mirth. Having been tricked, the important thing for me was to take my embarrassment in good spirit, to bounce back quickly and join in the joke, as being able to 'take a joke' was seen as a positive quality in this community. The other important lesson was that I was so willing to believe the misleading advice about avoiding eye contact, because, even as a junior ethnographer I was aware of the impediment poor 'body talk' could prove for my research.

The boxing sociologist

One ethnographer who took the task of a shared, intersubjective embodiment with his participants to an extraordinary degree is the sociologist Louis Wacquant. His study of a South Side Chicago boxing gym in *Body & Soul: Notebooks of an Apprentice Boxer* (2004) is a compelling ethnographic account. Wacquant trained in this Chicago gym for three years, sparring with the local boxers, and doing his best to learn all facets of boxing. As Wacquant says, he learned by 'assiduously applying myself to every phase of their rigorous preparation, from shadow boxing in front of the mirror, to sparring in the ring' (2004: 4).

Wacquant (who also works on ghettoisation and urban segregation in the USA) finds that 'slugging it out' in the boxing gym gives him an intimate understanding of the importance of boxing in the lives of the gym regulars. The boxing gym is therefore one of those potent sites within the larger context of urban segregation that Wacquant focusses on. Wacquant's three years of participant observation, being schooled in the 'sweet science' of boxing in the Woodlawn gym, culminate in him fighting in the amateur Chicago Golden Gloves competition. As a result of his dedication to embodied experience he develops a capacity to translate such a physically taxing experience to an audience unfamiliar with the boxing gym and the smell of liniment, sweat and blood.

Body & Soul has a three-part structure which shifts from scene setting and ideas ('The street and the ring,') to the more explicitly 'interior' spaces of the bout ('Fight night at Studio 104') and Wacquant's personal experiences ('"Busy Louie" at the Golden Gloves'). This flow effectively concentrates the reader's focus, and conveys something of the boxers' worldview as they strive to survive, train, compete and win. It also takes the reader on the journey from theory to knowledge, from analysis to the experience of being ethnographic. The density and detail of this text works particularly well to illuminate the boxers' lives and give a sense of their bodily being. Perhaps the most salient observation from this ethnography is that the gym is a site of morality and discipline in a chaotic world; it is not a denizen of ne'er do wells and drop-outs. It is a respite from the immorality of structural disadvantage and socio-economic marginality that characterises South Side Chicago. The gym is a space where work is rewarded and you are free to be as good as you can. The boxing gym, that beloved space of sports journalists, is also a wonderful site for ethnography. Archetypal characters, ritualised roles, magic and superstition, order and structure are all there to be richly described and analysed.

Furthermore, *Body & Soul* is replete with methodological insights. If you ever wanted to convince a budding social researcher of the value of ethnography, *Body & Soul* provides many examples of what it means to learn by doing. Yet the gym became a problematic space for Wacquant also, attractive to the point of distraction, he writes that he became so fascinated by boxing that:

In the intoxication of immersion, I even thought for a while of aborting my academic career to 'turn pro' and thereby remain with my friends from the gym and its coach, DeeDee Amour, who had become a second father for me. (Wacquant, 2004: 4)

Here we have a good example of getting close but not too close; friendship, kinship and shared body experience almost take Wacquant over the edge. Wacquant of course doesn't give up on ethnography, and the reasons are not simply to do with his dedication to his intellectual interests. If Wacquant wanted to continue boxing he would have to negotiate with the less than enthusiastic, and presumably immovable, mentor and trainer DeeDee. Wacquant returns to the gym after his losing bout in the Chicago Golden Gloves to be met by a congratulatory group of fellow boxers. But DeeDee has other ideas. These lines below are from the very last paragraph of the book:

I felt like a soldier going back to base camp after having been at the front lines, I'm so bombarded with high fives, smiles, winks, pats on the shoulder, compliments, and commentary on the refereeing. ... From now on I am fully one of them: 'Yep, Louie's a soul brother.' Ashante is eagerly inquiring about my next fight when DeeDee shuts the party down: 'There ain't gonna be no next time. You had yo' fight. You got enough to write your damn book now. You don't need to get into d'ring.' (Wacquant, 2004: 255)

While Wacquant has taken his embodied experience of the boxing gym to a high level, according to DeeDee, he didn't have the physical competence to make a career of boxing (this is no slight on Wacquant, as he tells the reader time and time again, this is possibly one of the most difficult physical skills to master). Yet this is exactly how it should be in ethnography; close, but not too close. Without that delicate 'social distance' management Wacquant would not have written this book and we would never get to have the transporting experience of reading ourselves into a space that most of us could never hope to 'inhabit' otherwise.

The dancing anthropologist

Anthropologist Kalissa Alexeyeff undertook ethnographic research in the South Pacific nation of the Cook Islands between 1996 and 1998. Alexeyeff was interested, among other things, in dance and ideas of femininity in the Cook Islands, and how these performative aspects of culture were negotiated as the Cook Islands engaged more and more with the global world through tourism. An influential dance troupe who regularly performed for tourists became a focal point for Alexeyeff's research, and along the way she was encouraged to join in on the preparation for the dance shows and partake in the dance lessons. Alexeyeff says she attended:

weekly rehearsals and also attended hotel shows twice a week where I became promoted from spectator to babysitter (of dancers' children) to operator of stage lights, a job that meant timing the lights with drum beats. I also assisted in costume preparation, which involved making fresh components of costumes on the days of performance, such as *ei* (flower wreaths) and *rautī titi* (leafy girdles). I also worked on bi-annual costume workshops, which involved treating pandanus in order to make *pāreu kiri'au* ('grass-skirts') and sewing, screen-printing and weaving other more permanent costume components. (2009: 23)

While the dance troupe was happy to have Alexeyeff participate in rehearsals, her performances in dance routines were restricted to Cook Islander-only shows which were staged outside of the tourist market. The dance troupe was keenly aware that tourists expected to see what they regarded as typical 'Islander' girls in these routines. Again, here we have an example of getting close, but not too close to an intersubjective experience of the embodiment of 'others', and yet again the restriction of just how far one can immerse oneself is not always the ethnographer's to make. In this case Cook Islanders were the arbiters of the degree to which Alexeyeff could immerse, their decision made against the reality of the tourist market and the expectations that come with paying customers at 'cultural' performances. The local Cook Islanders however enthusiastically engaged with Alexeyeff's performances outside the tourist shows, praising and critiquing her development as a dancer and acknowledging her growing understanding of Cook Islander dress, comportment and performance norms:

Learning Cook Islands dance was a frustrating and often humiliating experience. As well as learning the formal aspects of Cook Islands dancing, I also had to learn a great deal of contextual knowledge including how to dance, in what costume, in what style, with whom and when. Foreign representations of Polynesian sensual exoticness shaped my immediate understanding of Cook Islands dancing. The dancers were young and slim, scantily clad in coconut bras, grass skirts, shaking their hips in ways that seemed highly sexual. As I came to know Cook Islands norms of bodily display and movement the picture became far more complicated. While display of the upper thigh is viewed as immodest by Cook Islanders revealing the stomach is not. Young Cook Islands women will rarely wear a bikini in mixed company, and will go to great lengths to cover their upper thighs with pāreu or shorts. Similarly dancing styles—particularly the hip movements of female dancers—while certainly meant to be sensual in some contexts, also signify grace, skill and technical competence. (2009: 23)

In the examples from Wacquant's, Alexeyeff's and my own ethnography the idea of the ethnographer's body as a foundational tool of the research is made salient. And yet it's a delicate and tricky tool to use. An ethnographer needs to educate their body to local performative and attitudinal mores as part of the rapport building process and attempts at 'fitting in'. It is no easy task to inhabit the habitus of another group, because as Bourdieu tells us, habitus is not merely a frame that structures behaviour, it is also generative (1990: 52). In their attempts to be with people of differing dispositions, histories and behaviours an ethnographer has to, in real time, resolve tensions between two generative, historically informed habitus. Along the way there is much scope for embarrassment, frustration and 'body shame'. However the lessons which are imprinted on the body of the ethnographer, the appreciation that flows from attempts at embodied intersubjectivity, are enormously valuable if they can then be translated successfully into text, image or other forms of representation. They set the stage for the crucial ethnographic synthesis whereby an appreciation of what it feels like to 'be' with others is given explanatory ethnographic potency; when it helps to explain to readers or 'outsiders' how particular groups of people use their bodies to make social and cultural meaning. An ethnographic appreciation of embodiment is a central step in developing questions and answers of ethnographic consequence.

THE ETHICAL PARTICIPANT

This chapter so far has laid out an argument for a close, but not too close, approach to intersubjective embodiment in ethnography. The argument has coalesced around the ethnographic utility and instrumentality of being with other people, while preserving a sense of outsider-ness in order to disengage for the purposes of reflection, analysis and writing. In addition to these points, one must consider the ethical dimensions of being close to others in ethnographic research. In discussing these issues I don't intend to make anything of the distinction between ethical and moral practice and behaviour, or reduce this discussion to an obtuse cultural and philosophical argument about the relativity of human 'goodness'. While such an argument is a purposeful one, I will instead be working through this discussion with the concept of universal human rights as a guiding principle (while acknowledging that cross-cultural perspectives can raise many tricky questions about the idea of universal human rights).

Also, I will not be discussing the formal processes of obtaining ethics approval to undertake research with human subjects; this is a process that all universities, formal applied research institutions, government departments and other institutions have in place in order to vet ethnographic and other human research projects.

▬ TOP TIP 4.3 ▬▬▬▬▬▬▬▬▬▬▬▬▬▬▬▬▬▬▬▬▬▬▬▬▬▬▬

Ethical approval procedures can vary greatly across different institutions, so before you start your research, make sure to familiarise yourself with the statutes of all relevant organisations from whom you will need to seek ethical approval. For instance, if your university won't condone any research involving children, there's no point in setting up an ethnographic study within the local primary school!

While these formal approval processes are indeed about ethics at some level, they are also about managing 'risk' and avoiding the commissioning institution becoming liable to legal action as a consequence of the behaviours or research practices of an employed researcher. While institutional risk is a serious and noteworthy issue, I'm not going to be taking it up here.

What I will discuss in a general, common-sense manner are the issues of doing what is right by one's participants (a group of people with a series of rights in relation to research), doing what is right by oneself, the ethnographer (a person who has responsibilities, obligations and rights of their own to consider), and doing what is right by the discipline of ethnographic practice (which has codes of conduct, generally accepted norms and a future worth protecting against unscrupulous research). There is a great deal of overlap between these layers of ethnographic action, but there is also the possibility of tension between their various expectations; ethical ethnography is not always as simple as being a good person. Doing ethnographic research enters the ethnographer into various forms of informal and formal contracts. Beyond formal ethics approvals, a suite of informal contracts are struck with one's participants; participants who have rights in relation to research.

Rights and relationships

Participants in ethnographic research should not come out of it in a worse position than they went in with regard to their safety, welfare, economic position and health. Participants in ethnographic research have the right to know:

- what the intention and direction of the research is;
- what will happen with the data (Thesis? Publications? Other forms of dissemination?);
- that the data will be securely stored;
- whether confidentiality and privacy can be maintained;
- how much time and effort will be required from them;
- if it will negatively affect them in any foreseeable way;
- that they can withdraw from the research if they wish.

These sorts of guarantees are relatively easy to organise in the form of written or verbal informed consent processes, and should not pose a problem for any ethical ethnographer. Unfortunately ethnography has a marginal yet noteworthy history of leaving some participant groups in a worse position as a consequence of their involvement in research. And there are strong critiques which represent modernist anthropology as the hand-maiden of colonialism, suggesting that any and all anthropological ethnographic research was ultimately deleterious to groups who wanted to resist the influence of colonial expansion. Of course the real picture is more complex than this. One way to manage the larger responsibilities of ethical ethnography is to work hard on creating locally meaningful informed consent with one's participant group. Participants need to know as much about the intellectual forces that drive your research as they can assimilate – even if linguistic and knowledge-system barriers make comprehensive explanations difficult, one must try to encapsulate and explain one's research in terms the participants can genuinely understand.

An ethnographer can be both an asset and a burden to a group of participants, and an ethnographer needs to come to grips with just how burdensome their presence will be in the everyday lives of the participants. Think again of the anecdote I told earlier about staying in my main informant's caravan in his backyard. There was a distinct ethical dimension to this strategy, beyond the mere discomfort it caused; the fact of causing discomfort, or shame, or embarrassment or anger are ethical conditions that require resolution. Further, while ethnographers may be oftentimes welcome presences in the field, they may also cause problems for their participant group for political reasons. The investigative and revelatory nature of ethnographic knowledge is not always popular with governments and their agencies who may have oppressive or hegemonic relations with a participant group (for example, this could be true for indigenous peoples in tense relationships with settler-colonial states, or teenage gang members in relation to law enforcement agencies). The truthful telling of an ethnographic story (something we can represent as ethical from the point of view of the discipline) can sometimes be a very dangerous thing from the point of view of one's participants if that truthful narration is also politically naïve.

In these matters of tension between the rights of participants, ethnographers and ethnography, it is my practice to invoke a hierarchy of responsibility that has participants at the top, ethnographers second, and one's discipline third. With that in mind, we can say that no ethnography is worth more to the world than the lives of the people being studied or the safety of the ethnographer. To be less dramatic, no section or element of ethnography is worth more than the safety of a participant or ethnographer. And to narrow down the focus even further, no single bit of ethnographic data or single ethnographic point is worth more to the disciple or an ethnographer than the comfort participants have with the research processes.

Nevertheless, while this hierarchy of ethnical responsibility can be invoked in most ethnographic situations, ethnographers will encounter situations where the degree of human abuse, illegality or dangerous behaviour engaged in by participants is such that one has to stop prioritising research and tell someone in authority what is happening (either internal or external to the group). In such situations, ethnographers may find themselves turning to universal notions of human rights to help frame a response. Beyond that reference there is no more specific template or guide for when these decision-making processes are triggered, and like a lot of ethnographic experience, it becomes trial and error and relies on ethnographers keeping a sufficiently strong sense of their 'close, but not too close' ethnographic being to be able to make these decisions. Ethnographers also need to have considered the degree to which social or culturally relative ethical positions are going to influence their decision making and what will be the limits of their tolerance to different ways of being ethical in the world. These considerations of social and cultural relativity can clash with universalist views on human rights, so this is not always an easy decision-making matrix to form. The ethnographer appearing as interrogative 'body in the field' can have serious ethical implications for participant groups, but it can also throw serious ethical responsibilities back onto ethnographers.

Safety

If everyday life can be dangerous for participants, it's axiomatic that it can also be dangerous for ethnographers conducting participant observation. It is both common sense and ethical for an ethnographer to keep themselves safe. There are the obvious physical safety issues to consider, but sometimes the desire to experience life in a field setting can cause ethnographers to act with a carefree abandon that they would never display in their everyday lives (people on holiday are often similarly risk-attracted). Many ethnographers get injured doing fieldwork, using unfamiliar road rules and vehicles, undertaking potentially dangerous and unfamiliar tasks, overextending themselves in physical activities in order to keep up with participants, or being ignorant or dismissive of the risk of disease; there are innumerable ways to get injured or become unwell in the field. Of course, ethnographers should extend themselves, they should take calculated risks, that's simply part and parcel of being an ethnographer (see Jacobs, 2006). But bodies are fragile things so the risks ethnographers take need to be very well calculated. If in doubt, don't do it.

■■■ TOP TIP 4.4 ■■■

Physical harm is not the only type of risk you may encounter in the field. To minimise risk to your emotional well-being, keep your research and home lives balanced and separate, use buffer questions if a discussion becomes too heated, and keep perspective by examining facts and reframing experiences.

Many of the forces that could bear down in a harmful way on participant groups (state, military, police or others) will not be deployed against accredited researchers who are undertaking approved research. This is a point of relative power difference that ethnographers may be uncomfortable with, but can also exploit pragmatically to do better ethnography, as a certain amount of immunity from external threat can enable ethnographers to get closer to the lives of their participants. But one needs to be careful not to push things too far – in cross-cultural situations it is a brave ethnographer who thinks they know with certainty the minds of the potentially threatening forces that exist around and in their field site. A good ethnographer is a politically intelligent being who appreciates that their work is carried out in larger social-cultural contexts that may on a day-to-day basis seem remote from the lives of the participants, but can intrude with rapidity and force at other times. There has been a lot of work put into the construction of the ethnographer as some sort of 'hero'. One needs to be careful that one doesn't get taken in by this rhetoric to the degree that one becomes 'heroic' or 'brave' – a dead ethnographer does no one any good.

Now let's talk about sex. Sexual intercourse between ethnographers and partici-pants is a taboo topic in ethnography not just because there is a general ethnographic injunction against it, but more importantly because we all know it happens and nobody (with a few notable exceptions) talks publicly about it (see Coffey, 1999: 77–96). Sex can have a role in creating new and enduring relationships, or breaking existing relationships, and sex is generally thought of as a problematic practice for eth-nographers in the field. By and large that is a view I subscribe to and have practised. Sex is emotionally charged, is highly political and in many ethnographic contexts occurs across salient lines of power. At times during my ethnographic research I have been a single white male working in Australian Aboriginal communities. The history of Aboriginal and Whitefella contact over the last 200 years (with dispossession, vio-lence, rape and disease, being notable facets of this contact) has rendered the single white male a problematic category in Aboriginal Australia and I was accurately aware that at times Aboriginal people unsure of my ethnographic agenda were instead suspi-cious of me 'sniffing around' their communities. There was no way I could have an ethnographically unproblematic sexual relationship in this situation; the social, polit-ical and historical forces were too obvious to ignore, and to think otherwise would have been overly naïve and romantic. The simplest solution is to say, as with other forms of risk taking, if in doubt, don't do it. Yet such a proscription flies in the face of the many successful and enduring relationships that have come about as a conse-quence of romance in the field. Nevertheless, I suspect most seasoned ethnographers could point to many more failed relationships that began in fieldwork situations, so as a general rule of thumb, an ethnographer should not see sex as part of the shared embodied intersubjectivity of being ethnographic.

Disciplines and legacies

The final ethical commitment I want to mention in this chapter relates to the practice of ethnography and our attachment and responsibility to the disciplines that foster ethnographic research – anthropology, sociology, cultural studies, and so on. Earlier, I put a commitment to disciplines in the third tier of my ethical hierarchy, yet I don't want to suggest that this commitment is weak or insignificant. If ethnographic knowledge is worth going to all this trouble to acquire, if we truly believe that ethnographic insights have the potential to solve human problems and foster greater understanding between human groups, then the body of work compiled by ethnographers is worthy of an ethical commitment that seeks to ensure that future ethnography is undertaken in an ethical manner, and that past ethnography is critically analysed; criticised where it falls short, and valorised where it meets expectations. In short, an ethical commitment to ethnographic disciplines requires us to examine the ethical dimensions of theories and practices, to think ethically about the overall ethnographic project.

SUMMARY

Being with people by engaging in ethnographic participation is one of the more distinctive characteristics of being an ethnographic researcher. Participation is central to 'being ethnographic' and a cornerstone of ethnographic methodology. Participation can teach ethnographers a great deal about their participant groups, but also opens them up to serious relationships and responsibilities with their participants.

The classical portrayal of ethnography is as a long-term, co-residential practice that totally immersed the ethnographer in the culture and society of the participant group. While long-term fieldwork is still undertaken and is extremely valuable, the idea of total immersion is contradicted by the fact that ethnographers leave the field to produce their ethnographic texts.

However, a notable amount of contemporary ethnography is undertaken on a 'step-in-step-out' basis. Nevertheless, be it long-term or short-term ethnography, co-resident or 'step-in-step-out' ethnography, the ideal relationship between an ethnographer and their participant group is characterised as 'close, but not too close'.

Ethnographers' bodily experiences and their ability to understand the bodily experiences of their participant groups (embodied intersubjectivity) are important aspects of the participatory approach. There is a great deal of scope for learning and for making mistakes in attempting to do as others do. Wacquant's, Alexeyeff's and my own research experiences show that persisting with the tricky business of participation can be enormously rewarding and produce important insights into the lives of our participant groups.

Participation also involves the ethnographer in a series of ethical responsibilities. The rights of the participants and their safety are paramount considerations. However, the safety of the ethnographer and the professional standards of the disciplines which foster ethnography are also integral parts of an ethical decision-making matrix. The tension between moral and cultural relativism and universal human rights further complicates the ethics of being ethnographic.

QUESTIONS

Why is it, with all its contingencies, that participation in the everyday lives of people is seen as so important to ethnography? What is it about embodied experience that attracts the advocacy of ethnographers?

Conversely, could it not be argued that such intimate contact with the lives of participants leaves the participatory ethnographer in a poor position to critically understand the lives of others? Is it possible that ethnography is inimical to critical, objective research on the human condition?

How is it possible to get 'close, but not too close' to a participant group without appearing to be faithless or tricky? Isn't it attendant on ethnographers to immerse themselves as fully as possible in their participants' lives?

How should ethnographers balance the sometimes contradictory demands of universal human rights and moral and cultural relativism? Discuss with reference to ethnographies that you have read.

What duty do ethnographers have to their disciplines and professions? Is it ever possible for responsibility to a discipline to outweigh the responsibility an ethnographer has to their participants?

SUGGESTED READINGS

Wacquant's *Body & Soul* (2004) provides an engrossing account of participant observation taken to a high level; it also raises questions about the degree to which the ethnographer should appear in the text. Glesne and Peshkin devote Chapter 3 of their *Becoming Qualitative Researchers: An Introduction* (1992) to the topic of 'Being there: Developing understanding through participant observation'. For an in-depth review of the politics and boundaries surrounding going native in ethnography, students can review 'Going "native"' (O'Reilly, 2009) and Fuller (1999) in 'Part of the action, or "going native"? Learning to cope with the politics of integration'. Almost every book on ethnographic methods has a section or chapter on ethical ethnographic research.

Chapter 3 of O'Reilly's *Ethnographic Methods* (2005) is one of the better examples. Coffey's *The Ethnographic Self* (1999) drives home the point that to know others you need to know yourself, and raises the issues of self and other bodies along the way (see particularly Chapter 4 'The embodiment of fieldwork'). For an online account see the American Anthropological Association's page at www.americananthro. org/LearnAndTeach/Content.aspx?ItemNumber=12910. The Association of Social Anthropologists also offers substantive ethical guidelines for the research process at www.theasa.org/downloads/ASA%20ethics%20guidelines%202011.pdf.

BEING ETHNOGRAPHIC

Human beings are an intricate and sometimes tricky research subject. You need to be well trained in ethnographic methods to make the most of these interactions! Furthermore, by being ethnographic you have to critically take on this tricky role of being a human with your research participants.

FIVE

LOOKING AT PEOPLE: OBSERVATIONS AND IMAGES

CHAPTER CONTENTS

So far we have discussed talking to people, and being with people, and now to round off the final major element of the ethnographer's participant observation process, we will discuss how it is that ethnographers observe people. Ethnography is, to paraphrase Wolcott, a particular 'way of seeing' (2008). What do ethnographers 'see' and 'not see'? What ways do ethnographers train their observations to produce useful data? And what is particularly ethnographic about the simple act of looking at other people? In this chapter we will be dealing with the act of visual observation, the ethnographic 'gaze' if you like. In the next chapter we will move on to a discussion of how we write down our observations as primary fieldnotes.

The ethnographic 'gaze' is a term that is used to describe the specific way ethnographers have trained their observations on others. It is just one of many types of gazes we can identify in contemporary cultural analysis. Daniel Chandler notes that:

'The gaze' (sometimes called 'the look') is a technical term which was originally used in film theory in the 1970s but which is now more broadly used by media theorists to refer both to the ways in which viewers look at images of people in any visual medium and to the gaze of those depicted in visual texts. The term 'the male gaze' has become something of a feminist cliché for referring to the voyeuristic way in which men look at women. (Chandler, 1998)

As well as the ethnographic and male gaze, there are many other ways of seeing that are framed by the social conditioning of particular groups of people. The phrase 'ways of seeing' comes from John Berger's 1972 television show and book of that name. One of the main thrusts of Berger's argument related to the 'male gaze' and the way it co-opted women into masculine ways of seeing. This argument led to his famous proposition, 'Men look at women. Women watch themselves being looked at' (Berger, 1972: 47). According to Berger the male gaze is one directed from a perspective of privilege, and as such in most circumstances it is typically a 'white male gaze'; a way of seeing that combines gender and race as viewed from a 'dominant' social position. Thus we might also refer to a 'feminist gaze', a counter-gaze that seeks to unpack and critique the white male gaze (among other things). There is a 'colonial gaze', a 'gay gaze', a 'child's gaze', a 'tourist gaze', and so on (Chandler, 1998). Foucault explored the idea of the gaze as a form of coercive power and governmentality and wrote of the power of surveillance in institutions to normalise and order the behaviours of groups of people (Foucault, 1979). The point is that humans have ways of seeing that are perspectival and reflect their socialisation, relative social positions, politics, power and history. This is as true for ethnographers as it is for any other identifiable group of 'gazers'. Ethnographers need to pay attention to the fact that their observations of others are saturated with power, politics and history. A commitment to reflexivity, which I have argued is an important part of the ethnographic toolkit, is also a commitment to understanding how our ethnographic gaze registers and doesn't register aspects of field settings and human behaviours. Furthermore, having a critical and reflexive understanding of our own ethnographic gaze is an important component of being ethnographic; looking at people is not a simple or passive act, the manner in which we process our observations can tell us something important about how it is we generate our ethnographic being.

THE ETHNOGRAPHIC GAZE

The anthropologist Michael Jackson in *At Home in The World* (1995) had this to say upon his first visit to Alice Springs in Central Australia:

Someone I met in Sydney said that Alice Springs was the ugliest town in the world. But I hardly noticed the town. I was looking up at the quartzite escarpment of the Western Macdonnells [a low desert mountain range], inhaling the dry air of the desert. Inwardly I was celebrating something I has all but forgotten—arid places are where I feel most at home.

I ambled through the town like any other visitor, looking at Aboriginal art ... browsing through books on Aboriginal culture in the Arunta bookshop.

What struck me most about the Aboriginal people I saw in the street was the way they walked. Whites moved singularly and lineally towards their destinations, pressed for time, giving no ground. Aborigines dawdled, sauntered, strolled and idled. They circulated in groups. Eddies or whorls in a stream. (Jackson, 1995: 16)

To reiterate, ethnographic fields are actual social and/or geographic domains shaped by our interrogative boundaries. Ethnographic negotiations and conversations are real exchanges shaped by the instrumentality of ethnographers and participants. The ethnographer's body is a real body and yet a research tool charged with finding inter-subjective embodied understandings with the bodies of the participants. From this it follows that ethnographic observation is more complex than just looking at people. While ethnographers do indeed look at people, they do this in such a way as to frame the observations in relation to the interrogative boundaries, conversations and inter-subjective embodiment that comes with being in an ethnographic field. In the above quote from Jackson, brief though it is, we can see his larger contrastive and reflexive agenda; Aboriginal people look different to whites, it's not just a matter of skin colour, but is in their movement, stance, intent and public sociality. Indeed this difference at the level of initial observation is worked up in *At Home in the World* to argue that Aboriginal people have a different way of being in the world to Westerners. Jackson is also saying that he is 'at home' in this setting (this theme is also developed in the text). In one small quote we can get a sense of how an ethnographer's vision is framed by their interrogative boundaries.

Being ethnographic is really a rather strange way of being in the world that attempts to approximate naturalness. It follows that ethnographic observation is a 'strange' way of looking at people that attempts to approximate everyday observation. Staring, an intrusive and impersonal form of overt observation designed to take in as much infor-mation as possible without reference to the feelings of the observed, is a behaviour that many societies and cultures deem rude (but it's by no means a universal injunction), and yet that is just what ethnographers do in their field observations. Ethnographers have developed a 'stare' we call the 'ethnographic gaze' (notice the rhetoric here; 'gaze' doesn't sound as intrusive as 'stare', one can gaze longingly, but to stare longingly conveys a much less positive feel). Ethnographers have to work at developing a concen-trated form of observation, an information-hungry way of looking that is analogous to 'rude' staring, yet they must accomplish this in a manner that doesn't appear rude, overly interrogative or 'unnatural' with regards to the local social and cultural conventions related to observation.

■■■ TOP TIP 5.1 ■■

Many people tend to focus their looks on the scene of the action rather than silence and stillness (think of a teacher watching over a classroom), but the ethnographer's gaze should also include the background and the 'non-events' to ensure the picture of the field is complete and true to reality.

The ethnographic gaze and history

The ethnographic gaze, this disciplined and peculiar way of looking, has a history; we can track the shifting foci of the ethnographic gaze with reference to the dominant theoretical and intellectual paradigms of the day. Ethnographic observers are obviously trained to notice behaviours, events and occurrences which are considered theoretically important at the time of their engagement with the field, and this historically framed, evolving character of the ethnographic gaze is noteworthy. This highlights the fact that ethnographers once 'saw' things in a way that may now unsettle contemporary practitioners. The ethnographic gaze has attracted criticism in postmodern times because of the uncomfortable instrumentality recognisable in past ethnographic ways of seeing. The existence of discomfort with previous ways of seeing and the consolidation of the postmodern critique of ethnography does not mean that ethnographers no longer have a gaze. They do, *and should*. Just because previous intellectual epochs in anthropology and sociology 'saw' savagery, primitive isolation, exotica, cultures of poverty, entrenched disadvantage, and other standbys of modernist ethnography that seem passé and even unethical to the sensibilities of some contemporary observers does not mean that contemporary ethnographers should eschew the notion of a perspectival gaze. So while critiques of the ethnographic gaze often serve to chide previous generations of ethnographers for looking at people the 'wrong' way they can be ironic in that these critiques of earlier ethnographic gazes are themselves new forms of ethnographic gaze that have been disciplined and shaped by the post- or late-modern critique of modernist ethnography (see Clifford and Marcus, 1986; Manganaro, 1990). The ethnographic gaze is alive and well; it has expanded its horizons in the last 30 years, lifted its gaze to look not just at 'others' but back on its own ancestors, as is typical of the critical and reflexive aspects of more recent ethnography. Yet, a bit more attention to reflexivity would cause us to admit that being ethnographic at any time is about taking a particular interrogative relationship with a particular group of people, and that a historically and theoretically framed and disciplined way of observing those people is a necessary part of any ethnographic endeavour, regardless of time or intellectual and theoretical currents.

The point I want to make about the ethnographic gaze is that all ethnographers develop one; our vision is inevitably shaped by our theoretical climate, the people and questions that interest us, and our own experiences, predispositions and foibles. Each and every ethnographer has their own ethnographic gaze that will have similarities to others of their time and theoretical leanings, but will be in other ways unique to their research and their personal relationship to their research. The ethnographer's gaze is much more than the act of observation in a sensory way; it refers also to the 'mind's eye' of the ethnographer, the mental frame of reference through which a particular ethnographer views the world (Asad, 1994). The ethnographic gaze is a legitimate target of criticism, for ethnographers past and present, but it's nevertheless a key component of being ethnographic; as such we should attend to the ways in which we develop an ethnographic gaze, and do so critically and reflexively, such that we may be aware of the context for the production of our visions and their representations, and acknowledge that these may seem passé to future generations of professional ethnographic observers.

The acquisition of an ethnographic gaze, a systematic way of seeing, is something that I found challenging in my early fieldwork experiences. The familiarity of the landscape I was working in caused me time and time again to 'overlook' structures and behaviours, to miss the fact I was seeing things that were of ethnographic importance. As an ethnographer returning to a familiar field I was prone to reanimate a previous habitus, and with that came preordained and selective ways of seeing. In Chapter 2, in the section 'A tale of two homes', I discuss how the mutually familiar landscape of the coast in my ethnographic field was 'seen' rather differently by myself and my main participant. To expand briefly on that issue, when my key participant in my doctoral research first took me out to the Aboriginal settlement or 'Mission' where he was raised I found myself 'seeing' this place as problematic, a sort of rural ghetto, or a disadvantaged enclave in a sea of rural prosperity. My initial gaze was figured by the problematic relationship between my natal 'Whitefella' community and my participant's 'Blackfella' community; I wore history like a pair of blinkers. After hours of being shown around the Mission, visiting the formative sites in my participant's upbringing, having this domain described in terms of attachment, affection and nurturance, I began to 'see' the Mission differently. My vision of disadvantage was not totally elided (and nor should it have been as relative disadvantage was a social fact of this setting), but it was nuanced and tempered by a chance to look at a social space through someone else's eyes; I was able to also see a more complex and ambiguous relationship between people and place. Being reflexive about one's 'ways of seeing' was crucial in the development of my own ethnographic gaze.

So, how does one train an eye?

THE SYSTEMATIC EYE

While the development of an ethnographic gaze will reflect an ethnographer's intellectual and personal views of the social world they are interrogating, there's more to ethnographic observation than referencing one's background. Ethnographic observations are a systematised form of looking at others, that is to say, they are disciplined. In any given social setting, even a low-key and mundane setting, there is too much going on for the ethnographer to either observe or record in its entirety. One would need a barrage of video cameras and audio recorders just to track all the movement and noise in a confined social setting. But what of the temperature, the smells, the emotion, or the information that is conveyed by what people might *not be doing and saying*? In ludicrously non-technical terms, what about the *vibe*? No other recording device but the ethnographer can register this information, and as I say, there's so much of this data even in low-key interactions that no one ethnographer can see and record it all.

▬ TOP TIP 5.2 ▬▬▬▬▬▬▬▬▬▬▬▬▬▬▬▬▬▬▬▬▬▬▬▬▬▬▬

Ideally you should avoid relying solely on a digital recorder to capture information from the field, as certain information may be better captured by quick notes or scribbles on a pad (and nothing obscures good information like technical glitches). If, however, you cannot carry a notepad into the field, use dictation on your digital recorder to record your thoughts and observations in the moment so that you can register them in real-time.

So we must consider that ethnographic observation is partial, in both senses of the word (not complete, and framed by personal inclination). Ethnographers attempt to overcome the limitations imposed by the reality of observing people by bracketing off the observations in ways that will make the task of observation less daunting and more efficient.

There are two main domains ethnographers 'see' when watching people – structural elements and behavioural elements; the 'where' and 'what' of human social and cultural activity. In addition to these elements, ethnographers will attempt to quantify and qualify what they are seeing; to count and condition the structural and behavioural aspects of their observations. I want to take you through the same sort of observation exercises I did when I was studying ethnographic methods – an approach I still use today in my teaching.

Structures

Wacquant describes the urban setting of the Woodlawn boxing gym, where he undertook participant observation:

The gym ... is located on 63rd Street, one of the most devastated thoroughfares of the neighbourhood [South Side Chicago], in the midst of a landscape of urban desolation ... the section of the street where the gym stands has been reduced to a corridor of crumbling burned-out stores, vacant lots strewn with debris and broken glass, and boarded-up buildings left to rot in the shadow of an elevated train line. (2004: 21–2)

Reading this, one can almost see the street scene for themselves, but note also that in such a short quote there is nonetheless a lot of structural information, a street with burned-out boarded-up buildings, vacant lots and an overhead railway line throwing a shadow down onto the pavement. The ethnographer confronted with such a scene, has to see beyond the decay (but not ignore it) to see the physical structure that shapes the domain in her or his purview. Physical structures or settings are important elements of the ethnographer's gaze, and yet these non-human structures can be disarming. Despite the fact we might regard buildings, fields, houses, open spaces, closed spaces and other concrete and material objects as objective facts, ask two people to describe the same building or room and look at the differences. How might another ethnographer describe the location of the Woodlawn gym? The way individual humans apprehend space, the material in it, and the human activity associated with it can vary enormously. It may seem ridiculous, but one has to remember to 'see' these elements in a setting, as they are sometimes obscured in the hurly-burly of human social interaction. Here are some themes and questions to help break down the observations of structures and settings. The first point to consider is 'place'. Look at your surrounds as a location or site. How do you see it – in relation to other places or independently? How does the ethnographer want to begin their own task of 'place making' in these initial observations? Then think about 'appearance'. What qualities are you seeing in this setting? How do elements of the structure or setting relate to each other? Are there any special features? What are the 'social aspects' of this place: What sort of social place is it? Is it a mundane or ritual space? Is it likely that the structures of the setting and its constituent elements will affect social behaviour?

Once the ethnographer has considered the setting as a physical tableau, and moreover one that has the potential to influence human behaviour, then the eye can focus on the human activity within this setting.

Behaviours

It is an ordinary evening. Outside a light spring rain gives softness to the night air of the city. Inside Brady's the dim lights behind the bar balance the glow from the low-burning candles on each table. A relaxed attitude pervades the atmosphere. Three young men boisterously call across the room to the waitress and order another round of beer. ... A couple sits at a secluded corner table, slowly sipping their rum and Cokes, whispering to one another. An old man enters alone and ambles unsteadily toward the bar, joining the circle of men gathered there. The bartender nods to the newcomer and takes his order as he listens patiently to a regular customer who talks loudly of his problems at home. (Spradley and Mann, 1975: 1)

This is the opening paragraph of Spradley and Mann's ethnography *The Cocktail Waitress* (1975) in which they describe the human interaction in 'Brady's' the bar where they undertook fieldwork. In a few lines Spradley and Mann have recorded that they saw a suite of human behaviours. They noted attitudes were 'relaxed', conversation that was boisterous and loud. They conveyed how people were positioned; a couple sat, men gathered, another man ambled unsteadily. Some were old and some were young, and he noted numbers, both absolute and suggestive, such as 'three young men', 'a couple', 'an old man enters alone' and a 'circle of men gathered'. These are the sort of human behaviours that the ethnographer needs to train themselves to see in their field observations.

Structures, places, settings and environments; the concrete stuff of our world influences people's behaviour in obvious and subtle ways. Naturally, structures like corridors or plazas will channel and disperse people respectively, but light, shade, closure, openness, the ritualised and the mundane in structures can influence behaviour in myriad ways. Some human behaviour may seem to have little or no relationship to its surrounds. Ethnographers can systemise their observations of human behaviour and ask themselves the following sorts of questions. How does one 'characterise' the human activity before them? Are people standing, walking, running, sitting or lying down? Are they demonstrative, still, quiet or noisy? Are the participants friendly, hostile, passive or engaged? Are they close or distant to each other? Is it a socially intense or socially diffuse interactive domain? Are communications based on gestures, voices, mobile phones, the internet or all of these?

━━ **TOP TIP 5.3** ━━━━━━━━━━━━━━━━━━━━━━━━━━━━━━━━━━━━━━━

You may find it useful to consider a preliminary set of classifications or definitions surrounding behavioural characteristics you might expect to witness so that you can ensure your observations are standardised across time if you are in the field for an extended period of time or over different days. For instance, what will you define as a 'noisy' social interaction versus a 'quiet' one?

Then consider the many ways in which humans group and align themselves (or are grouped by others), and ask are there social divisions to consider? For example is the setting or activity gendered? Are there women with women, men with men, or cross-gender interactions? Are those interactions in themselves gendered in ways that are reflected in the postures and attitudes of the participants? Are there age groups to consider? Infants, youths, the middle aged and the elderly; are they segregated or intermingled? Are other social divisions or categories apparent such as class or ethnicity (taking into account that such designations are not always readily apparent)? Is one drawn to focus on some characteristics more than others? If so, what is ethnographically potent about these characteristics?

Can one observe intent and impute purpose to the interactions witnessed? Of course there are risks in attributing purpose to observations, particularly in unfamiliar settings, but are there any tentative analytical insights? Can one see effects of interactions or any causal link between one observation and the next? Or is it simply easier and more reliable to see what is unfolding, rather than try to hypothesise why?

Are there observable codes of conduct? Is there a sense of a normative framework shaping the behaviours? Conversely, is there any observable aberrant or unusual behaviour? Is there any behaviour that stands uncomfortably against the observable norms and codes of conduct witnessed? What about unusual or distinctive events, where 'events' refers to behaviours involving more than one person, which have a history and have socio-cultural consequence and are likely to be repeated (LeCompte et al., 1999: 99)? Can one observe unusual collective behaviour that could be read as a special event? If so what marked it off as special?

Quantifying and qualifying

Having considered the human and non-human elements of any particular ethnographic setting one is observing, an ethnographer can 'value add' to their observations by taking note of quantities and qualities. Oftentimes quantifying will involve estimation and in order to add to the estimation one will be drawn to a qualification, and this gets the ethnographer into the tricky area of the adjective, that is to say, how does one evaluate or qualify a setting without running the risk of passing a value judgement on it? Many textbooks on ethnography will caution the novice on the use of such descriptors, but in my view it is better to run the risk of the adjective and the qualifier, then to pay no heed to these elements at all. Pure, neutral description is a fine thing, but so much of what we remember of an observation will be reanimated later by the 'quality' of the observation, so I feel it's best for ethnographers to find a dialogue with their memory that suits the recall of the quality of human interactions. The issues of value judgements and biases in representation are not really a problem of memory, but of later textualisation, and can be dealt with then.

In looking at an ethnographic setting one can make note of the numbers of people. This is not always easy, and estimating crowds is the ethnographer's version of the guessing game, 'how many jelly beans in the jar?' Nevertheless, approximation is better than nothing, and qualifying these approximations can also help to give more reliable information. One may have made note of a setting, and estimated the numbers of people there, but then go on to observe that a room, or a field, or a dance floor, is 'crowded' or 'sparsely peopled'. Such qualitative observations help to fortify the approximations ethnographers make about numbers of people, or numbers of any other element in ethnographic fields (animals, buildings, trees, whatever).

In addition to numbers, and the way in which we might want to qualify approximate numbers, ethnographers should consider temporal aspects of the setting and human behaviours they are observing. One can pay heed to time, frequency and duration. So when did an observation or event take place? How long did it last? Is it recurring or unique, frequent or infrequent? Is there any discernible pattern? Times, dates, months, seasons, all these absolute measures of time are important to consider in our ethnographic observations, and like the disarming naturalness of the physical background to human actions, temporal matters can be easily forgotten in the act of ethnographic observation.

The ethnographer's gaze therefore looks out on scenes of human activity and sees elements that can be recorded as ethnographic 'data' (either as notes, or memories or embodied experience). What is registered as mundane or ritual or extraordinary in the lives of participants, will register similarly in the mind of an ethnographer who is attuned to a setting, but what also needs to happen is the registration of what is ethnographically important. So much in social interactions, cultural performances and the settings of human activity is relevant to ethnography, but we can't hope to 'see' all of this, hence the need to systematise observation, to render looking at people more ethnographically 'efficient' and in order to take as much in as possible. Much of what we have discussed in this section on the systematic eye has obvious relevance to note-taking strategies, indeed the ethnographer's eye is intimately linked to their hand as they record as much of what they see as they can. So we will be revisiting some of these issues in the next chapter when we talk about the act of faithful inscription. But before we move to inscription and text, we need to discuss the other visual element of ethnography – the images, photos or films that are part of textual ethnographies or stand as ethnographies in their own right.

VISUAL ETHNOGRAPHY

So far in this chapter we have discussed how it is that ethnographers look out onto their fields, and how they can train their eyes to apprehend the human and non-human elements of their fieldwork in such a way as to make 'seeing' ethnographic a constituent part of 'being' ethnographic. But we must also consider the impact of images and visual media in ethnography, for visual elements (photography, video and 'hypermedia') are being used increasingly in ethnography (Pink, 2014: 1). How is it that ethnographic subjects and settings 'look back' out of the text at readers and influence their comprehension of the ethnographic story at hand? What part does visual ethnography play in the larger ethnographic project? And what issues are particular to the visual realm of ethnography? In a common-sense way we all know that images can be powerful and affecting devices; they can move people to extremes of emotion, they can add a sense of validity in the way they allow a reader to see exactly what the ethnographer saw, they can pick a reader up and drag them into the text in a way that a purely textual strategy might not. And yet for all their obvious power, images (both still and moving) have not dominated ethnographic representation in the way one might expect from the assessment above. Why might that be so? Before we move onto the relationship between text and visuals in ethnography, we should attend to the types of visuals that are employed in ethnography.

For me, Image is a direct expression of the world we live in, of what we See and experience as participants in that world. Through my photographs and ethnographic explanations I try to provide viewers, if somewhat indirectly, a glimpse into that reality, but also of the surreal of the everyday that we often overlook as a part of our world. My lens and the ethnographic perspective it conveys attempt to provide eyes to the world as much as tools to describe it – its poetry, sadness, mystery and joy. They do not complete the picture nor provide a complete account of human experience, however, to the extent that this work helps to illustrate those small and often forgotten realities, I will feel these visual representations a success. (Ahmady, 2009)

In the above quote Kameel Ahmady neatly sums up the potential and limitations of visual ethnography; images offer tantalising insight, perhaps the sort of insights that could be gained by no other experience but being there. There is also a hint of the passionate commitment some ethnographers have for the use of visual media as a central part of telling others' stories and interpreting others' lives. Indeed this dedication has spread; both visual anthropology and visual sociology are growing rapidly, and in applied sectors there are texts presaging a greater role for the use of visual media in the problem-solving efforts of applied anthropologists (see Pink, 2009). We are perhaps reaching a point when the 'hegemony of the text' in ethnography will be challenged by the ethnographic image (see O'Reilly, 2009: 221). There are many technical and logistical aspects of ethnographic photography and film worthy of exploration, but we will come to some of those in subsequent chapters as we discuss recording data. For the moment I want to stick with the methodological and theoretical issues pertaining to ethnographic photography and film, and shift our attention from the outward looking, projective gaze of the ethnographic author to the inward looking, consuming gaze of the reader of ethnography. Entangled in this author/audience relationship are the participants in ethnographic projects who both look out of texts at readers, shaping their vision of the ethnography, and are already heavily contextualised by ethnographers, who attempt to get readers to see ethnographic participants in certain ways consistent with their view of them. This sometimes tense dialogic relationship brings both opportunity and challenge to ethnographers who use visual media in their work.

And in terms of visual information, the illustrative work of Alex Pavlotski wonderfully captures the movement and context of parkour, and does so in a way that readily transports the reader to the site of activity. Alex undertook a PhD project across Australia and various Northern Hemisphere countries looking at Parkour culture and practice, and his PhD thesis combined written and illustrative text to convey the ethnographic reality of his situations. An example of his illustrative output is shown in Figure 5.1 and more of his work can be seen at www.parkourpanels.com.

Figure 5.1 Pavlotski illustration

The ethnographic photograph

There is a well-worn cliché that says a picture is worth 1000 words. Perhaps, but ethnography is typically committed to expansive contextualisation as part of its explanatory and informative agenda. Ethnographers are known for being wary of 'shorthand' ways to portray social or cultural situations, preferring the long version of the story (a commitment that is related to the ongoing influence of holistic description and analysis in ethnography). Accordingly, a picture in an ethnographic text is more likely to *require* than replace 1000 words. Consider, for example, if one had never heard of the Trobriand Islanders but had seen Malinowski's photographs of their village life and seafaring ways. One could take these photographs in and imagine a tropical agricultural, fishing and trading society, perhaps using stereotypes of such cultures already assimilated in other reading. But the photo itself would convey little to the person new to the Trobriand Islanders. Malinowski did use photos in his *Argonauts*, and used them effectively because the images were heavily contextualised by dense detail, description and analysis, so that the appearance of a Trobriand sailing vessel in the text conveyed, illuminated, indeed amplified one's insight into the Kula trading ring. This is one common use of photographs in ethnography – as amplification devices for a predominantly textual product.

In some cases the photographs are used as simple reference points; an ethnographer describing the setting of their research might refer to a photograph of a village, or street corner, or house, or natural environment to 'value add' to the written description. Two responses are created in such uses of photographic image. Firstly there is empirical confirmation, so that when an ethnographer describes a village of thatched huts on stilts set in a dense forest and a reader turns to the image to see just that, a simple, yet fundamental authority of 'being there' is played out as the reader acknowledges, 'it's just like they said it was'. Such simple reinforcement should not be underestimated. The second response is for the reader to amplify their engagement with the ethnography by 'stepping into the picture' and being more readily transported to the scene though the power of an empirically informed visualisation. This is the safe form of ethnographic 'travel' where the reader can place themselves at the scene with the comfort of knowing it is a 'real' place, just as the photographs show. The same is true for photographs of participants in ethnographic research, perhaps more so. Photographs of participants allow for the reader to confirm the description of the people, to lock into their mind's eye how people 'really' appear, and then allow for a relationship to be built, for the reader to more readily visualise the embodied intersubjectivity that lies at the heart of ethnographic encounter, and which gives ethnography its 'being there' authority.

Photographs in books tell a reader that they are consuming non-fiction (at least I can't think of a fictional tale that uses unaltered photographs of people or settings to amplify a story). Unaltered photographs are commonly seen as empirical data, factual records, and therefore good data in an ethnography conscious of its claims to scientific validity. Of course the adage that 'the camera never lies' is hardly credible as dense contextualisation of photographs in ethnography can make images do the bidding of the text. By this I mean that the same photo of a participant laughing at the camera could be explained as enjoyment, derision, passive resistance or some other emotive state that generates laughter; it would all depend on the contextual strategy that was employed by the ethnographer at this point in the text. We might say that the camera never lies, yet we need to acknowledge that ethnographers can get one photograph to tell more than one story.

■■■ TOP TIP 5.4 ■■■

Use caution in treating photographs as objective evidence; they gain their ethnographic meaning not through what scene they reflect, but through the interactive context in which they are brought into existence.

Despite the issues one might point to with the need to contextualise photographs and the fact that they have a 'plastic' validity, they remain fundamental to the ethnographic toolkit. Moreover, we must not foreclose on the fact that photographs can be ethnography in their own right. A photo-essay is as valid an ethnographic form as text or film, although such presentation is 'courageous' in that it hands much more of the interpretive assessment over to the 'reader' of the photographs. The presentation of uncaptioned and/or un-contextualised ethnographic photographs could in fact raise the question, what makes them ethnographic? What questions about the human condition can un-contextualised photographs address other than those brought by the viewer? This point has also been made in reference to ethnographic film, as the anthropologist and ethnographic filmmaker David MacDougall says, 'much of the film experience has little to do with what one sees: it is what is constructed in the mind and body of the viewer' (1998: 71). With that in mind let's move our attention to moving pictures.

Ethnographic film

If photographs are a powerful amplifying and transporting device in ethnographic representation, then ethnographic film is perhaps even more affecting. Ethnographic films exist as discrete partners to particular ethnographic texts (Napoleon Chagnon's texts and films of the Yanomamo, for example) or as ethnographies in their own right, and increasingly with the rise of multimedia presentations, as coextensive with textual presentations of ethnographic material (ethnographic websites for example that may provide text, audio, photographs and filmic representations; or doctoral theses submitted with accompanying film footage). Ethnographic films and ethnographic texts, while being highly complementary, are also obviously different 'orders' of presentation and representation and do not easily translate one into the other (MacDougall, 1998). One of the key differences that we can discern between ethnographic film and text is the relatively reduced role the ethnographer has in controlling the way each form is 'read' or understood. To be sure, ethnographers can narrate, voice-over and steer the reading of a film in overt or subtle ways, but perhaps not to the same extent as is possible with ethnographic text. MacDougall says of this phenomenon:

Films are objects, and like many objects they have multiple identities. An axe-head to you may merely be a paperweight to me. Films that are inwardly dialogic, juxtaposing the voices of author and subject, may also be outwardly so, by appearing as something quite different to each of them. (1998: 150)

Of course, an ethnographic text may be read in differing ways, particularly if it is one that polarises opinion for theoretical or ethical reasons, but the meaning of the text (whether or not readers agree with it) will generally be less ambiguous than the meanings people take from ethnographic films. As with photographs, ethnographic films are 'courageous', in that they experiment with the authority of the ethnographer.

SEEING IS BELIEVING

The sum total of the ethnographer's gaze, systematic observation and the visual dialogue created between the ethnographer, participants and the reader through still and moving imagery allows us to now say something about the overall importance of ethnographic observation. Of course, by now it should be apparent; we are not talking merely about the sensory and physical act of observation, but also about the mental frames of reference that make these sensory experiences ethnographic. In a sense, we are talking about an ethnographic 'mind's eye' (after Asad, 1994) which has been trained by systematicity, theory and history. This develops an ethnographic perspective, which we can understand in relation to the act of visual observation, as well as in relation to the ethnographic project overall.

Perspective and point of view are terms one hears constantly in relation to ethnography. Ethnographers are constantly reminding readers about differing perspectives in order to fortify concepts of social and cultural difference and to strengthen the role of the ethnographer as the authoritative translator of social and cultural difference. As MacDougall writes:

Anthropologists have taken to heart, sometimes concurrently, Malinowski's famous injunction to 'grasp the native's point of view, his relation to life, to realise *his* vision of *his* world,' and Lévi-Strauss's dictum: 'Anthropology is the science of culture seen from the outside.' It is generally acknowledged that these perspectives are interdependent. (1995: 217)

While MacDougall goes on to problematise the relationship of these perspectives especially in the way it related to visual media in anthropology, I want to suggest that this comment is a worthy way to sum up the ethnographic task of 'seeing' others and understanding how others 'see'. Outsider and insider perspectives are not incompatible, they are simultaneously created and sustained as part of ethnographic fieldwork without the need for a sense of schism (this is usually imported later to enhance the translatory aspects of the ethnography). In the moments of observation, in the real-time of 'seeing' we can be both understanding and uncomprehending of what unfolds before us, we can be inside and outside, and so it should be. This is to be expected in the visual domain of the participant observer.

Ethnographic observation is a complex and theoretically challenging issue, not a mere sensory act, but a theoretical and political act of categorisation and attempted understanding. Like the contracts we enter into with participants in ethnographic conversations, there are visual contracts to consider also. The truth value that is ascribed to images is, I have suggested, debatable when perspective and position mean so much to how it is we see others. One photograph or film can become many photographs or films in the eyes of different observers.

SUMMARY

The ethnographic way of looking at people is no simple matter. It is a systematised and disciplined form of observation that is designed to efficiently gather reliable data. Ethnographers 'gaze' upon their participants and surroundings in a way that is historically, theoretically and personally defined. The ethnographic gaze has therefore evolved over the history of ethnography to reflect the paradigms and predilections of each phase of the ethnographic endeavour.

While previous ways of seeing in ethnography may discomfort or offend contemporary practitioners, each and every generation of ethnographers has an ethnographic gaze that needs to be developed and reflexively critiqued with the intention of understanding how it is ourselves and our theoretical climates, how it is our own ways of seeing, produce ethnographic representations.

For ethnographic observation to achieve its aims we need to train and discipline our observations to 'see' things that are ethnographically relevant and important. Ethnographers need to train their eyes to observe structures and behaviours and to note quantities and qualities of relevance to their project.

In addition to the way ethnographers observe their fields, we must pay attention to the way images and film of participants are presented by ethnographers and understood by consumers of ethnography. Visual ethnography is a growing part of ethnography and the presentation of ethnographic photographs, film and multimedia content is now fundamental to the ethnographic endeavour.

Yet the use of visual material also has its complications. Images and films are not neutral objective facts as they can be viewed differently by different people. Solid contextualisation of visual ethnography and becoming more comfortable with the idea of losing one's authority over the understandings people form with visual media are some ways that ethnographers are dealing with the challenges and opportunities thrown up by visual ethnography.

QUESTIONS

How would you describe the evolution of the ethnographic gaze over the last 100 years? What did Bronislaw Malinowski 'see' in the Trobriand Islands, and Robert Park and his colleagues 'see' in Chicago, that today's ethnographers might not 'see'?

How can we be sure that the problems and distortions we might see in the ethnographic gaze of previous eras are not being replicated in the present? What role does reflexivity have in this particular problematic?

Get together with a fellow student of ethnography and without consulting each other write a page of notes describing a mutually familiar physical setting (campus, library, suburb, etc.). Compare the results. What differences and similarities did your observations have? How do you account for the divergence and convergence?

Again, get together with a fellow student of ethnography and without consulting each other write a page of notes describing a mutually familiar event focussing on human behaviour (sporting event, festival, city centre at rush hour, campus cafeteria, etc.). Compare the results. What differences and similarities did your observations have? How do you account for the divergence and convergence?

Ethnographic photographs and ethnographic film are not 'proper' ethnography, and would have no relevance to the practice without textual ethnography to make sense of them. Discuss and debate this polemical statement.

SUGGESTED READINGS

Berger's *Ways of Seeing* (1972) is not an ethnographic text, yet it is a seminal study of the ways in which humans see and represent each other; it has relevance to the concept of the ethnographic gaze. Spradley and Mann's *The Cocktail Waitress* (1975) is another classic text to delve into; their vision of the cocktail bar is neatly captured in fine-grained description. Sarah Pink's *Doing Sensory Ethnography* (2015), *Doing Visual Ethnography* (2014) and *Visual Interventions* (2009) are useful additions to visual ethnography, while MacDougall's *The Corporeal Image: Film, Ethnography, and the Senses* (2006) is worthwhile for those interested more specifically in film and ethnography. For a sociological perspective, see the International Visual Sociology Association's online journal *Visual Studies* – www.visualsociology.org. The *Visual Ethnography* journal (http://www.vejournal.org/) publishes information on both digital cultures and the visual and digital ways in which they can be studied, and you can find more information about using visual ethnography in Oldrup and Cartensen (2012).

BEING ETHNOGRAPHIC

Gazing at any social situation can be disarming; remember to look for what is ethnographic about what you are seeing! Being ethnographic requires that you see the social in the scenes that surround you.

PART THREE

INSCRIPTION

DESCRIPTION: WRITING 'DOWN' FIELDNOTES

CHAPTER CONTENTS

In Chapter 5 the discussion on observation examined the ethnographic gaze, looked at how ethnographers systematise their observations, and examined the role and impact of visual media in ethnography. All of these ethnographic 'ways of seeing' have implications for the act of ethnographic inscription (seen either narrowly as writing or more broadly as the recording of ethnographic information – written, visual and otherwise). As such, some of the themes touched upon in the last chapter will be revisited here because of the way they relate to ethnographic inscription. What we 'see' as ethnographers we try to capture as information, so in a general sense these initial inscriptions are also 'observations', and as such these two types of observations are often spoken of as one. However, I think there is value in noting that seeing something and writing down something are different orders of observation with their own characteristics and problems which require some forethought to ensure they complement each other. The tried and traditional manner of capturing what we see is to write it down in the form of fieldnotes (although other forms of 'information capture' such as audio recorders cameras and video cameras are obviously important, and they will be looked at later in this chapter). The relationship between the act of participant observation and the fieldnotes that flow from it is a central part of ethnographic mythology. Ethnographic fieldnotes are seen as almost magical scribbling; raw, primary, unadulterated; a window onto real human lives and events. This is a myth worthy of a bit of close investigation and reflexive criticism, for fieldnotes are indeed very special things, but perhaps for reasons other than that which is implied by the previous statement.

WRITING 'DOWN'

Notes of any kind are generally said to be written 'down'. Journalists, police officers, accident investigators and other information gatherers write down notes at and about the scenes of incidents and events. This writing is not expansive, not interpretive , just a documentation of the 'facts' in the most efficient manner possible. 'Writing down' in a note-taking context means to be brief and factual (at least this is generally the manner in which we characterise notes which are to be *relied* upon at a later date). We would all be familiar with the image of a police officer giving evidence in a court room turning to his or her notes (usually flipping open a pocket-sized notebook) to verify details of the evidence given. The implication is that human recall of events taken only from memory isn't good enough, one must have notes. In ethnography fieldnotes are often presented as having these same qualities, and budding ethnographers are taught how to systematically, reliably and efficiently record factual information upon which they can base later analyses, interpretations and conclusions. This understanding of ethnographic fieldnotes as 'factual evidence' is such that in litigation arenas where applied ethnographers are employed as experts, ethnographic fieldnotes are often 'discoverable' evidence in trials. This may mean ethnographic fieldnotes can be subpoenaed and examined to ensure the conclusions drawn in the expert's report are based upon the 'facts' as recorded in the fieldnotes. It is not an overstatement to say that this view of fieldnotes suggests that they form the basis of what we can and can't say as ethnographers.

This myth of factual 'first sight' that attaches itself to ethnographic fieldnotes is, like most good myths, not entirely divorced from reality. Ethnographers should strive to be systematic in the manner in which they initially inscribe, and part of the sys-temisation should be the attempt to reliably record what they are seeing. *Fieldnotes can and should be faithful representations of real events*. However, initial inscription and note-taking is a part of the observation process, so like observation, note-taking is framed and directed by various instrumentalities and agendas, not all of which will be obvious to the note-taking ethnographer in the moment of inscription. Ethnographers cannot write everything down, so the choices they make to record or not record infor-mation are always strategic and sometimes subjective. Being as faithful a recorder as possible requires ethnographers to check for the filtering that occurs between the eye and the hand and to understand that their choices in recording some things and not others make the claim that ethnographic fieldnotes are 'raw' data, problematic at best, and misleading at worst (see Kouritzin, 2002).

▰▰ TOP TIP 6.1 ▰▰▰▰▰▰▰▰▰▰▰▰▰▰▰▰▰▰▰▰▰▰▰▰▰▰▰▰

Keep your observed facts separate from your interpretations or elaborations – when you are reviewing your fieldnotes later, you may not easily be able to remember what information is purely factual and what isn't.

Hand wringing about handwriting

While there are many other methods by which we can record ethnographic field data, handwritten notes remain a central method in ethnography, even though cam-eras and audio-recorders may seem to be better at capturing information and easier to use. There is a deeply personal aspect to one's own handwritten notes, and even though we might strive to keep personality or subjectivity out of some types of field-notes, ethnographers are very protective of them and are often shy of sharing them with others ('Oh, they are very messy, I'm ashamed to show them to you'). I have heard several ethnographers who were working in litigious applied anthropological arenas express deep anguish about their fieldnotes being subpoenaed. I have also observed that this reluctance is evident in students undertaking an ethnographic methods subject I teach. I require students to submit a sample of their fieldnotes for assessment; I am keen to see that they are taking notes in a systematic way, and are also building the analytic and interpretive value of their notes by beginning to code and organise them thematically. These students from the outset develop a protective attitude to their notes, asking many questions about how neat and tidy they have to be, regularly expressing concern that I will not be able to read their handwriting, and asking if they can type them up first before they hand them in. All this, despite my regular pronouncements in lectures that I want to see their fieldnotes in their original handwritten state and that perceived 'messiness' or illegibility are not going to be taken into account in the assessment process. Ethnographers have a lot invested in their fieldnotes, and this investment can manifest as a protective anxiety about sharing them with others, but it is also an intense relationship to one's data that I feel is worth experiencing.

This attachment and protective attitude towards ethnographic fieldnotes suggests that something more than the mere recording of observable facts is taking place in ethnographic note-taking. And that's because it is. In many ethnographic contexts fieldnotes are an extension of an ethnographer's internal dialogue. The notes are mnemonics, reminders, bits and pieces of important information, snatches of verbatim quotes, short descriptions, impressions and feelings that the ethnographer uses later to revivify the moment and more fully describe what was occurring at the time of the observation. The 'interiority' of fieldnotes gives them a private character and for a lot of ethnographers fieldnotes remain a private exercise, with notebooks carefully secured and kept to oneself. Yet this private aspect also alerts us to the role, for better or worse, subjectivity plays in the construction of ethnographic fieldnotes. Subjectivity is a matter to wrestle with for ethnographers but it's not a problem that requires exclusion, rather just a matter for appropriate management as all recorded observations are potentially useful in ethnography. However, one must know how to sort and manage these inscriptions so that a coherent analytical base can be built from these important field observations and impressions. It does no good to treat subjectivity in note-taking as a 'private problem', rather it is better to engage with the fact that the perspective of the ethnographer, their own personal ethnographic gaze, will inevitably shape and form their notes. It is then that one can make more or less from the embedded subjectivity of the notes; depending on the context and the constraints of the reporting process relevant to each ethnographic setting (we will discuss the particular problems of fieldnotes in applied settings in more detail later).

Learning to take handwritten ethnographic notes is something I think all ethnographers should do. We have entered the age of the 'digital native', a time when people are coming through education systems using computers to write and record information from early on in their education process and who are socialising and exchanging information regularly via digital technology. As a result many would say that typing notes directly into a laptop computer is now the equivalent of handwriting, and they are probably correct. At the risk of coming across like a methodological dinosaur, and despite the ready and willing uptake of digital devices to capture ethnographic information, I want to suggest that all budding ethnographers should at least try to come to grips with the task of compiling handwritten fieldnotes. It is a skill that doesn't require microphones, batteries, power supplies or technological savvy. I still feel that handwritten notes have a central place in the initial phases of observation and inscription; this may be due to some form of technological nostalgia, but there is also something about the embodied experience of writing that has a special quality. This is manifest in the protective attitude people will have for handwritten notes, an attitude that is not as strongly demonstrated in relation to typed-up notes. Handwritten notes convey the personhood, the embodiment of the ethnographer, and as such I find them magic and illuminating for what they can tell us about the ethnographer as much as what they say about the participants being observed. So in this chapter I will primarily focus on handwritten notes, but I suggest all the points I make about handwritten fieldnotes apply equally to computer note-taking that is increasingly practised by more and more ethnographers. Our task here is to work again through the themes we explored in the previous chapter when we looked at the 'systematic eye' and work up these points on visual observation into useful ways to consider the recorded observations and impressions that appear in fieldnotes.

■■■ TOP TIP 6.2 ■■

If you're in a hurry or are concerned about your penmanship, pay special attention to numbers and dates you record – words can be guessed, but interpreting a number incorrectly could drastically change your interpretation of your findings. If a number is incorrect, don't write on top of it; cross it out and write the new one next to it.

Digital or 'smart' pens

The digital capture of ethnographic information is increasing every year and with every ethnographic project being undertaken. Various digital recording devices are becoming cheaper and many are now within the reach of ethnographers, be they students or professionals. While I still think there is value in writing fieldnotes (they can capture some social interactions that are beyond any recording device, such as non-verbal communications or the 'feel' of a social exchange), there is a device that allows for the ethnographer to write what they see and feel as occurring, while simultaneously doing a sound recording (as a mp3 file) and scanning and saving the notebook page by page as a PDF file (this file saving option accords with my advice to back-up and save materials). These recording devices/pens are commonly referred to as 'smart-pens'. There are a number of different brands available that essentially do the same tasks, so I don't recommend one brand over any others, but I do see the potential for these devices to bridge the putative gap between physical and digital recording, while avoiding the tendency for ethnographers to rely too heavily on digital recording devices at the expense of one's own notes. As I know from my own practice, digital recorders can sometimes malfunction, and a session may be bereft of any data if the ethnographer doesn't take their own notes in addition to the recording. One word of caution in the use of these devices relates to ethics. These 'smart-pens' can look to participants just like ordinary pens, and they may not realise from the look of the device that they are being audio-recorded, or that the fieldnotes are being scanned and saved. It is important for ethnographers to clearly explain their methods including the use of any recording devices they employ. Participants have the right to know just how their data is both being gathered and ultimately how it will be used. An internet search for smart-pens will produce a range of results that can give the ethnographer options for purchasing smart-pens, should they wish to utilise these sorts of devices.

THE SYSTEMATIC HAND

Although recent scholars have written several volumes ... dedicated to understanding how personal meaning is made manifest in fieldnotes, researchers have made little or no mention of how to describe events, peoples or objects; how to use language(s) in description; how to use or avoid rhetorical strategies; or how to use or avoid linguistic strategies, and why. (Kouritzin, 2002: 120)

The above quote from Kouritzin is a useful point at which to begin a discussion about the way we can systematise our understanding of fieldnotes and the manner in which we record them. Like other ethnographic skills, taking fieldnotes is something that gets easier with practice and trial and error. Ethnographers should experiment with a range of note-taking strategies to find what best suits their style of participation and observation, and most importantly to find what best fits particular ethnographic contexts, as differing field sites and human groups can require quite different note-taking approaches. Perhaps the first question we need to ask of fieldnotes is what sort of data are they?

As I have already alluded to, fieldnotes are often portrayed as primary or raw data, a simple descriptive record of what was observed by an ethnographer. Of course, the choices individual ethnographers make, from the way they categorise and identify themes in their notes to the words they chose to write down, mean that fieldnotes can be rather idiosyncratic records. In reality, it is a given that ethnographers will influence fieldnotes in all sorts of different ways even when they strive to maintain an objective purpose for their inscription. This, of course, does not mean that fieldnotes are not primary or raw data, but that they are a primary record of a particular ethnographer's gaze, reflecting the strategic and personal inclinations of the ethnography as much as they tell us about the participants. In pointing to a suppressed subjective element in fieldnotes, I do not mean to say they can't tell us objective facts, because they surely do, it is just that these subjective and objective elements of ethnographic visions and recording are not easily separable, but are part and parcel of all ethnographers' understandings of the scenes they see unfolding around them. Don't forget, fieldnotes are, among other things, personal documents, and it is not a conceit or a slip into problematic subjectivity to consider one's own personality of foibles in finalising a note-taking strategy; rather one needs to employ a rigorous reflexivity to find a balance between the forces of 'self' that will always intrude in some way into ethnographic projects, and the forces and demands of professionalism and ethnographic information gathering which require us to pay attention to validity, faithfulness and efficiency of information gathering and recording.

Secondly, ethnographers need to understand why we take notes. This seems like the simplest of questions, but it becomes complicated when we look to the uses to which ethnographic notes are put. So, what purpose do fieldnotes serve? To answer this question we can categorise ethnographic fieldnotes into a series of identifiable types that are distinguished by the purposes they serve in the overall project.

Types of fieldnotes

There is a plethora of advice in textbooks on ethnography regarding the construction of fieldnotes, some of which is rather prescriptive. For example, Bernard asserts as a given that ethnographers will need to create a range of notes called 'jottings', 'fieldnotes', 'diaries' and 'logs', and we'll look at these forms in turn (2002: 367). In line with other aspects of what we have been discussing I do not declare that one *must* take fieldnotes in a certain way nor will I argue that ethnographic fieldnotes need to be defined by certain formal structures. Yet an overview of the way ethnographers organise fieldnotes is worthwhile in order to give the budding ethnographer a range of possible options to experiment with to enable them to find a note-taking strategy that is most appropriate for them and their setting (see also O'Reilly, 2009: 70–7).

Fieldnotes can be broadly broken up into two main types (excluding some other forms of note-taking that relate more to project management which we will discuss later). The first type of notes are those taken in the hurly burly of active fieldwork and participant observation (or very soon after) which concentrate on jotting down as much information as possible in as brief a form as possible. The second type is those which are taken at the end of a day's work or sometime soon after an event, which expand the description and might have a more reflective and/or analytical tone. The first category of notes has been called variously 'scratch notes' (Ottenberg, 1990), 'jottings' (Bernard, 2002), 'participating-in-order-to-write' (Emerson et al., 1995) and 'shorthand notes' (LeCompte et al., 1999). The second category of notes is generally referred to simply as the proper fieldnotes (Bernard, 2002; Ottenberg, 1990) or 'full fieldnotes' (Emerson et al., 1995). When most ethnographers refer to their fieldnotes they mean these more consolidated, end-of-day form of their notes. The key distinction is of course participation; the first type of notes are being produced in participatory contexts and the second are worked up from the first in non-participatory, reflective and often solitary contexts.

Participatory fieldnotes

Here we return to the supposed oxymoron; participant observation. How can one take notes when they are in amongst the action, eating, dancing, hunting, swimming, 'hanging out', or driving (in my experience ethnographers spend a lot of time in the driver's seat when travelling in the field, and while moving cars are a fantastic place to have informal interviews they make for dangerous places for a driver to attempt any note-taking). The short answer is that if you have your hands busy in your participation you obviously can't take notes, but in most field situations there are ample opportunities to jot down figures, names, impressions, short verbatim quotes and other snatches of data that are designed to prompt one's memory at the end of the day. In participatory circumstances ethnographers focus on shorthand versions of events, with dates, times, names, other lists, dot points, keywords and rough sketches or diagrams making up the bulk of participatory notes. Ethnographers can step in and out of events to record participatory notes, often within sight of the event as it continues. In some cases ethnographers have been known to schedule 'restroom' breaks or to manufacture some reason to step out of the action for a minute or two in order to jot down something of importance (the advantage of writing notes in a small notebook over typing into a laptop computer is obvious here). At other times note-taking can occur within the participation. As part of my ethnographic fieldwork I attended many community meetings of Aboriginal groups, meetings called to discuss land issues, service delivery and other formal aspects of community organisation. Note-taking in these circumstances was relatively straightforward as many participants in the meetings were also taking notes and the sight of me scribbling in a notebook did not appear the least out of place.

However, there does need to be caution exercised in participatory note-taking; oftentimes it is better to put the notebook and pen down and concentrate more fully on the activity in which one is engaged in order to appreciate the experience of being with others. Furthermore, constantly stepping in and out of participation to jot down notes can disconcert participants and give the impression that the ethnographer is distracted and not properly engaged with the participants (see the discussion on notebooks and reactivity below). In fieldwork ethnographers need to trust their recall on a daily basis, and be prepared at various times to focus on participation over note-taking. But ethnographic encounters can be so information rich that it doesn't do to stretch one's recall beyond the day of the event; there is too real a risk of losing the memory of the orders of events and the participants in them, let alone the nuances and impressions and other qualitative assessments that can be more fleeting than dates, times and names.

Consolidated fieldnotes

Participatory fieldnotes or jottings form the basis of the notes written at the end of the day. I refer to these end-of-day notes as consolidated notes. A classic, indeed cliched image of the ethnographer has them sitting in their tent tapping away on their typewriter, working doggedly into the evening to record the range of observations and events that they participated in during the course of the day. While the technology may have changed, the image of the tired ethnographer working on their notes at the end of the day is as relevant as it ever was, and a commitment to building up a large set of fieldnotes is also a commitment to working through tiredness and preserving moments of solitary reflection in fieldwork in order to get these consolidated notes down (this also challenges the notion of total immersion fieldwork we talked about in Chapter 3).

I make this point about consolidated fieldnotes from a position of regret. In my doctoral research I did not dedicate enough time at the end of each day to recording the day's events. As I was doing fieldwork in a familiar setting, of which I had already built up a rich image, I was relying more on memory at the end of the research process to reanimate the surrounds and the activities in which I was participating. While I did record names, dates, times, places and other quantitative material, I didn't do nearly enough expanding and reflective note-taking. To this day I look at the less than voluminous set of notes from this research and kick myself. However, later work in applied anthropological settings well and truly cured me of my laxity in note-taking, and it was in this professional practice that I really came to appreciate what a wonderful and reliable resource a good set of fieldnotes are. So much later work can be based on a good set of fieldnotes, and ethnographers may never know if they can return to the places and the people they are working with, so one needs to make the most of every research opportunity. Good ethnographers should bracket off enough 'step-out' time to produce a solid set of consolidated notes.

Consolidated fieldnotes are constructed with a number of approaches. Many ethnographers build their consolidated notes as an expanded version of their participatory jottings, in other words, one simply produces a longhand version of the shorthand jottings. Non-participatory notes are also built up by recalling periods of the day when the ethnographer could not take notes as they were concentrating on participation. And finally, there are ethnographers who for methodological reasons eschew the taking of participatory notes during the day to be able to dedicate themselves to active, unbroken engagement with the participants. This 'experiential' approach (Emerson et al., 1995) requires the ethnographer to be assiduous about having sufficient time at the end of the day to properly chronicle what has occurred. For some ethnographers this might mean they spent four to six hours participating in a day and four to six hours writing notes. I have heard that some ethnographers will also go for days without writing notes, and then spend blocks of time intensively recording all they can recall from the past days of participation. This may suit some field settings, particularly where the ethnographer cannot get the solitude required to write fieldnotes on a daily basis, but it is also a risky strategy, as one can never really predict with certainly in the ethnographic field that one will have the opportunity to put aside enough time to recall several days' worth of ethnographic experience.

■■■ TOP TIP 6.3 ■■

While you're in the field, concentrate more on recording descriptive information. Reflective information is easier to write down during your breaks or debrief sessions at the end of the day. However, if an important connection or analytical thought occurs in the field, write it down as soon as possible.

It is a much more sensible strategy to take consolidated notes on a daily basis, and personally I prefer those consolidated notes to be based on a mixture of participatory notes and recall of non-note-taking periods. The immediacy of the notes is greatly enhanced by a daily schedule, and should unforeseen circumstances interfere in daily note-taking (and in ethnography one can almost be guaranteed of being disrupted), the ethnographer at least has the chance to catch up using relatively fresh recall on the following day.

Other forms of fieldnotes

In addition to participatory jottings and consolidated fieldnotes, Bernard identifies two other forms of fieldnotes; the 'diary' and the 'log' (2002: 367). Bernard says the diary:

... is personal. It's a place where you can run and hide when things get tough. You absolutely need a diary ... It will help you deal with loneliness, fear, and other emotions that make fieldwork difficult. (2002: 369)

Many ethnographers find this advice compelling and do keep a separate diary dedicated to the more emotional, personal and subjective aspects of their experiences in the field. However, many ethnographers do not see the need to keep such thoughts separate from their consolidated fieldnotes, and do not see this type of information as a 'contaminant' (I certainly didn't feel the need to keep a separate diary). Indeed, depending on the aims and theoretical influences of the project (an overtly reflexive approach for example) such information may be best placed in the consolidated notes. As such, ethnographers do not absolutely *need* a diary, but many find them a useful device for managing the potentially tense relationship between their ethnographic being and their private being. If extreme emotional experiences and feelings threaten to 'contaminate' the ethnographic experience, then by all means keep a diary, but also be wary of the assumed therapeutic quality of taking the 'writing cure' to dissipate or manage negative feelings. Committing discomfort, negativity or fear to paper does not necessarily cause the conditions that created these feelings to dissipate. If ethnographers have real and substantive fears in relation to their field, they need to do more than write them down; they need to mitigate them through negotiation, by building up more trust or by removing themselves from danger.

The 'log' is a form of daily tracking device that measures progress in fieldwork against the plans that were entered at the start of the fieldwork. As Bernard says a log helps to keep a systematic approach to the gathering of ethnographic data. As with the diary a log is not something that I have used in fieldwork, as I have always entered my planning and outcomes as part of my consolidated notes. But in certain situations where the ethnographer has to regularly report to an employer, university or funding agency on the progress of field research, a separate log that can be disseminated without disclosing the rest of the, sometimes sensitive or confidential, field data is a very useful record. Again, this is a 'horses for courses' situation – it is not a given that every ethnographer will need or want to keep a log – but if your research requires a marker of research progress and a ready tool for research grant acquittal then a log will accomplish these tasks.

The 'one notebook fits all' approach

As I have alluded to above, there is more than one way to build up fieldnotes, and my practice has been to keep the process as simple as possible by having a single notebook that includes all of the participatory, consolidated, reflective and planning aspects of fieldnotes. As I said earlier I prefer to handwrite my consolidated notes, although I realise that many ethnographers will take the opportunity to enter their consolidated notes straight into a word processing program or indeed into qualitative software.

In the case of large long-term ethnographic projects the advantages of digitising notes earlier rather than later are evident; they are far easier to index and search in this form. Obviously ethnographers will often find it advantageous to have a small pocket-sized pad for the participatory notes, but in these cases I would cut and paste these notes into my notebook (or type in the jottings before expanding the consolidated notes if I were using a computer). I like to see the jottings immediately preceding the consolidated notes in my work as I can look back at a glance and see how I expanded upon particular jottings and whether after some time there might be more (or less) I would want to make of these participatory notes. I like to have the evolution of the notes as apparent as possible, hence my preference where possible to have them in the same notebook. Some might be concerned to see all the 'eggs in one basket', but I generally found it more user-friendly and less unwieldy to carry one notebook instead of four. However, notebook security is particularly pertinent with this strategy (as it is with all fieldnotes). I will look at this aspect more fully in the next chapter when I talk about data management, but as a prelude one should develop a mantra that goes something like: BACK-UP, BACK-UP, BACK-UP, COPY, COPY, COPY, SAVE, SAVE, SAVE, SECURE, SECURE, SECURE.

Notebooks and reactivity

Another thing to consider, particularly in relation to participatory fieldnotes, is that participants can view notebooks differently than the ethnographer. Reactivity describes the fact that participants may 'react' to the ethnographer or the ethnographer's technique of recording information (notebook, camera, microphone, etc.). These reactions are seen as a problem because they typically affect the natural flow of events that the ethnographer was trying to capture. As such ethnographers should try to minimise these reactions. Reactivity is an issue with all forms of technology ethnographers bring to the field. In certain contexts technology such as cameras and audio and video recorders can cause a great deal of reactivity, ranging from anxiety about their presence to people 'acting up to' or behaving in an exaggerated way in the presence of these types of recording devices. But such problems are not limited to recording devices; something as simple as a pen and a piece of paper being used in the presence of participants can radically affect the tone of the interaction and limit the ethnographic value of the exchange. Once I was undertaking an informal interview with an Aboriginal participant and I had my notebook inside a clipboard, which to another Aboriginal person who walked in on the interview looked too much like a 'police interview' or interrogation. He became rather defensive about my presence and it took a bit of explanation to settle the situation down (in fact, being regularly mistaken for an 'interrogator' meant that one of the first Aboriginal words from my field site that I learned was the term for policeman – *Djungah* – so that I could say in these situations, 'don't worry mate, I'm not a *Djungah*').

However, negative reactivity is not always the problem, as I have sometimes begun informal interviews without a notebook seeking to ease people into 'chatting' with me, only to be asked why I wasn't writing everything down and taking lots of pictures. Some informants 'react' to ethnographic situations by becoming exaggerated ethnographic characters whose every word and gesture must be recorded. One can't always be sure how participants will react when faced with a notebook, but an ethnographer who wants to keep a positive interaction with a participant has to be prepared to put down the pen and paper, and in some cases, to put the notebook out of sight in order to continue their ethnographic conversation.

WHAT GOES INTO NOTEBOOKS

Here we need to revisit the systematic approach to ethnographic observation we discussed in Chapter 5. The act of 'seeing' structure and behaviours of ethnographic importance also requires us to think systematically about how we might jot down or consolidate a description of structures and behaviours. What ethnographers aim for is the ability to inscribe their ethnographic gaze, and while this might seem to be a relatively straightforward process of description, the ways we see the world do not always translate easily into ways we might write about it. In my experience it's best to think about a descriptive language that can accommodate the list of attributes we discussed in relation to the ethnographic gaze. A descriptive toolkit is something the ethnographer will need to take with them into field settings, but they also need to be prepared to add to or subtract from this toolkit as the process of trial and error clarifies the best ways to record what they are seeing. Regardless of what you as ethnographer write down, always leave a good margin in your fieldnotes so that in subsequent analysis you can write in topical codes and indexing information without overwriting the original fieldnotes (we'll look at codes and indexing in Chapter 7 when we deal with data analysis).

TOP TIP 6.4

In addition to leaving decent margins in your notes, make sure to record the date, time, page number, and name of participant at the top of every page to preserve the chronological order if they get jumbled or confused with another day's notes.

Structures

We have already mentioned that physical structures or settings can be disarming in that they have a taken for granted quality, that is to say, they can be difficult to 'see' ethnographically. It is one thing to say that some human activity is taking place in a building, field, house, open or closed space, but an ethnographer needs recourse to language that gives more of the character and quality of the setting. Of course adjectives and adverbs are the obvious place to start, but here the different styles of fieldnotes ethnographers chose to create will influence decisions on this matter. If one is keen to separate any value judgements out from their consolidated notes then buildings might be 'tall', 'brown', 'brick and steel edifices' or 'built in the style of Frank Lloyd Wright', for example. However if one were to write fieldnotes in a way that didn't filter out more subjective and value-laden expressions, then buildings might be all of those things just listed as well as 'ugly', 'imposing', 'old fashioned', or 'beautiful'. Time and time again ethnographers will be told not to bring value-laden language into any part of their fieldnotes, analysis and writing up. However, I don't necessarily have a problem with this as far as fieldnotes are concerned. If the ethnographer sees the fieldnotes as personal documents, as long as they are aware of the problems value judgements make for ethnographic analysis and conclusions, I don't have a problem with them forming part of a fieldnote strategy. The reason is because these familiar, introspective and value-laden judgements make for good shorthand mnemonics. An ethnographer is in dialogue with themselves through their fieldnotes and will know exactly what they mean when they see their description of an 'ugly brown old-fashioned Frank-Lloyd-Wright-type of building'. So, as an extension of our discussion on how to 'see' ethnographic structures and behaviours, ethnographers need to think about how best to 'write' them.

Behaviours

Because human behaviour is socially and culturally coded, because different human groups and individuals see behaviour differently, the description of behaviours is both a writing and cultural challenge. To borrow the title of an influential collection of essays on anthropological writing, it is a 'writing culture' challenge (Clifford and Marcus, 1986). In writing about human behaviours we need to pay attention to sorting the winks from the blinks, the grins from the grimaces, and finding the right words to convey such differences. Typically ethnographers are encouraged to find as neutral and objective a language as possible in order not to project their culturally framed appreciation of body gestures and comportment onto the human behaviours being recorded. This is sensible advice and developing a language that avoids the pitfalls of ethnocentrism is something all ethnographers have to do at some stage, so they may as well start with their fieldnotes. However, once again I caution about being overly prescriptive in this regard. While one certainly doesn't want to see biased and negative characterisations of other humans' behaviours contaminating fieldnotes, subjective description of human behaviour need not be ethnocentric or problematic, indeed recourse to more subjective or personal portrayals of human behaviour may be the best way for the ethnographer to initially inscribe and then reanimate these behaviours later when they are writing up. One simply needs to be able to distinguish between these positive and negative forms of subjectivity.

Describing human movement is particularly difficult to do without highly qualitative language that could be seen by some as subjective of judgement. When an ethnographer sees people standing, walking, running, sitting or lying down, one could be forgiven for describing that they are standing forlornly, walking stiffly, running wildly, sitting comfortably or lying lazily, for example. In this context the evocative adverbs 'forlornly', 'stiffly', 'wildly', 'comfortably', and 'lazily' will convey much more of the scene to the ethnographer when they come to revisit it, and yet these terms are also potentially culturally loaded, and may miscast the observed people in a negative light. As long as this language was part of the initial fieldnotes, as long as the internal dialogue an ethnographer has with their notes appreciates such terms as providing useful mnemonics, and as long as such phrasing wasn't transposed into the later writing up texts without due critical consideration, I wouldn't have a problem with this language in fieldnotes, especially if such terminology enabled the ethnographer to better recall the nuances and subtleties of human behaviour and the corporeal ways of the participants. Ethnographers are culturally and socially formed humans just like any other, and in the rush of fieldnote taking one shouldn't be too hard on oneself if subjective language finds its way into the notes, but one should be alert to uncritical and baldly biased phrasing making its way up through the inscription process.

Diagrams

One way to complement the words that are in fieldnotes is to add diagrams that can help reinforce descriptions of structures, movements and behaviour. Quickly sketched plans of physical layouts and the spatial relationships of structures to each other and to people, can add a great deal of descriptive value to fieldnotes. One doesn't need to be overly mindful of scale or perspective or spatial accuracy; the diagram simply needs sufficient detail to take the ethnographer back into that space or behavioural context, and sufficient detail to remind the ethnographer of the relationships between objects and people. The places people take relative to each other when they come into a room and sit down, the ways people move across an open space (use arrows and pointers), the spatial relationships between houses in a small community or village, the patterns on clothing, the topography of the landscape, all of these visual facets can be easily sketched as diagrams and in a way that allows for a much better quality written description later on. Of course, such diagrams are much more easily and quickly drafted by hand, so even if an ethnographer is entering fieldnotes straight into a computer, one should have pen and paper ready to jot down diagrams (these can be scanned and later entered into the electronic fieldnotes as image files).

Photographs, audio and film

Cameras, audio and video recorders should be considered as part of one's fieldnote strategy, and ethnographers need to think critically about using these technologies in the field. Cameras, audio and video recorders can be used to amass huge amounts of ethnographic field data; as such I will have more to say about them in the next chapter when we look at data management, but there are a few things to note about these technologies and the way they can complement my old-fashioned approach to handwritten fieldnotes. The key term here is 'complement', for many times I have seen ethnographers treat cameras and recording devices as alternatives to fieldnotes, so that when the camera or recorder is switched on the ethnographer somehow feels they can switch off. Nothing could be further from the truth. Again, this is a lesson learnt from bitter experience. In my case I was prone to forget to take notes of my own when I was audio recording informal interviews. While the tape captured all the content and tone of the verbal exchanges (a lot of data in itself), the recorder could not capture body language, posture, facial expressions, or my feelings and sense of my participant's feelings. All of this non-verbal communication, which is such an important part of the way humans communicate, is lost to an audio recorder. So switching on an audio recorder is not an opportunity to put the pen down.

What of film? It's true that a video recorder observing an informal interview or other human behaviour will capture a lot (but not all) of the non-verbal communication that takes place between humans, but it won't record what the ethnographer is thinking about the participants, and there is no guarantee that watching a film again will transport you back to the same frame of mind, to reproduce the same questions and impression you had originally. Well shot raw ethnographic footage is an undeniably rich source of data, but for all its power it cannot compete with the ability of the human mind to capture the nuance of experience. So, as with audio recorders, it is best to take notes when filming, as fieldnotes are an extension of the mind of the ethnographer in a way an audio or video tape can never be.

Photographs are perhaps less likely to hijack the fieldnote-taking process than audio or video recording, as typically ethnographers see photographs as complementary field information. However, photographs are sometimes used as an alternative to drawing sketches. This is a habit I would refrain from, for the reason that sketches, like fieldnotes, are an extension of the ethnographer's mind in a way that a photograph can never be. By all means do both, as the combination of photographs and hand-drawn diagrams builds up a valuable record of the visual and spatial aspects of the field setting, but remember that a sketch or diagram allows the ethnographer to stress or exaggerate aspects of the setting or behaviour that they most wish to be reminded of. Sketches can be partial and discriminatory, including only what the ethnographer wants to 'see' in a scene. They are potentially better mnemonic devices than photographs because of the mental and physical effort that goes into constructing them. At the very least a note should be made of where and when photos were taken so they can be placed in the proper context of the fieldnotes at a later stage.

FIELDNOTES IN APPLIED ETHNOGRAPHIC SETTINGS

So far I have been encouraging ethnographers to take a personal approach to finding a fieldnote strategy that works best for them and while I have offered a few prescriptive comments of my own, my general approach is to think of 'rules' relating to ethnographic fieldnotes as suggestions. Ethnographers should survey the range of possible fieldnote strategies and find an approach that best suits them and the participants. While I hold that this is appropriate for most ethnographic research, there are professional settings that require the ethnographer to be a stickler for the rules, and to exercise a good deal of caution in taking fieldnotes.

In some applied ethnographic contexts (such as the Australian Native Title Application processes I have worked in) anthropologists, historians and linguists are called upon to write 'expert' reports, may be required to give 'expert evidence' to tribunals, governments or courts, and may be cross-examined in the litigation process. The subjective and personal 'stick it all in one notebook' approach I favour in non-applied research is not a suitable fieldnote strategy in these contexts. Expert reports and evidence that has in any way 'relied upon' the ethnographer's fieldnotes (which in the normal course of events it most certainly would do) can render those notes discoverable or able to be subpoenaed in court cases. As such these notes cannot be treated as personal documents; they must be constructed and formed with the knowledge that they may become public documents. Of course different applied settings to the Native Title domain I am familiar with will be more or less litigious, and more or less likely to require disclosure of fieldnotes, but ethnographers working in applied or professional settings where even the faintest whiff of litigation is possible need to be fully aware of the legal status of their fieldnotes before they begin any fieldwork and inscription. This is a matter of ethics that is both pertinent to protecting the ethnographer and protecting the information given by the participants.

In these settings an ethnographer should rely on one set of notes only, that is the fieldnotes proper. They should all be in the one notebook with numbered pages and with no pages having been removed. They should adhere to the neutral, objective style of note-taking, and should at that stage concentrate on describing and documenting factual information. They should not be overly speculative or interpretive, leave that for a later consideration of the whole of the data. In some ways this form of 'applied' notes is a counter-example of the personal and subjective note-taking I prefer. But this corrective is necessary, as applied settings have serious constraints and demands operating in them that ethnographers are foolish to ignore. If you want to work as a professional expert in an applied ethnographic field, you need to learn the 'facts, and only the facts' approach to note-taking.

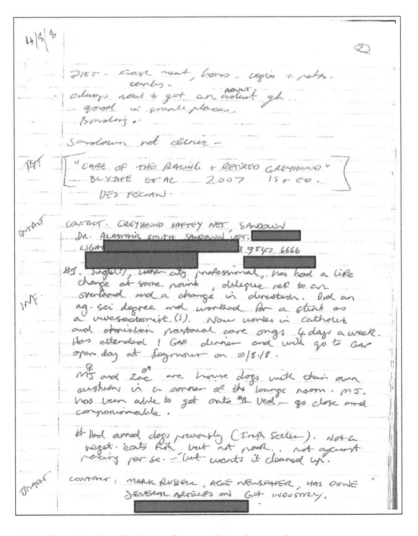

Figure 6.1 Example of my fieldnotes from greyhound research

Examples of fieldnotes

Figures 6.1 and 6.2 show two examples from my fieldnotes on my research on greyhound adoption and an Aboriginal employment scheme. They have all the required aspects for good notes, but they are also messy and idiosyncratic; as notes can be. They do function, however, to record data and to recall situations. In this way they have ongoing value for ethnographic reflection and analysis.

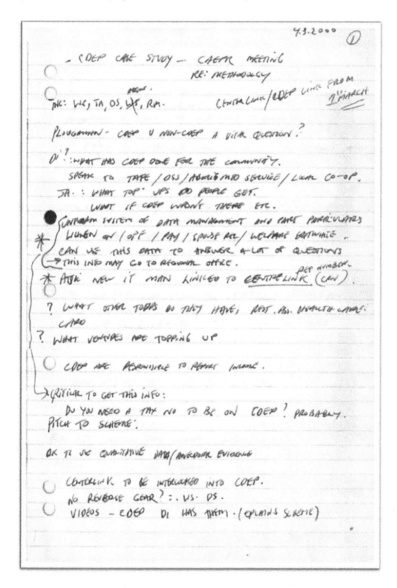

Figure 6.2   Example of my fieldnotes from an Aboriginal employment scheme

SUMMARY

Fieldnotes are intimately connected to ethnographic observations, but they are not one and the same. Ethnographers need to think carefully about the strategies they use to convert their observations into valuable ethnographic inscriptions. I argue that handwritten fieldnotes are still an important way to record participatory fieldnotes and I encourage ethnographers to learn this skill and form a relationship and dialogue with their notes.

Writing down fieldnotes should be a systematic act that ethnographers will need to practise and refine to suit their particular circumstances. Broadly speaking there are two main types of fieldnotes: participatory notes taken during active fieldwork and daily consolidated notes which are an expanded form of the participatory notes usually taken at the end of each day. Increasingly, ethnographers are entering their consolidated notes directly into word processing or qualitative software programs. However, I still prefer to create handwritten consolidated notes.

Fieldnotes may also include notebooks dedicated to diary entries and a log book for noting plans and research outcomes. My personal strategy is to combine all these fieldnote elements into one notebook, but, again, ethnographers should experiment to find the best strategy for their circumstances. At certain points in the fieldwork experience the best strategy may be to not take notes at all. This can occur when participants become overly reactive to the presences of notebooks or other recording devices.

Fieldnotes should contain descriptions of structures, human behaviours, and qualities and quantities that help capture the ethnographic setting. Caution should be exercised in using value-laden language in notes; however, such language is often more evocative and a better mnemonic device for the ethnographer. Diagrams, photographs and film should all be considered part of the fieldnote toolkit, but ethnographers need to remember not to 'switch off' their own note-taking when other recording devices are switched on.

An important corrective to the advice given in this chapter comes from the domain of applied ethnographic research. Ethnographers employed in professional and potentially litigious settings need to be well informed about the legal status of their fieldnotes. In many contexts fieldnotes may become publicly available through legal discovery processes. In these settings a 'just the facts and only the facts' objective and neutral form of note-taking is required.

QUESTIONS

Ethnographers are often protective and sensitive about their fieldnotes. Does such personal attachment to fieldnotes impair their value as a record of ethnographic events?

What are some of the advantages and disadvantages of handwritten notes compared to other methods of recording (for example, computers, cameras and audio recorders)? Is the argument for handwritten notes justifiable in the age of digital devices, and when digital recording devices are so efficient, portable and affordable?

Is it not the case that the values placed on a shared experience of being with participants mean that ethnographers would be wise to focus their attention in the field entirely on participation and leave the fieldnotes until they have finished in the field?

What are the key descriptive issues facing the ethnographer as they attempt to inscribe the structure and behaviours of their field setting? How should one deal with subjective or value-laden language in fieldnotes?

What are the issues facing ethnographers working in applied and potentially litigious contexts that challenge some of the advice on fieldnotes given in this chapter?

SUGGESTED READINGS

Emerson and colleagues', *Writing Ethnographic Fieldnotes* (1995) provides discussion about ethnographic inscription, and together with Sanjek's *Fieldnotes: The Making of Anthropology* (1990), they provide plenty to read on this aspect of ethnographic research. Kouritzin's article, 'The "half-baked" concept of "raw" data in ethnographic observation' (2002) is a worthwhile critical examination of the way ethnographers construct knowledge from fieldnotes. Again, Bernard's *Research Methods in Anthropology: Qualitative and Quantitative Methods* (2002) has a useful discussion on the types of fieldnotes used by ethnographers. Gibson at *Anthropod* has an online section on fieldnotes that is useful – see https://anthropod.net/2013/08/14/a-template-for-writing-fieldnotes/. Tricia Wang at *Ethnography Matters* discusses digital and contemporary forms of 'open ethnography' note-taking at http://ethnographymatters.net/blog/2012/08/02/writing-live-fieldnotes-towards-a-more-open-ethnography/. For a set of quick tips on honing your fieldnote techniques, see Pat Thompson's blog at https://patthomson.net/2014/10/06/practice-writing-field-notes/.

BEING ETHNOGRAPHIC

The increasing accessibility of digital recording devices does not excuse the ethnographer from writing data down – this is still a very useful activity! The act of writing causes you to think more critically about being ethnographic.

SEVEN

ANALYSIS TO INTERPRETATION: WRITING 'OUT' DATA

CHAPTER CONTENTS

ORGANISING PRIMARY DATA

At this point we turn from the language of experience, and recording that experience, to the language of data, and securing, managing and organising that data to get the most out of our analysis and interpretation. In Chapter 6 we looked at the ethnographer as the creator of ethnographic data, principally fieldnotes, but also we considered that sketches or diagrams, photographs or film are also part of this 'primary production' process, noting as we did that these early inscriptions are formed through the strategic and instrumental frameworks of the ethnographer. As such, claims that fieldnotes are 'raw' data are best dealt with critically. A generalisation we can make about ethnographic data is that all good ethnographic projects start with a successful embodied experience in the field, and the subsequent recording of these experiences as fieldnotes, diagrams and other forms of data is the beginning of all good ethnographic data sets. However there are many more forms of data in addition to these primary forms that typically feed into an ethnographic understanding. While the experience of the field is central and characteristic, beyond that point ethnographers are rather like bower birds when it comes to data, they will pick and choose all sorts of interesting bits and pieces of information that complement and support their interrogative structure. From project to project this data can vary markedly; some ethnographic projects draw heavily on historical or archival material, others make use of statistical or census material, some employ secondary visual material in addition to that captured by the ethnographer, and others use newspapers, magazines, literature, the internet or other forms of mass media that are relevant to a particular field setting. Of course there are also ethnographic projects that will use all of these data forms. This can amount to a lot of data, and before one can begin the process of analysing this data one has to have a system for organising it and understanding its relationship to the primary ethnographic data. Moreover, the act of organising data is not just a filing exercise; organising data is the first step in its analysis and interpretation.

We have two broad categories of data to consider, primary ethnographic data (fieldnotes, diagrams, audio recordings, photographs, film and memories) and the secondary or complementary data that ethnographers amass as a part of pre- and post-fieldwork research. As I said, this secondary data can vary from project to project but we can say in general terms that an ethnographer has to consider secondary information such as existing published research on the participant group or setting. This could include, but generally won't be limited to, published ethnographies, histories, linguistic studies, government reports, news accounts, relevant biographies and autobiographies and even fictionalised accounts of the group or setting in question. There is also publicly available archival material related to the group or setting to consider. This could include such things as government or state agency records (police, migration, demographic or census material), the archived accounts of missionaries, development or aid agencies that worked in the area, unpublished local histories or personal accounts, archived photograph or film collections, and much more besides.

━━ **TOP TIP 7.1** ━━━━━━━━━━━━━━━━━━━━━━━━━━━━━━━━━━━━━━

Publicly funded sources prepared for public use are the most straightforward option for accessing secondary data. Organisations like the Cornell Institute for Social and Economic Research, the Mass Observation Archive, Statistics South Africa, the US Census Bureau, and the UK Data Service might be good places to start for existing social research data.

In some cases, restricted material not available to the public may also be of relevance, and as such ethnographers need to be willing to negotiate with the holders of sensitive or restricted material and make a good case for their access to that material. Generally, participant groups need to be aware of the desire of the ethnographer to investigate this material in case they have specific concerns about access to material. If these concerns are ignored or inadvertently overlooked, it could threaten the trust relationship between the ethnographer and the participants which can ultimately affect the viability of the project. There is generally a good reason why some information is restricted, and as such it is axiomatic that ethical issues will surround access to restricted material. Restricted or archival material is not simply a store of objective facts about people from times past. When such material is brought out and exposed to researchers and participants in the present, these documents can be seen as highly charged in a political and cultural sense.

Securing primary data – keeping it close and away

Ethnographers go to a lot of effort to record good fieldnotes; they experiment with different styles and different fieldnote formats, weigh up the pros and cons of jottings versus consolidated note-taking, and wrestle with the reactivity notebooks can sometimes cause. Oftentimes ethnographers sit up late into the evening, tired after a busy day of participation, writing up their notes. These are hard won bits of information, so the first organisation principle of fieldnotes and primary ethnographic data is to think about how to secure them. As I mentioned in the last chapter, ethnographers need a mantra of back-up, save, copy and secure running through their head every time they look at their notebooks. It is common to hear of horror stories of lost, stolen or destroyed fieldnotes in ethnography, and yet it is also common to run into the attitude, 'it won't happen to me'. If there is one indisputable law of ethnography it is 'Murphy's Law' which dictates that if something bad can happen to your notebooks or computer, it will. And it will. Fires, flood, theft, forgetfulness and foolhardiness are ever present threats to your fieldnotes. In the first instance ethnographers need to find ways to keep fieldnotes secure in the field, so carry them at all times, keep an eye on them during those periods of non-note-taking participation and make common-sense judgements about the equipment you will need to do this. A small back pack or a bag you can sling over your shoulder will allow you to keep your hands free to write and/or participate.

In the second instance regularly copy or back-up your notes and send them off site so that should the worst happen you haven't lost *everything*. If possible find a photocopier, and visit it regularly. If you are using a computer, save copies of your fieldnotes to your hard drive and then to a portable hard drive. But don't just do this, also email them to yourself or to a trusted college or supervisor for safe storage, or copy them to disk and post them back home. As a last resort one should print and send hard copies home as well. If you have access to a computer and email, but not a photocopier, think about taking a portable scanner with you, and copy and send your notes via email as digital images or burn to disk and send home. There is also an array of internet servers that allow you to upload and store information on them; investigate these options if they suit your situation. Whatever the method, and whatever the contingencies of copier and computer access in your ethnographic field, just remember to keep the originals safe and close to you and a copy at a safe place away from you. That should protect against the loss of a notebook or a 'beyond retrieval' computer incident (theft, damage, software meltdown). And once more; don't say 'it won't happen to me,' because one day it will.

The same goes for photographs and film taken in the field. The current generation of digital cameras are relatively affordable, have impressive storage capacity and are becoming more reliable and robust; they are a great ethnographic tool. But don't treat your camera like a portable hard drive; do not leave hundreds of un-copied ethnographic images on the camera, as that is almost certainly the time the camera will choose to crash or find its way into someone else's possession. These digital image files can be very large and may be difficult to email home regularly, so copy them to a disk and post them home regularly. As for primary ethnographic film, copies may be difficult to organise, but in such cases one should send them off site to a trusted colleague or supervisor. Depending on where you are working, most postal services will offer premium or registered services that are very reliable, and in most cases it will be better to trust to this system than the contingencies of the field. Again, use your common sense and develop local knowledge to weigh up the risk of each strategy, but think of data organisation firstly as a risk management exercise.

■■■ TOP TIP 7.2 ■■

There is no such thing as 'too many backups' when it comes to your fieldnotes and research records! Always back up your records in at least two different sources.

Coding fieldnotes

Organising ethnographic fieldnotes is also the first step in the analysis of ethnographic data, as the manner in which the ethnographer indexes and codes their notes will in part reflect the interrogative frame of the project. Coding of fieldnotes does not refer exclusively to the encryption of data (although that may be the case with respect to personal identities and places that the ethnographer wishes to keep confidential in their participatory and consolidated notes). In large part the coding of fieldnotes refers to the manner in which we index and identify themes in our notes which are of relevance to the questions we wish to ask in our ethnographic project. There is a potential for tension here between the idea that data are facts that will speak for themselves and data are information that we actively create meaning from as a consequence of our own intellectual and theoretical predispositions. In my experience neither of these definitional poles of ethnographic data is accurate. Rather, most ethnographers hold to both these approaches in varying degrees and use both simultaneously to organise and find meaning in their data. There will be objective facts recorded in fieldnotes that can be indexed and there will be latent meaning in fieldnotes that will only emerge as manifest evidence once the ethnographer has identified the themes and issues that he or she sees as important in their data set (needless to say, individual ethnographers will 'see' a different set of facts and themes emerging when presented with the same data set).

In suggesting that ethnographic fieldnotes have both facts and discoverable or variable meaning in them, that they are both 'solid' and 'plastic' with regard to meaning, I am reiterating the point made in Chapter 6 which suggested it is uncritical to see ethnographic fieldnotes as simply 'raw' data. The data has already been partially 'cooked' by the choices the ethnographer made in the primary inscription process, and this latent framing only becomes more evident as the ethnographer 'sees' and 'doesn't see' certain themes and issues emerging from the fieldnotes (see Kouritzin, 2002). This idea of 'finding meaning' in fieldnotes may strike some as dangerously subjective or too idiosyncratic to be seen as systematic, in that the ethnographer can chose to make whatever meaning of their notes that they feel is relevant to the questions that drive their overall ethnographic project. What is the point of being systematic and faithful and ethical about one's fieldnote inscription process if one can plasticise meaning in the notes to the extent that the data is made to speak for the ethnographer (as opposed to the ethnographer speaking only on the basis of the data)? However, we should remind ourselves of the critical reflexivity I mentioned earlier in this text. If we acknowledge, as I think we should, that all sorts of subjective choices and influences will impact upon even the most objectivist of fieldnote strategies, then it is silly at this stage to treat ethnographic notes as a simple set of objective facts or observations. The meaning-making process has already begun at the point the notes were written. Beyond that point it is a matter for the ethnographer to make the choices as to how they extract more meaning from their data through the way they organise, index and name the bits and pieces of information that make up their fieldnotes. To do otherwise, to say that the facts in the notes will do the talking, is to abdicate responsibility for analysis and interpretation, and what qualitative social scientist in their right mind would want to give over the power of analysis and interpretation to 'data'? Making meaning from data is a rewarding process, and the ethnographer is responsible for it. In sum, one can get a more objective account out of their fieldnotes if they acknowledge and manage the fact that there are subjective elements in them.

So why raise this concern with subjectivism and objectivism in relation to the coding of fieldnotes? The themes we choose to code our fieldnotes with are a matter of ethnographic choice, a choice that is informed by the obvious facts we encounter on returning to our fieldnotes, and the hypotheses that are emerging as we review them. Coding fieldnotes is about indexing what did happen in the field and what this might mean for questions you may want to ask later. As such, coding fieldnotes is a matter of organising the concrete and interpretive or hypothetical aspects of the primary data. Balancing 'fact' and the beginnings of hypothesis in fieldnotes is potentially tricky, but is rendered less difficult if one sees the coding of fieldnotes not as a singular act of interrogation but as an unfolding and ongoing process that will become more refined as the analysis and interpretation become more resolved. For this reason I do not enter pre-formulated and conventionalised codes for human behaviour in my fieldnotes as I am taking them, such as the masses of OCM codes used to topically code the world's largest ethnographic archive, the Human Relations Area Files at Yale University (see Bernard, 2002: 378, 483). As I have said I concentrate my fieldnotes on personal descriptive strategies that mean something to me and only attempt to code them more systematically after I have left the field.

━━ **TOP TIP 7.3** ━━

If you want to note themes in your fieldnotes quickly while you're still in the field – and save the systematic coding and category identifications for later – try using highlighters or symbols in the margins to identify which theme each passage touches upon or relates to.

The audio and visual material one collects in the field will also need to be indexed and organised with reference to the fieldnotes, so as general and more specific themes are arrived at, organise images in relation to these themes (keep a general folder of all images arranged in terms of date taken, and then copy images into folders organised in terms of themes of relevance). Obviously, images will often have relevance to more than one theme and as such will appear in more than one thematic folder. As with film, once a set of themes is established, watch the film and make notes at which point in the film various themes are instanced, and as with photos certain scenes will be of relevance to more than one theme at a time. With audio recording of informal interviews or ethnographic conversations, if possible have these transcribed fully as then they are much more easily searchable for themes, but if one hasn't the time or resources to transcribe audio recordings fully at least do as one does with ethnographic film and create an index of the time on the tape the various themes appear. In other words, treat your visual and audio images as you would your fieldnotes and break them down into thematic pieces that can indicate to the ethnographer both the relationships between certain themes and the frequency with which certain themes appear in the data.

The order of themes

The thematic codes we use can therefore be as generic and broad or as complex and minute as we want them to be, but typically they will evolve more complexity as the ethnographer mines the data for more and more information. A code is simply a term that tells the ethnographer that a theme or issue of interest is to be found at this point in their fieldnotes. This is easily done with computer files (either with qualitative ethnographic software or in a simple word processing program) and is also easily accomplished as a secondary act of inscription in handwritten fieldnotes where the thematic codes and potential questions are entered in the margins of the notes. Codes can be large sociological categories that overlap (for example, age, class, gender or status) or discrete behavioural observations that have meaning in the project context (for example, handshaking, eye contact or mother-in-law avoidance). Different ethnographers will of course make differing choices as to what themes and codes they want to use, and this would be the case even if they were analysing similar data. A set of codes for your fieldnotes are meant to be the best fit for your interests in your data and the aims of your project. If one were to return to the same data set in later projects and re-interrogate it, then of course both existing and new codes would help unpack the material. There is much 'mystification' about how we find meaning in fieldnotes, but with a guiding question (or questions) an ethnographer can sensibly think of a series of general issues of relevance. With a series of general themes coded and some patterns and early hypothesis emerging from the reading of the data, more refined thematic codes that add complexity to the analysis can be entered until one reaches the point where one feels they are familiar with their fieldnotes as both a record of a time spent with others and as a repository of ideas and issues which one wants to interpret more fully. This familiarly with your data is the key to unlocking what meaning the fieldnotes will have for your particular project. A theme is what you make it – it could be a large sociological category, a group behaviour, an individual behaviour, an aspect of the physical setting or an observation of a mood or feeling – it all depends on the way in which the ethnographer wants to interrogate or 'unpack' their data as to which themes, codes or topics will be chosen to identify and organise their data.

Themes originate from the specific codes and categories your data provides – not the other way around. You will certainly begin to notice patterns as you work through your notes, but try to avoid setting your themes before you carefully review and code the data so that you don't force it into certain categories.

To give a concrete example of the simple beginnings of a targeted thematic coding process I will relate a case of coding I was involved in when working on an applied ethnographic project. In this case a historian and I were working through a large pile of transcripts of ethnographic interviews from Aboriginal people who were involved in an Australian native title land claim. The interviews ran to about 200 pages of printed material. We were working to a very tight timeline and had to provide the case manager of this project with an opinion and overview of the relevant anthropological and historical evidence for this case in a matter of days. This overview was based on identifying and indexing instances where the interviewees commented on a number of themes relevant to the case such as: their historical and living connection to traditional lands, the transmission of traditional knowledge, traditional authority and the system of respect for Elders in the community, sanctions for transgressors of traditional laws, and the use of natural resources from the application area. We thematically coded these as 'connection', 'transmission', 'authority', 'law' and 'resources' respectively. These are rather generic, 'first order' themes that we expected to find instances of across most, if not all, the interviews. What we did as a stop-gap measure to meet the deadline was to get several packets of variously coloured adhesive notes that are used to mark texts or documents, and assign a particular colour to a particular theme. We quickly read through the interviews, posting a blue note for authority, a red note for connection, and so on. What we ended with was a pile of transcripts that on visual inspection could be seen to have concentrations and/or patterns of colours related to themes. We found this a very useful temporary measure to take this pile to our meeting with the case manager and talk about the frequency of themes, patterns in the themes, relationships between the themes, all the while referring to the colour-coded transcripts to drive home our initial analysis of the evidence in the interviews.

Of course I hasten to add that this was just a temporary measure that was driven by the need to gain a quick overview of a number of relevant themes, and shortly after this the transcripts were more thoroughly coded with more narrow second and third order themes which were entered into an electronic data base (this made them cross-searchable by themes and instances). The point of relaying this story is that the process of beginning to code ethnographic notes need not be overly complicated.

One could have a large selection of data and begin quite simply at first with a series of generic themes, and this process can be accomplished rather quickly. The generic or first order themes should be constructed with reference to the overall aim of the project; thinking about the reason you started the ethnographic research in the first place should help you decide if class, gender, age, ethnicity, religion, socio-economic status (and so on) are the first order of themes of relevance to your project. There is no universal template for this process; themes will emerge differently from project to project. From that point the patterns and relationships, or lack thereof, between your first order themes should alert you to a series of associated issues or themes that could also be coded and identified in the material. Socio-economic status, for example, may show an interesting relationship to fashion or styles of dress. Perhaps one is working in a community where people's relative wealth or poverty has a direct relationship to the clothes they wear. Or perhaps an ethnographer is initially confounded by the fact that there is an inverse relationship between socio-economic status and clothes, such as relatively impoverished kids wearing really expensive footwear. Either way a second order theme to look for in one's ethnographic data might be 'clothes' or 'footwear' or perhaps 'status fashion'. Having noticed something interesting about clothes or footwear, the ethnographer may suddenly 'see' behavioural aspects noted down in relation to these themes, the manner in which clothing or footwear might be displayed in social settings for example, and as such a third order of themes may emerge. Second or third order themes may not be apparent at first glance through the data and an ethnographer may be forgiven for thinking that codes are somehow 'hidden' in their data and wonder how ethnographers actually begin the analysis when the meaning in the data can be so elusive. But just like observation and inscription, one needs to tackle early coding and analysis systematically. Start at the generic or first order level, even if this seems crude and obvious, for in doing so one will see second and then third order themes that will build the complexity, analytic and interpretive value of your fieldnotes and other data to the point whereby the relevant meaning for your ethnographic project can be extracted from the data and become part of the storied reality of an ethnographic account. There is no way to say for certain which themes will belong in which order of analysis, again that will be different from project to project. What is important to consider is that coding, indexing and thematically organising fieldnotes and other primary data is something that evolves over the time of the analytic and interpretive phases of the project; ethnographers should not expect to get 'answers' from their primary data all at once. The deeper aspect of the illumination will come with patient dedication to looking for relationships and patterns (and non-relationships and lack of patterns) in one's data. At that point the ethnographer can say they have an analytical understanding of their primary ethnographic data which they can now articulate with secondary data to arrive at interpretations and ultimately some sort of conclusion.

ORGANISING SECONDARY DATA

The manner in which one organises the complementary or secondary data will be determined by the thematic coding and early hypothesis one draws from the primary data and by the theoretical or intellectual frame one brings to bear on an ethnographic project before and after the experience of the field. So the published sources, archives or restricted information one brings to an ethnographic project will be a matter of reconciling the pre- and post-field appreciations of the situation; that is to say taking stock of the ethnographic analysis as against other existing and relevant material. Ethnographers typically engage in pre-fieldwork research where they gather sufficient background information on the setting and the people they wish to work with in order to construct a sensible and informed ethnographic project. Histories and previous ethnographies of the group (if they exist), are read as well as theoretical and methodological works which help shape the scope and intellectual direction of the research. Comparative ethnographic material is looked at, as are archives or other material that can help the ethnographer become as informed as possible without actually meeting the people yet. Ethnographers may also wish to have conversations with others who have worked in the area. After fieldwork however, what is typical is that while this background research was a useful process and helped the ethnographer to hit the ground running, there was much in the material that was challenged by the ethnographic experience and as such these sorts of materials are often revisited to make sense of the differences before and after fieldwork. This is an important part of melding the influence of the ethnographic perspective into the broader disciplinary boundaries that have informed and framed the ethnographer's interest in the first place. The task is one of marrying primary and secondary data so that a resolution between the 'tribal' (fieldwork) and 'scribal' (academic) domains can be accomplished (after Boon, 1982).

Pre-fieldwork data

I want to step out of the chronology for a short time and take us back to the stage of planning and preparation for entering the field. It is not particularly common to hear of published ethnographic accounts, theoretical treatises, histories or press clippings treated as 'data' in ethnographic discussions, as the data we create in the field setting tends to dominate (understandably). However, what has already been written and is of ethnographic, theoretical or historical relevance is indeed data; it's just data that was created by someone else. As with the ethnographic data, this secondary material needs to be organised and systematised to complement or challenge the project at hand. The two main tasks that ethnographers wrestle with before they get into the field are literature reviews and theoretical positioning. These two tasks can be characterised as learning about what's already been done and deciding where you stand in regard to the existing literature, therefore combining to create a single critical perspective. This pre-fieldwork priming might be seen by some as problematic. Why would you want to form a perspective on a group or situation before you go there? Wouldn't the ethnographer be best advised to enter the field as *tabula rasa*, as a blank slate, so that the ethnographic experience could inscribe itself on the ethnographer without the filter of existing literature or theoretical perspectives? As I have already stated, I think that a view of the ethnographer as a neutral, apolitical, objective data capturing device is inadequate and does nothing to deal with the interplay that exists between subjectivity and objectivity in ethnographic thought and practice. Whether or not an ethnographer critically examines relevant works of ethnography and theory, they will take socially and culturally informed understandings into the field with them.

■■■ TOP TIP 7.5 ■■

There is no such thing as a blank slate in the ethnographic imagination. Take the time to inform yourself about relevant information about your ethnographic setting ahead of your field research.

Given this, the ethnographer is better served to fill their head with relevant and potentially useful information about their ethnographic setting if it is available. Even if one comes across what one regards as inappropriate or misleading ethnographic or historical accounts of relevance, consume them (as opposed to letting them consume you); they will give you something to bounce off as you reflect on them after fieldwork.

But what should an ethnographer read before heading into the field? Again, this will depend on the vagaries of each individual project and the intellectual and theoretical disposition of the ethnographer as to what sort of material one will critically examine and consume before they enter the field. In the case of my doctoral research I looked at a number of relevant topics. In terms of historical material, I looked at archival and published accounts of European/Aboriginal contact and conflict related to my study area. I examined the history of government policy in relation to the Aboriginal people in the Australian state of Victoria. I analysed oral histories related to Aboriginal groups and individuals of relevance. From an anthropological point of view I looked at existing studies of Aboriginal communities in more closely 'settled' areas of Australia like the area I was focussing on, and how that related to the dominant corpus of anthropology of remote Aboriginal Australia. In a more purely theoretical vein I enquired into debates about concepts of culture, tradition, resistance and accommodation, reflexivity and ethnography and autobiography. And I continued to revisit and expand on this material during and after fieldwork period(s). This grounding in historical, ethnographic and theoretical material of relevance was important for me in the course of my PhD, and even though I didn't really have a settled theoretical position on issues like the concept of culture as I was doing my fieldwork, I was glad I exposed myself to debates about such issues as they arose again and again in my fieldwork and I was at least familiar with the historical, social and cultural forces that were producing such debates. The point of gaining critical pre-fieldwork perspectives on the existing literature is not to form the ethnographer in such a way that they can automatically 'judge' what they experience – that would take the experimental aspect out of ethnography and devalue its reason for being. The point of pre-fieldwork reading, writing and reviewing is to educate and alert the ethnographer to the themes of possible relevance they may encounter and which they may wish to pay particular attention to.

Post-fieldwork data

The experience of being ethnographic can variously confirm, challenge and complicate the thoughts and expectations the ethnographer has developed before entering the field. As such, one of the first tasks that confronts an ethnographer after they have completed a preliminary analysis of their field data is to revisit what they thought they knew and see if 'they still know it'. One of the most important aspects of all ethnographic settings is that they are particular and experimental, and as such ethnography can be guaranteed in some way to challenge expectations. This remains one of the most valuable reasons for sticking with the ethnographic approach to understanding other humans. But it also behoves the ethnographer to be robust and rigorous enough to accommodate the fact that the meaning they may find in the articulation of primary and secondary data may be a long way from what they expected. Again, there's a Murphy's Law for expectations; if they can be dashed, they probably will. But this should be regarded as a good thing; it reinforces the transformative nature of the ethnographic experience. So ethnographers returning from fieldwork do not simply analyse their data and write it up. They have to re-engage with the relevant literature to continually expand and refine their understanding of the place of their work in relation to the disciplines of anthropology, sociology or cultural studies (or whatever named discipline they identify with). This is why I refer to data organisation and analysis as 'writing out' data.

WRITING 'OUT' DATA

Data is often conceived of as being 'crunched', compressed and shaped by analytic forces that 'reduce' it to patterns and relationships that can lead the analyst to interpretation. I see this process rather differently. To use a manufacturing phrase, I think data organisation and analysis is not crunching or reducing, but 'value adding'. I like to see this process as the beginning of fattening up the story. Writing 'out' gives the sense that a broadening of perspective is engendered by the process of analysis.

■ TOP TIP 7.6 ■

Avoid telling your story in the chronological way in which you gathered the data; successful writing of data means transforming what happened to you into an account of what your data shows.

To be sure, those who speak of crunching data do not mean to imply that they are lessening or thinning out the value of the data, they are in fact working with a metaphor of 'concentration' or perhaps 'distillation', and that's not such a bad way to view the task. However, I like the more expansive language of broadening, and to me it better conveys the sense that there is a systematic job to be done that is another part of the inscription process. The shift from organising data to analysing it is made by undertaking more reading, more thinking, and especially more writing.

From analysis to interpretation

Separating analysis from interpretation may seem like splitting hairs but as an ethnographer understands the overall picture of their ethnographic data (primary and secondary) they will sense they are making a movement from idea to explanation, from data to story, and in many cases from confusion to meaning. Of course the distinction is never clear cut, but analysis and interpretation can be characterised in ways that see them as distinguishable aspects of the larger ethnographic process. Analysis then is a systematic synthesis between the disciplinary intellectual frames that begat the ethnographer (the relevant literature and institutional training) and the ethnographic experience that further initiated and remade the ethnographer. Understanding the coming together of the 'tribal' and 'scribal' domains of knowledge leads to the point of interpretation; that time where the ethnographer can say of their data that it points to a particular meaning or set of meanings, that it has evolved as a consequence of its repeated interrogation, that it has some explanatory power. LeCompte and Schensul write of this process as the move-ment from seeing patterns in data (which create some understandings) to viewing the relationships between these patters as 'structures' in the data which create explanations (1999b). It is the ability of organised and analysed data to answer questions posed by the ethnographer that marks this analysis-to-interpretation shift.

Let's return to the example of my doctoral research about the relationships between the Aboriginal community and Euro-Australian community in my home-town area in Australia. As I said, in preparing for my fieldwork I read up on issues such as European/Aboriginal contact and conflict, the history of government policy, oral histories related to Aboriginal groups and individuals of relevance, existing stud-ies of Aboriginal communities in more closely 'settled' areas of Australia and debates about concepts of culture, tradition, resistance and accommodation, reflexivity and ethnography and autobiography. When I completed my fieldwork, I had gathered information that in varying ways confirmed and challenged the history and theory I had read before I set off. For example, I had consumed a good deal of theoretical material that was critical of the concept of culture and how it had been employed in anthropology over the course of the twentieth century. It focussed my attention on the idea that in anthropology a relative view of culture as something which positively differentiates people might in fact be a 'gilded cage' for local Aboriginal people in that they would have to invest a lot of effort into being culturally 'different' from the local Whitefella community in order to be seen as authentic. Aspects of what I observed in my ethnographic fieldwork did in fact support this argument about the practical pitfalls of a well-meaning, dominant concept. But other aspects made me resist agree-ing totally. By being ethnographic with Aboriginal people and Whitefellas I was able to experience the amount of positive energy and commitment people put into seeing themselves and wanting to be seen by others as culturally different peoples. This was not mere false consciousness, I observed many people who moved back and forth across the 'cultural divide' with ease, and one could have dismissed the relevance of the concept to understanding this particular situation. But I also saw the intense investment people had in the idea of differing cultures that could not be dismissed easily; it was an experiential fact of their being. People in their everyday lives were making much meaning out of 'culture' in this setting. And so the synthesis of the theoretical and ethnographic experience of 'culture' caused me to temper my original theoretical position and to see culture not as something that marked people as dif-ferent, but as a strategic process that was more or less strongly activated as a marker of difference depending on who was partaking in the human interactions I observed.

I make this point about the role of the concept of culture in my reading and ethnog-raphy in order to reinforce how it is we shift from analysis to interpretation. I had to reconcile the theory and ethnography of this concept in order to understand in the first instance that the two didn't neatly meet; it was this analysis of 'what' people were doing which suggested a problem or question. Then I continued to interrogate this aspect in order to come to an understanding of how people employ the concept in their lives. This allowed me to resolve the apparent contradiction that I first met in analysing my data. As such, this was interpretive and explanatory; I had moved to 'why' people were activating culture in the way they did. Understanding the relationships and patterns in 'what' people do leads to a position where we might be able to suggest 'why' they do it. This leaves us at the point in our ethnographic journey where we have to consider the textual (and other media) strategies for writing 'up' our ethnographic explanations.

Qualitative software

Ethnographers need to think carefully if they need any qualitative software as part of their methodology, and if they decide that they do wish to utilise qualitative software, the best option is to talk with researchers already using such tools and to look at the data outcomes of engaging with qualitative software. I have not used any qualitative software in any of the ethnographic projects I have been engaged in, and I do not intend to use it in any projects I have ongoing, as qualitative software would not make a difference to the sort of projects I have been engaged in, and in the end I feel that I need to do the interpretation of the ethnographic data, and no amount of organising of data with qualitative software avoids the ultimate step of the need for the ethnographer to interpret the data themselves. Qualitative software can help you organise and discuss ethnographic data, but it can't make that final interpretation of the data for you. Nevertheless, despite my lack of experience in using these tools, I have seen others use qualitative software to advantage, especially in large projects that produce a lot of data that needs systematic organising. There is a place for qualitative software in some ethnographic projects, but these options do not absolve the ethnographer from having to 'own' their data. This book will not be recommending any particular qualitative software for ethnographers as there are a number of options available. If ethnographers choose to use these sorts of tools, they need to consider carefully that they have the best option for their projects. As in any ethnographic methodology, the methods need to be sympathetic to the sorts of data collected.

SUMMARY

One of the first acts of data analysis is to organise the material in such a way as to make it possible to work through it systematically. Analysis and interpretation do not spring magically from ethnographic data sets, they are illuminated through a patient and systematic process of working through the data.

However, data is also fragile, susceptible to damage destruction or loss. Ethnographers need to constantly back-up, save, copy and secure their data. Always keep your primary ethnographic data (fieldnotes, film, photographs) with you and a copy at a secure place away from you.

Fieldnotes are thematically coded in order to index the data and to show the relationships (or lack of relationship) between various themes of importance in the data. Ethnographers will arrive at a set of thematic codes by reference to the question or questions that are driving their research project.

These themes have a relational order or hierarchy that shifts from the generic to the more specific as the ethnographer works through the analysis; the more specific level of themes will emerge as the ethnographer assesses the relationships between the broader generic themes. This shift also begins the process of moving from analysis to interpretation.

Apart from their self-generated primary field data, ethnographers must accumulate and analyse secondary data in the form of pre-fieldwork background reading and theorising, and post-fieldwork synthesis of primary and secondary forms of data. The relationship between the primary and secondary data helps to locate the ethnographic project within its discipline and helps to demonstrate the contribution the research is making to our knowledge.

I call this approach to data analysis writing 'out', by which I mean a good analysis should value-add and 'fatten up' an ethnographic data set. At this point the analysis of the data is now well and truly shifted into interpretation and the scene is set to discuss how one should write up the interpretive ethnographic story.

QUESTIONS

Why is it so important to secure one's ethnographic data? Couldn't one simply rewrite their ethnographic notes from memory if they were to lose them?

How do ethnographers arrive at general and then more specific thematic codes for their projects? What role do these differing orders of coding play in the analysis and interpretation of ethnographic data?

The fact that the thematic codes used to analyse ethnographic data can be derived from the ethnographer's particular research interests, without reference to other ethnographic coding, leave such analysis open to the charge of idiosyncrasy and subjectivism. Discuss and debate.

What role does a comprehensive examination of secondary ethnographic data play in an ethnographic project? Why is it important to find how one's project sits within the broader discipline or study area that spawned the project?

How does *Being Ethnographic* characterise the difference between analysis and interpretation? Is this a useful or defensible distinction?

SUGGESTED READINGS

Chapter 4 of Brewer's *Ethnography* (2000) gives a good account of the analysis of ethnographic data, and LeCompte and Schensul's, *Analyzing and Interpreting Ethnographic Data* (1999b, Vol. 5 of their Ethnographer's Toolkit), provides a wealth of information on this subject. Chapter 7 of Agar's *The Professional Stranger* (1996) discusses 'Narrowing the focus' in data analysis and interpretation. Those with an interest in health care and addiction issues might be interested to look at a text by Miller and colleagues called *Addiction Research Methods* (2010). For a manual on all aspects of coding qualitative data, students may find Saldaña's *The Coding Manual for Qualitative Researchers* (2016) useful. For a collection of resources about ethnographic data management and writing, see http://sru.soc.surrey.ac.uk/SRU5.html.

BEING ETHNOGRAPHIC

Good ethnographic interpretations are built on good data, thoroughly analysed. You cannot skip any of the ethnographic data-handling steps in compiling your storied reality! To truly be ethnographic you must work through these processes systematically.

EIGHT

INTERPRETATION TO STORY: WRITING 'UP' ETHNOGRAPHY

CHAPTER CONTENTS

THE STORIED REALITY

Now we shift our focus to textual and representational issues, and one aspect of representation we will wrestle with is 'creativity' – that 'X-factor' in writing that is impossible to quantify, and even difficult to qualify. As we talk about writing structures and styles I will attempt to systematise some of those less tangible elements of ethnographic writing into a string of advice. So, we can try to de-mystify the writing process, and show that style and creativity in ethnography are not in opposition to, or somehow removed from, methodology, analysis and interpretation, but rather good writing springs from good data, properly gathered – there's a link between the systematics and practicalities of fieldwork, data gathering and organisation and the niceties of writing good ethnography. Doing the practical stuff properly makes finding your ethnographic muse a whole lot easier. Evocation, thick description, persuasion, beauty, and a nice turn of phrase are so much easier to accomplish when you've got the data organised and marshalled behind you. If you have a flimsy data base, if you are trying to paper over the cracks, it's hard not to betray a lack of confidence in your material. Ethnographic writing is at its most elegant and persuasive when it exudes a sense of confidence in its fieldwork-based foundations, and can focus on textual strategies that reveal a particular socio-cultural reality. Ethnography doesn't command attention and interest if it's distracted by attempts to obscure the fact one doesn't have an immediate sense of a particular socio-cultural reality.

In Chapter 7 we looked at the organisation, analysis and interpretation of ethnographic data, noting as we did that organising data is the first step in the analysis. As the analytical depth of the ethnographer's understanding of their data increases, as they get 'on top of' all their data, ethnographers can see a shift from the data that tells them 'what' people do to data that tells them 'why' people do things; this is the shift from analysis to interpretation. But we also noted in the last chapter that analysis and interpretation are ongoing and unfolding aspects of interrogation of the ethnographic data. This is true for the writing up stage too, for the act of writing is more than simply reporting on the interpretations that spring from the primary and secondary ethnographic data. The act of ethnographic writing is a form of collating, reporting and interpreting at the same time; it is both systematic and artful, hence the anxiety many ethnographers have about the writing process. It is in the writing of ethnography that we finally realise what it is we want to say about our ethnographic experiences. So an ethnographer does not need to feel they have all the answers, or to be fully reconciled to a certain form of interpretation before they start writing up; these final resolutions are sometimes, in my experience, to be found in the process of writing. In this chapter we will look at structure and style in ethnographic writing and stress again that there are no hard and fast rules for this part of the process, rather, ethnographers need to experiment and find their own ethnographic structures and styles to best represent the facts of their ethnographic experience and the thoughts and theories they have about these experiences. It is axiomatic that differing ethnographic contexts, with differing aims and audiences will generate differing styles of ethnographic representation. Finding a context-specific, balanced and resolved combination of science and art, of substance and style, is what makes for good ethnography.

As we mentioned in Chapter 1, ethnography, as a component of the social sciences, finds itself, methodologically speaking, in between the humanities and the natural sciences. In order to write in a way that conveys information and produces an accessible and believable portrait of a culture or society, ethnographic writing, as with ethnographic methods, has to find that 'sweet spot' in between these meta-disciplines in order to both present a sense of 'validity' and to answer the literary challenge that is rich and persuasive description. This is the balanced approach I call the 'storied reality'.

AUTHOR AND AUDIENCE

So far in this book we have considered the ways in which the ethnographer relates to the people and setting of their ethnographic project, and the ways in which the ethnographer relates to themselves in considering reflexivity and debates about the role of subjectivity and objectivity in ethnography. But when we consider ethnographic writing, we also need to consider a third party to the ethnographic endeavour, the audience (readers, viewers, listeners), because all ethnography, large or small, accessible or obscure, has a target audience in mind. It can be a textual strategy, a visual strategy or some combination or both, but ethnography must find a way to connect to its audience. And while all ethnographers may wish to be true to themselves in the way in which they represent their ethnographic stories, they also know that reporting issues will influence the way in which they present their material. Talking about writing is often dominated by talk of writers, but to say something about the writing process more broadly one has to remember the readers as well (and viewers and listeners in the case of audio-visual ethnography).

■■■ TOP TIP 8.1 ■■■

Before you start writing, make a list of all of the possible audiences for your research. Having a visual reminder of all the people to whom you intend to communicate will help you structure your paper – especially your concluding chapter – appropriately.

In order to consider these writing issues systematically, and move beyond (but not leave behind) the issues of reliability and validity, we need to consider more than just data and its uses. We need to look to its reception. According to Van Maanen, a discussion of ethnographic writing needs to consider a few elements in order to understand the way the story comes across. Van Maanen says we need to look at:

(1) the assumed relationship between culture and behaviour (the observed); (2) the experiences of the fieldworker (the observer); (3) the representational style selected to join the observer and observed (the tale); (4) the role of the reader engaged in the active reconstruction of the tale (the audience). (1988: xi)

This means we need to look at research, reflection, writing and reading in an overall understanding of ethnography. There are a wide range of issues to consider here, and as we have looked at the 'observed' and the 'observer' already in this text, in this chapter we will examine the 'tale' and the 'audience'. The key issue to stress in Van Maanen's four points is that in addition to research/fieldwork we must take reflection, writing and reading into account as methodological issues for ethnography. This reflexive and literary turn is something that any student of ethnography will be familiar with given the pervasiveness of 'witting culture' type texts – texts that have been around since the late 1980s. So if the textual strategies, narrative or rhetorical conventions assumed by a writer shape ethnography, just as the methods chosen to undertake the research shape ethnography, then ways of personal expression, choice of metaphor, figurative allusions, semantics, decorative phrasing, plain speaking, textual organisation and structure (and so on) all work to form a cultural picture. The varied ways in which these textual devices can be employed, mixed, matched and discarded, mean that ethnography can be a many splendid thing. However,

This raises the question among fieldworkers and their audiences as to whether ethnography (of any sort) is more a science, modelled on standardised techniques and reporting formats, or an art, modelled on craftlike standards and style. (Van Maanen, 1988: 34)

I hasten to restate that this is not a question that needs an 'either/or' answer, it is possible to have our cake and eat it. You can be scientifically 'valid' and rhetorically 'persuasive' in the same text; these are not mutually exclusive categories, but striking this balance isn't easy.

WRITING AS THE CONTINUATION OF INTERPRETATION

I have mentioned that the act of interpreting ethnographic data has sometimes been seen as a mystery, an act that relied on moments of inspiration to allow for an insight into the data, to see something in it that wasn't visible before. This view of interpretation (interpretation as a light bulb coming on, cartoon-style, above someone's head) is, to my mind misleading. It is in the systematic and repetitive revisiting of ethnographic data that we find meaning. It is in the ordering of the data in the first place that allows us to see patterns and relationships that convey meaning. It is not magic. The same is true, indeed more so, for writing. If there is one process that creates mystique, ritual and anxiety more than any other in ethnography, then it is writing. Everybody has heard of 'writer's block'. The best (and most annoying) advice I ever received about writer's block was to simply write your way out of it. Just write. This has turned out to be most annoying because it is true. While there is something ineffable about the writing process, while it does lend itself to romanticisms like 'inspiration', 'illumination' and 'mystique', it is when the systematic ethnographer commits a version of their ethnographic story to paper that they finally come to understand what it is they really want to say. Such a process has been seen as revelatory, but really it is just the logical and obvious outcome of the gathering, organising and pondering on the primary and secondary ethnographic data.

I am aware that there are people who plan, plan and plan what they intend to say in ethnographic writing before committing a draft to paper; they are the super-organisers who map in point form and in great detail the flow of ideas, facts and interpretations before they stitch it all together into an ethnographic account. But even for the most well-planned projects there is an interpretive element evident in the act of writing. For some of us (myself included) the best laid plans are not what we end up with because the act of writing up causes us to reflect, to alter, to reconsider what we had in mind before we wrote 'up'. The first draft of an ethnography is therefore something that we need to simply sit down and do. It is when we have this first draft that we fully appreciate what it is we want to say, and that is why I see the interpretation process continuing on from the analysis of the data and into the writing up. The act of writing is not just reporting, it is a systematic-cum-creative act that helps to arrange our thoughts on ethnographic issues into a coherent story. Having pondered the primary and secondary ethnographic data, having made a shift from the 'what' of analysis to the 'why' of interpretation, and then having committed oneself to writing a draft of an ethnographic story, the ethnographer must consider the issues of structure and style.

STRUCTURE IN AN ETHNOGRAPHIC STORY

Ethnographic accounts, these storied realities, have a number of common elements to them. Big or small, academic or applied, student or professional, ethnographic stories can be broken down into a number of key identifiable elements that we can apply to our own writing. I see the key elements as:

- Firstly, explaining the project's driving question or reason for being 'there';
- Secondly, furnishing an ethnographic description and using the authority of 'being there';

- Thirdly, engaging with the analysis and interpretation;
- Fourthly, substantiating the reason for being there, that is to say, the resolution or conclusion of the project.

The broad steps of aim, description, analysis, interpretation and conclusion will by no means be new to most people; anybody familiar with academic writing will already have come across these steps for presenting, debating and arguing ideas. Moreover, if we acknowledge that these steps may be typical in ethnographic accounts, we can also see that they may arrive in an order different to the prosaic sequence laid out above. It is common, for example, for sections of evocative description to come before the problem setting in ethnographic accounts – these are the so-called 'arrival scenes' we looked at in Chapter 2. In other cases, the ethnographer may wish to obscure the driving question of the research to reveal it later in the ethnography as a moment of sudden interpretive clarity. Indeed, ethnographers could conceivably start their story with the conclusion and retro-analyse and unpack it in such a way that they arrive at a key question. But regardless of how different ethnographers will arrange these elements, most, if not all, ethnographies will have these common elements in them. And yet it is their very commonness that invites me to refer to them as I feel that they are so obvious as to run the risk of being overlooked in the minds of people dealing with their masses of ethnographic data. It's as if the flood of interesting information one gathers from the field swamps the ethnographer and they are left wondering how it is they are to deal with all this information; how can they find the ethnographic story that lies within. By being systematic and going back to basics like the simple generic structure outlined above, a 'path to a clearing' can be found.

■■■ TOP TIP 8.2 ■■■

Struggling to stay on topic? Write the overall thesis, mission statement, key question, or target goal of your ethnographic story on a piece of paper and keep it next to you when you're writing. Make sure every paragraph is relevant to that statement.

The guiding question and the reason for being 'there'

But how does an ethnographer start the writing process? The first step is to continue the interpretation of the ethnographic data by arranging the meaning and explanation that you have formed thus far into a flow of ideas that tells a larger story, answers a larger question and gives an overview of the aims and outcomes of your particular ethnographic project. One needs to develop a plan for the order in which one intends to present one's ethnographic findings. As I have said, this order will of course vary from project to project and depend on the scope of the project. But regardless of whether one is writing a term paper or a university essay, a post-graduate dissertation or thesis, an expert report with a brief from a commissioning organisation, or is constructing a photographic essay or ethnographic film, one has a meta-question in mind that drives and frames the overall project. The reader or audience needs to be aware of this question, of the interrogative frame of reference, in order to understand the way in which the ethnographer presents the ethnographic story. A good ethnographic story therefore needs a good reason to exist. It is not a story for story's sake; it is an account of a human group, institution or setting that has a legitimate human purpose. This reason for being can be illusive, and sometimes ethnographers are not really sure why it is they are doing what they are doing until they approach the end of the process. In my ethnographic methods teaching the first task I set for my students is for them to think of a question that can drive a small 13-week ethnographic project for their class exercise. In this situation the students' key question often begins as a vague interest or a statement of general curiosity, such as, 'I want to look at a homeless shelter as I see homeless people on the street every day and I wonder how they survive?' When I encounter this sort of general interest in a particular human group, I try to focus the student's attention so that it will lead to a small project that is able to be acquitted in the allotted time. In this case I might suggest that the student look at the social relations between volunteers and recipients in a soup kitchen, for example, and I might suggest a guiding question such as, How does Mauss's theory of 'the gift' help us to understand the social relations of a soup kitchen?

As we have already discussed, doing ethnography is in many ways a personal journey as well as an examination of the life ways of others. Working up an ethnographic question from the point of view of a genuine interest (and not simply because a problem sounds exciting) is one way to find a project that can maintain your enthusiasm for the length of the project (although it's no guarantee). Converting a personal interest into an ethnographic setting or group, and then seeing that interest and group as a question to answer, begins the process of an ethnographic appreciation right from the outset.

The problem of setting a question to an as yet incomplete ethnographic project is how can one know if they are asking the right question? Isn't this a form of hypothesising that is detached from ethnographic reality? Like the process of analysis and interpretation which begins early in the life of the data, and is revisited and refined through the project, a guiding question is something that is regularly revisited and challenged and changed through the life of an ethnographic project. Yet despite the fact that it is subject to change I still feel that a guiding question is a necessary step to beginning the data gathering, analysis, interpretation and importantly the writing process. One has to have something to write towards even if it changes on the way through. There are safe and justifiable hypotheses that can be formed as questions to begin the ethnographic process – we already have these in our thoughts as motivating factors behind why and where we want to study particular ethnographic situations. The trick is to simply imagine these curiosities as questions, and don't get too attached to them as they will inevitably change on the way through. Again, one of the strengths of ethnographic engagement is that it can challenge and change our preconceived notions, ideas, curiosities and hypotheses, so we need to be prepared to embrace this aspect of the ethnographic perspective. But a question, as opposed to a statement, will impel the ethnographer towards an explanatory form of writing, and as such I prefer to see the ethnographic process as a quest in search of answers.

The description of being 'there'

A reader or audience then needs detail. They have to be 'transported' to the group or setting that is the focus of the ethnography, and this is a form of travel best achieved by good quality ethnographic description. An ethnographer needs to find a way of writing that can describe human groups, institutions or settings in such a way as to both convey concrete truths about them, and evoke them beyond the reach of mere factual description. As such, qualitative ethnographic description is a beginning to the process of 'narrativising' participants into real characters that readers or viewers can engage with. Note here characterisation is not caricature or a device of fiction, it is a storied portrayal based in observed facts. This is where those hard won descriptive fieldnotes become central and drive the ethnographic story. In a textual sense this is a straightforward play for the audience to believe what they are being served up. A storied reality needs to make the most of the authority of 'being there' and not to be shy of exercising this textual power. The reflexive turn in anthropology in the 1980s (as evidenced in Clifford and Marcus's *Writing Culture*, 1986), made a critical positive out of exposing the tenuous authority of the modernist ethnographer as someone who creates that sense of 'being there'. I for one have no issue with playing this textual card, and think it remains not as a weakness in ethnographic representations but as a potential strength, that when parlayed reflexively, can both confront the politics of authorial power in representation, and yet convey something real of the life ways of other humans. So, while the fact one was there and saw real events doesn't in itself convey any answers or create any ethnographic authority; the power of veracity and faithfulness in ethnographic description will ripple throughout the writing and fortify the account as not just a good description but as a description that serves to answer a question. Authors and readers of ethnography have to strike a trust; one that says the goods on offer are the product of faithful representation. Ethnography cannot fulfil its descriptive and explanatory role if both authors and readers fail to engage in a faithful exchange (hence the intense hatred in the social sciences for falsified ethnographic accounts).

The analytic and interpretive engagement

The story now needs to see the descriptive reality engage with the interrogative purpose so the facts of people and the setting have to come up against the questions that frame the project. In large monographs this could lead to a series of themed chapters that consecutively explore important issues against the ethnographic reality. For example, in Spradley and Mann's classic ethnographic account *The Cocktail Waitress* (1975), they work through chapters dedicated to setting up the problem of women's work in a masculine environment ('Bars, women, and culture'), then move to description of the scene and participants ('Brady's girls'), then turn to theoretical and analytical issues ('Division of labour' and 'Social structure and social network'), they then spend more time on descriptive and analytic accounts of the ethnographic scene as a structured behavioural space ('The joking relationship', 'The territorial imperative' and 'How to ask for a drink'), all of which leads back to the opening problem of woman's work in the final chapter ('Woman's work in a man's world'). Analytic and interpretive engagement dominates the middle sections of this text, and this is one common way to present analytic material.

The process of analysis and interpretation can also unfold throughout the text. In her ethnographic account, *Laughter out of Place: Race, Class and Violence in a Rio Shantytown*, Donna Goldstein (2003) presented chapters that dealt with 'black' humour, class and race-based domination, race and sexual politics, shantytown childhood, state and gang terror, sexual desire and transgression, and rape in order to explore her key problem of the way in which *favelados* (shantytown residents) use humour to cope with what appear to outsiders to be strikingly un-funny social situations. Each chapter posed an ethnographic problem or quest in its own right, but each problem built brick by brick a deep and moving account of the role of humour in disadvantaged lives. Either way, with sections on description followed by sections on analysis and interpretation, or with analysis, interpretation and description appearing side by side, the point is that the sense of 'being there' created by good ethnographic description is also the bedrock of a convincing and reliable analysis and interpretation. Ethnographers have to present enough of a portrait of their settings and participants to make transparent their route through the analysis and interpretation to a conclusion. Analysis and interpretation are not merely mental processes that occur 'behind the text', they should be seen as defensible outcome of thought processes related to the presentation of ethnographic realities. The point of all this is to say that while we might identify ethnographic description and analysis and interpretation as separate events, they must never be divorced from each other in the writing of ethnography. Articulating the 'being there' with the 'thinking about being there' is an important core task in any good ethnography, be it a monograph, an essay or term paper, or an applied ethnographic report. This means that analysis and interpretation should be worked through in a way that makes the argument clear to the reader.

The conclusion – substantiating the reason for being 'there'

To suggest an ethnography has a vital 'reason for being' can sound a little dramatic; it's as if an ethnography has a life and sense of purpose of its own. This, of course, would be a form of reification that might be best avoided. It is *ethnographers*, not ethnographies, which need to take responsibility for the shape and purpose of ethnographic stories. Nevertheless, we do need to acquit our ethnographic accounts against our initial aims and we do need good reasons for doing ethnography (in both the ethical and intellectual senses). So concluding an ethnographic account is more than simply saying the 'answer to problem X is Y'. If we look back to the example I provided from Spradley and Mann, their structure has an overt return to beginning form, namely from 'Bars, women, and culture' to 'Woman's work in a man's world' (1975). By returning to this theme overtly, the authors were able to say something particular about women's work at Brady's and expand on the subject of women in the workforce more generally.

Again, this is a feature of a lot of good ethnographic conclusions; they often take the form of a series of resolutions of particular and localised intellectual questions, personal questions and interpersonal questions, yet in so doing throw light onto a broader field of vision.

TOP TIP 8.3

A good conclusion is not just a summary of your work, but a discussion of the relevance and limitations of your work as well as what applications and/or implications it can carry from here.

This allows ethnography to pose predictions and hypothetical scenarios and to raise many more questions. Indeed it is common to see an ethnographic account arrive at an answer to an issue, only for that answer to pose a whole new series of questions that open the conclusion out onto larger issues. And so it should. Ethnographic conclusions are not 'proofs'; humans are too complicated to submit to mathematical type resolutions. However, while this level of indeterminacy is typical, that doesn't mean that ethnographic conclusions don't find a way to sum up their human stories. By reiterating the original problem, by revisiting the key points of the analysis and interpretation and by passing an ethnographic assessment of that process, ethnographies do indeed find an end to their particular project. It's just that such ends are never really neat and typically throw up a whole new series of questions. Ethnographers should not be disconcerted by this; all projects have more or less limited scopes and general questions, and to a greater or lesser extent reflect the intellectual motivations of the ethnographer. They are meant to be particularistic accounts; that is their strength. Their other strength is that by arriving at partial truths, by saying only so much and not too much, ethnographies remind us that there is more to do. This is not to say that they only have a purpose in creating more ethnographic writing and research; rather it is a taken-for-granted aspect of contemporary ethnography that we cannot paint the whole picture, so we must make a strength out of particulars.

STYLE IN ETHNOGRAPHIC WRITING

The flow of ideas, the way in which we choose to present ethnographic questions, data and conclusions is a matter of structure, but the manner in which we might choose to experiment with tone of presentation or genre, is a matter of style in ethnography. However, style is not something that can be easily separated from questions of structure. Style and structure go hand in hand to cohere and form an ethnographic story into a convincing account. They are textual elements in a co-dependent relationship. However, there are a number of issues we can deal with under the rubric of style. For example, Van Maanen's *Tales of the Field* (1988) discusses three genres of ethnographic 'tales': (1) realist, (2) confessional and (3) impressionist tales. While these genres overlap in the writing of many ethnographers (particularly realist and confessional approaches), they are a useful breakdown with which to begin an examination of style in ethnography. The overwhelming amount of ethnographic accounts can be categorised as realist or confessional (or a mixture of both) using Van Maanen's schema and, as such, I want to concentrate on these two genres. Impressionist accounts, where textual strategies most commonly associated with fiction writing are employed (such as dramatic control, plot twists, strong characterisations and narrativisation [Van Maanen, 1988: 101–24]), are far less common in ethnographic writing, and will not be pursued here, other than to say that while I regard this form of ethnographic writing as important, I see it as a genre ethnographers might arrive at after first spending time honing their writing skills in realist and confessional accounts. Writing good fiction is difficult at the best of times but writing good ethnography using the conventions of fiction is a very difficult task for the budding ethnographer. A number of my students have found this out when they have tried to tackle this genre in their student ethnographic projects. In most cases they retreated to more conventional forms of ethnographic reporting after realising the difficulty of acquitting a writing task that must resolve some of the contradictory conventions of ethnography and fiction.

Realism and confession

Van Maanen suggests that the realist genre is the most common and popular form of ethnographic writing. It is a genre that can be found across a number of contexts; from student projects to doctoral theses to applied ethnographic reports, realist tales dominate ethnographic representations. The dominant feature of this genre is that it attempts to represent ethnographic situations in a manner that causes the account to be read as reliable, valid and authentic. Van Maanen points to a number of ways that such accounts achieve these aims. The realist account will typically employ a 'dispassionate third person voice' which implies or assumes an *audience* and use four 'tell-tale' conventions:

- 'Experiential Author(ity)', where the fieldworker's 'being there' experiences produce authority and credibility and the author writes with a 'studied neutrality' to offer explanations about what the studied group said, did and thought, based on their observation of said behaviour.
- 'Typical Forms', where the 'actions and words of singular persons are minimised in favour of what typical "natives" do, say and think. This process is accomplished through thorough categorisation'.
- 'The Native's Point of View', where the emic perspective is utilised to enhance the sense of the ethnographer being at the scene of the action. This is usually achieved with 'extensive, but closely edited, quotations' from the participants which are contextualised in such a way as to support the argument or motivations of the ethnographer.
- 'Interpretive Omnipotence', whereby the ethnographer, after marshalling the facts and observable realities of their ethnographic encounter, authoritatively interprets the material through established theoretical frames and resolves the account (after Van Maanen, 1988: 45–51).

These characteristics come together to form a powerful and persuasive writing trope, and in following Van Maanen in unpacking the realist ethnographic writing I don't see these conventions as tricky or necessarily problematic; on the contrary, I am still indelibly wedded to most of these core principals, that is, marshalling evidence, managed objectivity, weighty and minute description, interpretive authority, if not quite omnipotence, and overt theoretical framing. I am unashamedly 'convinced' by such textual strategies, and I feel we should continue to use them in our ethnographic projects. The idea is to use realist strategies *critically*. In fact, my preference is that these realist qualities be reconciled with a methodologically reflexive approach that comes out of more 'confessional' accounts, to produce what I referred to in the introduction as the storied reality. For an example of a realist account I return to Evans-Pritchard's *The Nuer*:

I do not make Far-reaching claims. I believe that I have understood the chief values of the Nuer and I am able to present a true outline of their social structure, but I regard, and I have designed, this volume as a contribution to the ethnology of a particular area rather that a detailed sociological study and I will be contented if it is accepted as such. (1940: 15)

Confessional accounts, on the other hand, have:

… highly personalised styles, and self absorbed mandates. … Stories of infiltration, fables of fieldwork rapport, mini melodramas of hardships endured (and overcome), and accounts of what fieldwork did to the fieldworker are prominent features of confessions. (Van Maanen, 1988: 73)

Van Maanen breaks down confessional ethnographic conventions in the following way:

- The disembodied third-person ethnographer is brought into the first person and, as a consequence, into the text.
- There is mention of the biases, character flaws, or bad habits of the ethnographer as a way of building an ironic self-portrait with which the reader can identify.
- There is often a 'conversion experience', whereby the ethnographer comes to a startling realisation that helps them resolve their account and they arrive at a perspective close to that of the participants.
- There are claims to authority through the testimony of personal experience, a reflexive kind of 'being there'. That is to say, it's not just a matter of what the ethnographer objectively observed in the field, but also what they subjectively felt by being in the same social space as their participants.
- They often end up on an up-beat, if not self-congratulatory, note. (1988: 73–81)

These confessional characteristics are also persuasive in the manner that they bring the ethnographer into the text and work up a sense of authority, in part, by illuminating the relationship between the participants and the ethnographer. Those who adhere to the view that ethnography is more a science than an art may well be annoyed by confessional textual strategies because of their perceived subjectivism, but for a more general readership these devices tend to work well at engaging the reader in the lives and experiences of the participants and the ethnographer. For an example of a confessional account I quote my own work from 1999:

I need to outline my working model of home. From my perspective: Home is familiar. I know it very well, it is a geographical region within which streets, highways, back-roads, houses, sheds and other buildings, and landscape are known. Home is parochial. It is a place that elicits an almost defensive stance from me despite all its faults. Home is discrete. I know where it starts and ends, in both a geographical and social sense. I have it mapped out in my mind. Home is habitual. Old habits of speech, manners, attitudes and moods, come back to me when I go home. One could say that my personality changes when I go home, or conversely, that I just become myself again. Home is permanent. After well over a decade of living in Melbourne, I still go down 'home to the country'. Home is birth. It is where I spent my childhood, and also my youth. As such, it has played a large part in the construction of my adult personality. Home is death. It is where family members and relations are buried. From the hilltop house I grew up in, my father could look out one window and see the house he was born in, and look out another window and see the cemetery where he lies buried today: from the cradle to the grave. And finally: Home is ambivalence: Home is a place I felt the need to leave, and yet the need to return. The more time I spend in the city the more home tends toward the euphemistic and becomes somewhat sanitised in my mind; a bucolic idyll, a Steinbeckian world of simple values, of struggle and hope. I sometimes romanticise about returning home to live yet I know that I would run away from its closeness again, back to the comforts and sociality of the city. It is a problematic, yet attractive domain. Perhaps its attraction for me lies in its ambivalent status? (Madden, 1999: 261)

As I mentioned earlier, it is often difficult to say with certainty that an ethnography is exclusively realist or solely confessional, indeed these attributes are often found in the same work. To my mind some of the more attractive ethnographies have both realist and confessional aspects. They find ways to combine authoritative objectivity with engaging subjectivity, detailed dispassionate human portraits with empathetic intersubjectivity and a solid sense of the participant group and the ethnographer who produced the work. In this way what I regard as 'good' ethnographies can be seen to be a product of both their ancestral intellectual traditions, and the natural sciences and humanities, producing a literary and scientific style of social science writing.

Owning more than one style

Ethnographic style is a personal matter, and typically one's style might be seen as an extension of one's personality and intellectual predispositions. However, this point needs a corrective. If ethnographers are working in different contexts with different writing demands (essay questions, PhD topics, expert report briefs) then they are in fact not the same ethnographer at all times and they need to be able to write in varying styles in order to meet the task of producing faithful accounts in line with the expectations or demands of those who commission and consume them. The contemporary ethnographer will typically need to have a number of voices or styles at their command. The point of reiterating Van Maanen's breakdown of ethnographic styles is that while we might be able to identify these as discrete styles, in many cases they will overlap, or just as importantly, an individual ethnographer will find that they need to write in one style or another depending on the context. My doctoral research was written up using a mixture of realist and confessional styles and I have presented conference papers that lean more towards the impressionistic style outlined by Van Maanen. However, my applied ethnographic reporting is done very much within the realist style. Indeed the use of a passive voice and the omission of anything that could be regarded as unsubstantiated opinion or subjective interpretation are by and large weeded out of applied ethnographic writing where the ethnographer's expertise is part of the authority of the piece. It's a case of 'horses for courses'; one needs to be a flexible enough ethnographic author to write for these different contexts of ethnographic writing. What the ethnographer has to assimilate is that being ethnographic is not an absolute condition; it's a relative form of being that produces differing expressions or outcomes depending on the context. The variation in the expression of our ethnographic being is clearly displayed in the various writing styles ethnographers produce for differing audiences or contexts. This is not to suggest ethnographers are merely shaped by their context and not their intellectual intent; rather that being ethnographic is not a singular state of being, it is a way of being that must be sensitive to its surrounds, and developing a selection of targeted ethnographic writing styles is an important aspect of practice in this reality.

SUMMARY

Ethnographic writing should aspire to meet the challenge of conveying an interesting, accessible and believable portrait of a culture or society, and to do so it has to find a balance between the duty to facts and validity and a literary voice that conveys rich, evocative and persuasive description. This is the balanced approach I call the 'storied reality'.

Discussion of ethnographic writing must move beyond the appreciation of participant groups and the role of the ethnographer to appreciate the role of the audience. Questions of audiences' appreciation of texts are as much methodological questions as those that deal with fieldwork and data analysis. Writing is part of the ethnographic method, not an addendum to it.

Ethnographic writing continues the process of data interpretation. Ethnographic writing is often more than simply reporting on the outcome and resolution of the research project. Writing typically creates meaning as it is undertaken and thus it is only through actively engaging in the writing 'up' process that ethnographers will realise the conclusions to their storied realities.

The structure of ethnographic writing will typically involve elements dedicated to explaining the project's driving question or reason for being 'there', furnishing an ethnographic description and using the authority of 'being there', engaging with the analysis and interpretation, and substantiating the reason for being there, that is to say, the resolution or conclusion of the project. These elements may or may not appear in this order but are fundamental aspects of an ethnographic project driven by an interrogative approach.

Style is an important consideration in ethnographic writing. The realist and confessional genres (after van Maanen, 1988) have dominated the practice of ethnographic writing and offer their own forms of persuasive authority to make their storied realities credible accounts. Today it is common to find these genres used in tandem or overlapping to the degree it is difficult to distinguish them. However in certain contexts, such as applied ethnographic domains, adherence to a realist style of ethnography will be required. As such, ethnographers should learn to 'own' more than one style of ethnographic representation.

QUESTIONS

Is the approach to ethnographic writing labelled 'the storied reality' too artistic and not scientific enough? Is the literary turn in ethnography diminishing its scientific value?

What role, if any, does the audience have in shaping an ethnographic text?

Are considerations of style in ethnographic writing beside the point? If ethnographic writing conveys reliable information about other humans what difference does the style it is presented in make?

Why can't ethnographers use an impressionistic style of representation in all contexts? What difference does it make if one is writing or reporting in an applied ethnographic context?

SUGGESTED READINGS

Van Maanen's *Tales of the Field: On Writing Ethnography* (1988) fleshes out the debates about genres and style in ethnographic writing and Fetterman's *Ethnography: Step by Step* (1989) dedicates a chapter to ethnographic writing titled, 'Recording the miracle'. In order to pursue issues related to the 'literary turn' in ethnography, go back and look at a couple of seminal texts: Clifford and Marcus's *Writing Culture: The Poetics and Politics of Ethnography* (1986) and Manganaro's *Modernist Anthropology: From Fieldwork to Text* (1990). Narayan's *Alive in the Writing: Crafting Ethnography in the Company of Chekhov* (2012) offers practical exercises to help students grasp writing about story, theory, place, person, voice and self. Coffey's *The Ethnographic Self* (1999) has a chapter on 'Writing the self' which is worth a look. Bethel College has an online account of writing an ethnography at www.bethelcollege.edu/users/blowers/Writing%20an%20 Ethnography.htm. For a guide to putting ethnographic writing in context, see Seth Kahn's chapter 'Writing spaces: Readings on writing', Volume Two, at http://writing spaces.org/sites/default/files/kahn--putting-ethnographic-writing.pdf.

BEING ETHNOGRAPHIC

Write, write and re-write. It is hard, but writing gets better the more you do it. This is how you find your ethnographic voice! All your hard work with data will not translate into being ethnographic unless you work determinedly at the writing process.

PART FOUR

EXPANDING ETHNOGRAPHY

NINE

CONCLUSION: ETHNOGRAPHIC HORIZONS

CHAPTER CONTENTS

REVIEW

Let's summarise Chapters 1 to 8 in order to consolidate what we have discovered about ethnography thus far and to set the stage for a discussion on pushing the boundaries of ethnographic research and inquiry. Chapter 1 looked at ethnography as both a research practice and a textual product. From a combination of research and writing ethnographers build theories about the human condition. Participant observation, a key feature of ethnography, makes ethnography into a whole of body experience that requires a good grasp of the role of reflexivity. Ethnographers employ their methods like tools, but a strong philosophical and intellectual justification of one's methods defines good ethnographic methodology. There is remarkable methodological continuity in ethnography from the time of Malinowski and Boas to the present day. Ethnography doesn't have an ethical element – ethnography is an ethical commitment from the very outset, and through all phases of ethnographic research and writing.

In Chapter 2 we examined the complex relationships between humans and places, and the manner in which each shape and form the other. Through a variety of relationships humans imbue places with meaning. Ethnographers also instil places with meaning, but do so in very particular ways. Ethnography turns someone's everyday place into a thing called a 'field'. An ethnographic field provides an interrogative boundary we can use to map onto a geographical and/or social and/or emotional landscape that is inhabited by a participant group. An ethnographic field, therefore, helps to set up a problem or series of problems to investigate. A field is not always what you expect it to be, and any place, from the most mundane to the most extraordinary can be looked at with the ethnographer's investigative gaze. Through this gaze places come into their own as ethnographic fields.

In Chapter 3 we noted that successful negotiation in ethnography relies on both political and linguistic skills; it is not a matter of simply having the 'gift of the gab'. Rather, it is a matter of being able to explain one's research project in lay language and in a way that properly discloses one's intentions and engenders a sufficient level of trust to gain the permission of the participant group for the research to go ahead. All cultures have right and wrong ways of negotiating and exchanging information, so asking questions is rarely a straightforward matter, and successful ethnography requires the ethnographer to appreciate the do's and don'ts of negotiating and questioning. Ethnographers also interview participants, and conduct those interviews on a scale from less to more formal. The informal end of the spectrum, the 'ethnographic interview', is a key form of verbal exchange in ethnography. Learning how to structure these interviews, how and when to pose questions within this structure, are fundamental skills that ethnographers need to develop.

In Chapter 4 we discussed how engaging in ethnographic participation is one of the more distinctive characteristics of being an ethnographic researcher. Participation can teach ethnographers a great deal about their participant groups, but it also opens ethnographers up to profound relationships and responsibilities with their participants. While long-term fieldwork is still undertaken by many ethnographers, and is extremely valuable, a notable amount of contemporary ethnography is undertaken on a short-term or 'step-in-step-out' basis. Regardless of the time spent in the field, the ideal relationship between an ethnographer and their participant group is characterised as 'close, but not too close'. Participation also involves the ethnographer in ethical responsibilities. The rights of the participants and their safety are paramount considerations. However, the safety of the ethnographer and the professional standards of the disciplines which foster ethnography are also integral parts of an ethical decision-making matrix.

In Chapter 5 we discussed ethnographic observation and concluded that the ethnographic way of looking at people is no simple matter. It is a systematised and disciplined form of observation that is designed to efficiently gather reliable data. Ethnographers 'gaze' upon their participants and surroundings in a way that is historically, theoretically and personally defined. The ethnographic gaze has therefore evolved over the history of ethnography to reflect the paradigms and predilections of each phase of the ethnographic endeavour. For ethnographic observation to achieve its aims we need to train and discipline our observations to 'see' things that are ethnographically relevant and important such as the structure and behaviours that shape particular human lives. In addition to the way ethnographers observe their fields, we must pay attention to the way images and film of participants are presented by ethnographers and understood by consumers of ethnography. Visual ethnography is a growing part of ethnography and the presentation of ethnographic photographs, film and multimedia content is now fundamental to the ethnographic endeavour.

In Chapter 6 we saw that fieldnotes are intimately connected to ethnographic observations, but they are not one and the same. Ethnographers need to think carefully about the strategies they use to convert their observations into valuable ethnographic inscriptions. Writing down fieldnotes should be a systematic act that ethnographers will need to practise and refine to suit their particular circumstances. Broadly speaking there are two main types of fieldnotes; participatory notes taken during active fieldwork and daily consolidated notes which are an expanded form of participatory notes usually taken at the end of each day. Fieldnotes may also include notebooks dedicated to diary entries and a log book for noting plans and research outcomes. My personal strategy is to combine all these fieldnote elements into one notebook, but, again, ethnographers should experiment to find the best strategy for their circumstances. Fieldnotes should contain descriptions of structures, human behaviours, and qualities and quantities that help capture the ethnographic setting. Diagrams, photographs and film should all be considered part of the fieldnote toolkit. Ethnographers employed in professional and potentially litigious settings need to be well informed about the legal status of their fieldnotes. In many contexts fieldnotes may become publicly available through legal processes.

In Chapter 7 we looked at data analysis, and saw that one of the first acts of this process is to organise the material in such a way as to make it possible to work through it systematically. Analysis and interpretation do not spring magically from ethnographic data sets; they are illuminated through a patient and systematic process of working through the data. As ethnographic data is fragile and susceptible to damage, destruction or loss, always keep your primary ethnographic data (fieldnotes, film, photographs) with you and a copy at a secure place away from you. Fieldnotes are thematically coded in order to index the data and to show the relationship (or lack of relationship) between various themes of importance in the data. Ethnographers will arrive at a set of thematic codes by reference to the question or questions that are driving their research project and as the ethnographer works through the data the shift from analysis to interpretation begins. This approach to data analysis I call writing 'out' data, by which I mean a good analysis should value-add and 'fatten up' an ethnographic data set.

In Chapter 8 it was suggested that ethnographic writing should convey an interesting, accessible and believable portrait of a culture or society. This is the approach I call the 'storied reality'. Discussion of ethnographic writing must move beyond the appreciation of participant groups and the role of the ethnographer, to include an appreciation of the role of the audience. Ethnographic writing continues the process of data interpretation and is more than simply reporting on the outcome and resolution of the research project. Writing typically creates meaning as it is undertaken and thus it is only through actively engaging in the writing 'up' process that ethnographers will realise the endings to their storied realities. The structure of ethnographic writing will typically involve elements dedicated to explaining the project's driving question or reason for being 'there', furnishing an ethnographic description and using the authority of 'being there', engaging with the analysis and interpretation, and substantiating the reason for being there, that is, the resolution or conclusion of the project. Style is also an important consideration in ethnographic writing. The realist and confessional genres (after van Maanen, 1988) have dominated the practice of ethnographic writing and each offer their own forms of persuasive authority to make their storied realities credible accounts. In current times it is common to find these genres used in tandem or overlapping to the degree that it is difficult to distinguish them. However, in certain contexts, such as applied ethnographic domains, adherence to a realist style of ethnography will be required. As such, ethnographers should learn to develop more than one style of ethnographic representation.

Ethnography has been (somewhat conservatively) characterised in this book as a research and writing practice that is fundamentally shaped by the value ethnographers place on being with people in their everyday situations. I have done this quite deliberately because I still see much to value in this approach, and feel we should acknowledge such before moving to reflect more critically and explore the horizons of ethnographic practice. Face-to-face, direct research in the form of participant observation has formed the core of ethnographic methodology for over 100 years and for good reason; this approach in concert with ongoing engagement with social science theory continues to produce valuable insights into the human condition. Being ethnographic is indeed a tried and tested way to know others and answer questions about others. But what happens when the people you are interacting with are not in the same physical 'face-to-face' space as you the ethnographer? What if one's interlocutors and participants are virtual people or real people inhabiting virtual communities? What happens when one studies a situation where companion animals, for example, form kinship with humans, have agency in human lives and actively shape human emotional, social and physical landscapes? How should ethnography deal with these non-human participants in seeking to understand the human condition? In order to discuss what happens to ethnography when we don't have face-to-face contact with other humans in the field setting we'll take a brief look at the world of cyber ethnography and technology mediated sociality. In order to discuss what ethnography can say about non-human others who are in social relations with humans we'll quickly delve into the world of anthrozoology to test the applications of ethnography beyond the human. These two brief case studies will not settle the issue of the future of ethnography, but they will pose questions that will illuminate the potential and problems that will arise as ethnography seeks to deal with emerging social forms that are part and parcel of the contemporary human condition.

CYBER ETHNOGRAPHY

Cyber ethnography is a term used to cover a broad category of research approaches. The shared characteristic we will focus on is the form of ethnographic enquiry that is interested in technology-mediated sociality. Of course, one could say the telephone, now an old form of technology, creates a technology-mediated sociality, but I'm more interested in those forms of human communication and exchange that occur in the relatively new social domain of the internet where the shared characteristic is that these situations involve people who are not in face-to-face contact with each other. Cyber social researchers can look at a range of social relations that take place 'on' the internet. They can also get involved in the exchanges themselves via participant observation, thereby undertaking research from 'within' the internet.

━━━ TOP TIP 9.1 ━━━━━━━━━━━━━━━━━━━━━━━━━━━━━━━━━━━━━

If you plan to do any sort of cyber ethnography, make sure to define clearly who and what you want to study. The internet opens doors all over the world, so without clearly set parameters for your study, you could end up with more raw data than you can handle!

For example, Alex Broom undertook sociological research on the way in which survivors of prostate cancer used the internet to share their experiences and to refigure and challenge the doctor/patient relationship by accessing information on their condition through internet sites and 'chat rooms' dedicated to the topic (Broom, 2005a; 2005b). In this case we have a qualitative social researcher interested in the impacts of technology on a set of existing social relations (masculine interactions, doctor/patient interactions), and this is done from the perspective of an external observer of these interactions. Further, Helen Lee conducted research on the manner in which the Tongan diaspora debated and discussed issues related to the Tongan language via email and on various websites, internet fora and message boards (2006). Lee noted that these discussions were not simply a virtual recreation of Tonga on the internet, but an extension of existing diasporic networks that worked to strengthen the sense of Tongan community across the geographically dispersed groups (2006: 156). By observing these interactions, and also engaging in email exchanges with participants, Lee undertook cyber research that was dedicated towards understanding Tongans 'on' the internet and participated in the process of exchange 'within' the internet. Lee's research is part of a host of internet-based research being conducted in indigenous communities, and appeared in an edited volume called *Native on the Net* (Landzelius, 2006), which presented cases studies from remote Australian indigenous communities, First Nation people of Canada, Zapatistas of Mexico, Tamil groups in Sri Lanka and much more besides.

Perhaps most interestingly from the ethnographic point of view is the full participation of the ethnographer in online communities. Jonathan Marshall (2007), for example, had a decade-long ethnographic encounter as a participant observer on the internet mailing list 'Cybermind' (a list created to discuss the philosophical dimensions of cyberspace). Marshall documented the ways in which participants built, sustained and managed their cyber relationships, paying particular attention to the concept of authenticity in cyber relationships. Furthermore, Tom Boellstorff's ethnography, *Coming of Age in Second Life* (2008), is an account of an ethnographer's participation in the online world, 'Second Life'. Boellstorff pays homage to some seminal anthropological texts in this work, deriving the title from Margaret Mead's *Coming of Age in Samoa* (1961), and recreating Malinowski's famous arrival scene from *Argonauts of the Western Pacific* (1961[1922]) as his opening paragraph:

Imagine yourself suddenly set down surrounded by all your gear, alone on a tropical beach close to a native village while the launch or dinghy which has brought you sails away out of sight ... You have nothing to do, but to start at once on your ethnographic work. Imagine further that you are a beginner, without previous experience, with nothing to guide you and no one to help you. This exactly describes my first initiation into field work in Second Life. (2008: 3)

The manner in which *Coming of Age in Second Life* references classics of the modernist ethnographic canon makes an important claim about cyber or virtual sociality.

Boellstorff argues that a firm distinction between 'real' and 'virtual' sociality is unsustainable when we look to the operation of concepts like 'culture', which have always had a virtual element, an imagined binding force that exists beyond the concrete. In moving beyond the real/virtual binary, Boellstorff also argues that virtual social worlds can submit to the classic form of ethnographic methodology which centres on participant observation and ethnographic interviewing. In other words, Boellstorff's references to Mead and Malinowski are more than playful, they also invoke a serious rhetoric that suggests that the virtual is real and the real is virtual, and as such cyber worlds like Second Life are proper ethnographic fields which should be examined by ethnographers with the same tools they would use in any other field setting.

Social media and context

If an ethnographer chooses to use some form of qualitative software or social media in their ethnography it is incumbent on them to retain a critical disposition to these forms of data. These data are created and gathered in a particular cultural context that has historical, social and political influences they may or may not shape the data in particular ways. It is appropriate to remember that some of the apparent hope for change that can be suggested in the early phases of social media driven reforms may in time be overtaken and co-opted by more quotidian political and ideological forces, reining in what might have looked like a real opportunity for social change. All apparent social changes should be seen against the backdrop of the politics and ideologies that are in force in any given place.

Real social worlds and the lessons of cyber ethnography

In Chapter 1 we discussed the role of embodied experience in ethnographic research, and I argued that the ethnographer is an organic recording device who, by sharing an embodied intersubjectivity with others, can gather all sorts of interesting data and develop reflexive knowledge about the lives of the participant group. Being with people enables the ethnographer to share the experience of sights, sounds, smells and touch of the participants' everyday worlds. Being with people also builds an ethnographic authority based on first-hand observations and eye-witness accounts. This combination of subjective and objective experience is cited as a particular strength of the ethnographic approach. Surely then, not having this embodied exchange impoverishes cyber ethnography? Doesn't losing the first-hand real life experience diminish cyber ethnographic claims to authority?

While the subjective and objective dimensions of being in face-to-face contact with others in real worlds are very important elements of ethnography, they do not totally define the practice. If we critically assess what is of most importance in ethnography we can see the key characteristics of ethnography in a form of hierarchy, as different orders of importance, some of which have priority over others in the practice. In this case cyber ethnography causes us to pose a question about a hierarchy of methodological importance, namely, is it more important for the ethnographer to do as others do, to participate? Or is it more important to be in face-to-face contact with participants? Of course it is a truism to suggest that cyber ethnographers will see the act of participation as more important; in a setting characterised by virtual social contact the ethnographer, in being true to the dictum, 'do as others do', should engage in virtual social contact in order to get an insider sense or emic perspective of the operation of this form of sociality. However, I argue that this hierarchy is true for 'real life' ethnography more generally. While in practice 'real life' ethnography makes it axiomatic that participation and face-to-face contact are concurrent experiences, this is not to say they are the same order of event, or as important as each other. I argue that doing what others do and learning through shared experience is more important methodologically than face-to-face contact. I would also suggest that this has been true for ethnography from the outset, and is not a latter-day definition of convenience whipped up to meet the challenge of virtual sociality. The central position ethnographers give to the emic or insider perspective is not about looking participants in the eye; rather it is an attempt to see the world through their eyes. In short, a shared sense of participation has always had more methodological importance attached to it than the desire to be in face-to-face contact with participants.

■ TOP TIP 9.2 ■

The important position ethnographers give to the insider perspective is not about looking participants in the eye; rather it is an attempt to see the world through their eyes.

In short, a shared sense of participation has always had more methodological importance attached to it than the desire to be in face-to-face contact with participants (Madden, 2014, but cf. Hammersley, 1992: 145).

If cyber ethnography is not necessarily diminished or invalidated by criticisms that it lacks a face-to-face real world dimension, then what can we say of the sociality and social systems that cyber ethnographers explore? Again, these questions throw into relief the putative distinction between 'real' and 'virtual' sociality, and in doing so it also causes us to question what the 'social' might encompass. As noted above, Boellstorff has pointed to the 'virtual' dimension of culture, and we might extend this thought to include concepts like community, ethnicity, society or nation. While there are material social facts attending to particular manifestations of these concepts, there is also a dimension of them that is 'imagined', to use Anderson's (1983) terminology. Communities, ethnicities, societies and nations have always had a virtual element that exists only in the minds of humans. From this perspective such groups are no more 'real' than the society that coalesces in places like Second Life.

Furthermore, if we return to the perspective of those who inhabit these cyber worlds, the real/virtual distinction is again challenged by the fact that participants in online social worlds experience their sojourns in such spaces as real social interaction. Apart from the fact that people will buy, sell, barter, go to parties and form friendships and sexual relations within online worlds, they also experience real emotional states as a consequence of their virtual sociality (Boellstorff, 2008). Affection, love, disappointment, anger, intrigue, repulsion, belonging and culture shock are all experienced as real by participants in cyber societies. Such real experience utterly problematises the value judgements that flow from a view of 'real' society as authentic and 'virtual' society as fake. There is nothing fake about online sociality. It matters little to cyber participants that there is a level of technological interface between them and their fellow online social members when so many other authentic social relations are technology-mediated; they see and feel their experiences as real – because they are. In attempting to understand this insider perspective ethnographers have to take the reality of cyber sociality seriously. So, if we should treat cyber worlds as we would any other ethnographic field, bringing the same methodological toolkit to bear on the 'virtual' as we would the 'real' (and in the process dissolving the distinction to a large degree), then what of ethnography and animals?

The lessons of cyber ethnography for human and animal studies are that sociality is not predominately a matter of flesh and blood humans in the same space and time. Rather, sociality in postmodernity is increasingly a series of communicative networks, loops and technologically-mediated exchanges that include humans together in space and also together in 'virtual', diasporic and digital communities of humans, meta-humans, machines, avatars, cyborgs and animals. The relevance of this set of propositions is that animals are an integral part of an expanded posthuman vision of sociality and to treat animals seriously as ethnographic subjects we must do more than simply be with them; rather we should explore if there are ways to know what it feels like to be them. Furthermore, if cyber ethnography tells us that technology-mediated sociality is not 'fake' as a consequence of its 'virtuality', then ethnographers need to consider the potency of the sociality between animals and humans. Animals are not surrogate humans, animals and humans are not forming pale imitations of the social relations between humans, they are real actors and inter-actors (Alger and Alger, 1997; 1999; Sanders, 2007) with real lines in an age-old social drama. The animal turn has, like cyber-sociality, expanded our view on what constitutes the social. The posthuman implications and applications of cyber ethnography have a resonance with anthrozoology; what one once thought of as beyond the scope of classical modernist ethnography (the virtual) has been shown by Boellstorff (2008), Marshall (2007) and others as core business for a programmatic ethnography that is interested in the ways humans relate in our times.

NON-HUMAN ETHNOGRAPHY

Animals have long been used as a means to understand human society; myths and storytelling featuring animals have used symbolism, metaphor, allegory and analogy to illuminate the human condition – take George Orwell's well known and powerful anti-communist allegorical *Animal Farm* (1951) for example. Anthropology has long examined human/animal relations through the lens of totemism whereas sociologists and historians have sought to understand this association through frames of reference such as enlightenment and urbanisation (Thomas, 1983), manners, taste and attitudes to violence (Elias, 1986; 1994), and analyses of pro-animal discourse (Tester, 1989; 1992), to name but a few. However, study of the more directly social aspects of human/animal relations (anthrozoology) is more recent and emerging as an important line of enquiry in the social sciences (see Franklin, 1999; 2002; 2006 for example). This more recent research has focussed on issues such as animals and leisure culture, animals as companions, animal welfare, and debates about the so-called human/animal divide. These investigations are indicative of a shift in the manner in which the sociality between humans and animals is now understood. Humans in industrialised societies have generally become more 'distant' from some animals (food animals and working animals) while at the same time they have become 'closer' to other animals (companion animals). This shift towards companionability has brought issues of animal welfare and animal rights to the foreground in human/animal relationships and has also raised the issue of a new kinship between humans and animals. Animals are now thought of as more than symbols of humanity, they are seen to be in real social relations with humans. Animals shape the domestic everyday spaces of humans, they influence the running of households, they are treated as family members, given funerals and named as benefactors in wills, therefore they are more than passive elements in human social systems; they are undoubtedly dependent on humans in many ways yet they have an agency that is both interesting and problematic for an ethnography dedicated to understanding the complexity, variety and richness of the human condition. But can animals be studied ethnographically?

Animals as good-to-think: The greyhound example

I have been engaging with the emerging research into human and animal relations by undertaking research on the relationship between humans and greyhounds

(Madden, 2010). There are a suite of human/greyhound relations that interest me. Gambling on greyhounds, animal welfare and the anti-greyhound racing movement, Greyhound Adoption Programs, and the complicated bond between greyhound trainers and their greyhounds are some of the aspects of interest in this relationship. The tensions between groups with differing interests in greyhounds provide a rich vein of representation and counter-representation to analyse. I have focussed initially on the greyhound adoption programmes that seek to house ex-racing greyhounds as domestic pets and thus avoid their culling at the end of their racing careers. There is much debate around this particular aspect of the human/greyhound relationship. The greyhound racing industry is often characterised as having a questionable attitude to the welfare of greyhounds and in addition, training, racing and betting on greyhound races is commonly characterised as a working-class pursuit. Against this, animal welfare proponents have sought to use deep historical representations of the greyhound in an attempt to represent it as a dog with 'high' pedigree and noble origins. These representations characterise the greyhound as a regal and venerable breed with millennia of faithful service to humans, a 'track record' that demands a more respectful relationship than that putatively shown by the greyhound racing industry and gamblers (see Branigan, 2004 for example). Straddling these two contesting domains are greyhound adoption schemes. Greyhound adoption schemes are actively supported and promoted by the greyhound racing industry, yet they also foreground animal welfare issues that were once solely the preserve of anti-greyhound racing advocates. The Greyhound Adoption Program is a critical site of contestation over who has the best interests of the greyhound at heart; who can claim to 'own' greyhound welfare. Greyhounds are not typical working dogs, servants or food sources (cf. Cassidy, 2002: 141), but in this changing dynamic they are caught somewhere between working class totems and companions of the leisure class. The way that greyhounds are transformed from utilitarian racing dogs to domestic companion pets strikes me as an interesting topic in its own right, and appealing also as a test of the limits of ethnography. Furthermore, companion animals have the most overtly 'social' relationships of any animals with humans; can this companionable relationship be understood with an ethnographic approach?

Animals as humans

Previous studies of human/animal relations have typically occupied the poles of the generalist-to-particular spectrum. That is to say, there have been broad theoretical studies on the human/animal relationship (for example, Franklin, 1999) and specific case studies examining the associations between a single animal species and a particular category of humans, such as an occupation set, age cohort or recreational group.

Cassidy, for example, has produced an excellent case study of England's Newmarket thoroughbred racing complex, focussing on the relationship between horse breeders and thoroughbreds in order to discuss the operation of class in this domain of English society (2002). Most of these studies have looked at the influence of animals on human activities and attitudes without necessarily treating the agency of animals in shaping human lives as a focal point. This is not to say they have overlooked animal agency, rather that they haven't posited it as a subject for particular ethnographic analysis. But if we see the companion animal as a social actor that is something more than a part of the furniture, as a force that actively shapes the social aspects of the ethnographic field, then how should ethnographers approach this curious, human-like participant?

■■■ TOP TIP 9.3 ■■■

Literature and other creative arts have often considered the animal 'other' in society. If you're planning to undertake a non-human ethnography, consider balancing first-hand experience with secondary accounts of animal–human interactions and spaces.

Let's pursue an irreverent example in order to say a bit more on this issue. There are two theories on the origin of the human/domestic dog relationship. The most well known suggests that 'wild' dogs followed humans and scavenged from their kills, in the process getting more and more used to humans and over time becoming domesticated. The alternate version suggests that it was 'wild' humans who followed dogs, scavenging from dog kills and over time becoming more and more domesticated. I won't expand on the likelihood that one of these two theories is the correct one; that is beside the point. We do know that over time humans and dogs have formed symbiotic relations that have benefited both species and in which both species can be seen to have agency. Typically, however, it is the humans who are seen to have the overwhelming power in these relations. Dog owners will joke that their dog owns them, but by and large, humans are said to own their dogs. What the 'dogs domesticated humans' theory does is to illuminate that such an unevenly weighted view of human and animal agency might cause us to miss possibilities. It may be that dogs have had a far more profound impact on human evolution than is admitted by the idea that 'we domesticated them'. The extension of this proposition into our discussion about the possibilities and limits of ethnography is that if companion animals, like dogs, have a hitherto unrecognised degree of agency in shaping human lives, and if, as a consequence of this, people treat animals as 'other' humans, as kin (even if there is a certain partiality to that recognition) then it is arguably part of the ethnographers' job to also interrogate the animal as we would humans, with the approach of taking it all seriously.

Think of Jackson's set of propositions on intersubjectivity (outlined in Chapter 1) as applied to a human and animal exchange. How does the instability of intersubjectivity, with its acts of recognition and common goal setting, framed by the habitus of the participants, how does this fragile heart of ethnography map onto human and animal sociality? When Sanders (1999) describes the human–animal developmental exchanges in puppy training classes he alerts us to the deep social co-constitution and co-recognition we share with canines. When Alger and Alger (1999; 2003) describe the cat and human culture of a 'no-kill' cat refuge they alert us to the possibility that intersubjectivity need not be defined by language alone. When Haraway (2003: 1) describes how her dog licks her, we have a tangible sense of the intimacy of the exchange, the literally warm and fluid nature of their co-constitution. When Derrida (2008) describes being watched by his cat we have a tangible sense of the ambiguity and anxiety in a putatively intersubjective interspecies moment. We have in these sorts of exchanges the range of intersubjective ambiguities that Jackson documents for human exchanges, but I am left with a nagging concern about the last of Jackson's points: 'how can empathy, transference, or analogy bridge the gap between [human] me and [animal] you' (1998: 10)? Can we move beyond the sense that we are standing on the outside of animals looking in (after Fine, 2004: 642; Madden, 2014)?

Interspecies ethnography?

Why can't animals expect to have the same methodological rigour applied to their research participation as we have typically applied to humans over the course of the last 100 years? What is it about the explicit and implicit othering of animals that creates a fantasy space where one is free to be anarchic or anti-programmatic (after Hayward, 2010; Kosek, 2010)? Would such an approach be seen as ethical or legitimate if it were applied to a human community? I am suggesting that the ways that the consideration of 'writing' interspecies ethnography has perhaps been given more attention than 'doing' interspecies ethnography – I have a sense that we are not yet fully resolved with being ethnographic in the interspecies contact zone. How can we build a reliable system of knowledge that at least treats animals as potentially knowable and interpretable without paying more regard to the systems and programs, the methods, with which we build our knowledge? And what of the tricky business of intersubjectivity (Madden, 2014)?

Of course, we do indeed have qualitatively rich intersubjective exchanges with animals, especially those we are in close contact with such as companion animals and farm animals. Animals are able to communicate a range of desires and states of external and internal being to us (hunger, aggression, fear, affection, longing and disregard) as we can to them. The cognitive ethologist Marc Bekoff, who has produced a large and influential body of research and writing, is probably the strongest proponent of the practice of characterising these states of being as emotions, and using labels previously used exclusively to characterise human emotions to describe these animal states (see for example Bekoff, 2007; 2009). What is clear is that Bekoff (and others like him) have made it impossible to ignore that we do indeed have high orders of communication with animals and we should not overlook a series of works that have taken a programmatic approach to human–animal ethnography and the problem of interspecies intersubjectivity. Of particular importance here is the writing of anthrozoological sociologists who have taken a post-Herbert Mead approach to human and animal symbolic interaction such as Alger and Alger (1999; 2003), Sanders (1999), Irvine (2004b) and Arluke (2006); they have seen animals as active social agents who are able to engage in symbolic interaction and who have a rich non-linguistic intersubjective exchange with humans. While the positions are well argued and supported, there is, to return to the series of questions posed above, the issue of the quality of this intersubjective contact zone – is it sufficient to form the core of a reliable ethnographic methodology? How can we know? I wonder if such ethnographies are continuing to wrestle with the 'problem' of anthropomorphism, allowing us, for example, to appreciate what it is like for a human to be a cat rather than what it is like for a cat to be a cat (after Fine, 2004: 641). Fine writes of the Algers' *Cat Culture*:

As outsiders we might understand what our informants cannot but not entirely what they can. *Cat Culture* as a dual ethnography—both of cat and of volunteers—operates with a bifurcated epistemology. We can place considerable trust in the depiction of the emotional register of volunteers, while this is not the case of the claims of cats to happiness, security, or community. The Algers read volunteers from the inside out and cats from the outside in. (2004: 642)

The ethnographic animal?

Despite expanding views on personhood, despite advances in research on animal cognition (for example Bekoff, 2007; 2009; Bekoff and Jamieson, 1996; Bekoff and Pierce, 2009; Bekoff et al., 2002), despite all the posthuman 'natureculture' (Latour, 1993: 7) work towards de-centering species, the problem of knowledge remains a methodological problem for interspecies ethnography. While I disagree that animals 'have no thoughts as such to grasp' (contra Ingold, 1998: 94) because symbolic interactionalism has given us a range of useful cognitive 'grasping' strategies, I do feel that their thoughts, however constituted, are not able to be grasped in a manner that could *exclusively* inform a reliable, trustworthy ethnographic methodology. There are simply too many grey areas to suggest animals can readily assume the place of humans as ethnographic subjects. The concern I have about interspecies ethnography mirrors a concern I have about modernist human ethnography's disjuncture between method and theory. Modernist human ethnography dedicated its field practice, its methodological heart, to finding commensurability, communion and intersubjectivity with what was supposed to be radical human difference. It accomplished this task successfully with uncounted numbers of ethnographers living with, and coming to know intimately, other humans all over the globe, because in truth they were never really *that* different. And yet all this 'tribal' commensurability that was the hallmark of successful fieldwork was typically elided in the 'scribal' realm (Boon, 1982), rendered into ethnographic portraits powered by the desirous rhetoric of human racial and cultural difference, with the ethnographers, Hermeslike, authoritatively translating cultural gaps and adumbrating the fantasy space/time of the human 'other' (see Boon, 1982; Fabian, 1983; Crapanzano, 1992). At this point, Sperber's comments on relativism (read as 'cultural similarity and difference') are apposite:

The best evidence against relativism is, ultimately, the very activity of anthropologists, while the best evidence for relativism seems to be in the writings of anthropologists. How can that be? It seems that, in retracing their steps, anthropologists transform into unfathomable gaps the shallow and irregular boundaries that they had found not so difficult to cross, thereby protecting their own sense of identity, and providing their philosophical and lay audience with just what they want to hear. (Sperber, 1985: 62–3)

It strikes me in the posthuman and postspecies moment (see Weil, 2010 for a useful overview of the 'animal turn'), an inverse activity might be occurring; that interspecies 'ethnographers' are running the risk of writing away real difference and incommensurability. Are we in fact dissolving boundaries and positing human commensurability with our non-human others despite not having a sufficient quality of intersubjective exchange, despite the ongoing problem of knowledge, and despite not having a resolved methodology that allows us to confidently grasp the animal as an ethnographic subject? The potential for ethnographers to write fantastic animals as they want them to be, rather than what they might (intangibly) be, is problematic (see Madden, 2014).

The themes of interdisciplinarity, intersubjectivity (Jackson, 1998), empathy (Shapiro, 1990), and affect (Rutherford, 2012) all point to the fragile relational process at the heart of interspecies knowledge production. I suggest we embrace this fragility and ambiguity and continue to question existing approaches (Shapiro, 2002: 335) in order to better discern the less than fully tangible interiors of minded animals. An interdisciplinary, critical and programmatic approach to interspecies empathy, intersubjectivity and affect might allow a 'good enough' (Scheper-Hughes 1992: 28) ethnographic knowledge to be produced; one that allows us to gain a rich and empathetic appreciation of animal sociality, mindedness and meaning-making, without pushing the issue of ethnographic trust to breaking point (Madden, 2014).

It is at this point that we have more than likely reached the limits of the ethnographic horizon we are exploring. It strikes me as self-evident that animals, particularly companion animals living in close contact with humans, are 'real' social actors. They act as, and are treated as, members of households and families. However, I can't see the methodological framework of ethnography, one which is relatively unproblematic to apply to virtual domains, being applied *in toto* to the study of animals as social actors. Animals-as-human are a different sort of 'virtual' human to those encountered in cyber societies. The intersubjective experience that lies at the heart of all good ethnographic encounters becomes problematic if one were to treat animals as fully fledged ethnographic participants. Having said that I nevertheless feel there is a great deal to be learned about the human/animal nexus, and the human condition more broadly by paying ethnographic attention to the roles animals play in shaping human lives. And while we may be able to objectively observe the impact of animals on human social systems, I doubt that we are at the point of a human/animal intersubjectivity that allows us to see the world through their eyes. It is perhaps a task for a unified methodology drawn from ethology (the scientific study of animal behaviour) and ethnography to take up this task.

SUMMARY

Some of the key points one can take from this text are that ethnography has been remarkably robust over time, methodologically speaking, and the approaches valued by ethnographers have changed little from the time of Malinowski to now. Participant observation, being with people in their everyday lives, and learning systematic ways of conversing, observing and recording people have persisted as the most favoured ways to gain the objective and subjective experiences that make up the contemporary ethnographer's knowledge bank.

The concept of the ethnographic field is also central to our understanding of ethnography. This text has argued that despite the shift from a more geographically defined version of the field (the 'isolated tribe' scenario) to a more interrogatively based definition (the field is framed by a question applied to a group of people), ethnographers have always been 'made' by the field; shaped into trained investigators of the human condition by the fact of fieldwork.

Writing (in the form of fieldnotes, analysis and ethnographies), film and audio ultimately cast ethnography as a project of representation. In this representational space science and art come together to produce a 'storied reality', a representation of a group of humans that should aspire to be factual, engaging, entertaining and informative. Ethnography should also be thought provoking, it should cause debate, theorising and counter-theorising.

In order to test the limits of our understanding of contemporary ethnography we looked briefly at two ethnographic scenarios; cyber ethnography and the ethnography of human/animal relations. Taking Boellstorff's (2008) ethnography of Second Life as a template, we were able to further define our understanding of what matters most to ethnography by discussing the distinction between face-to-face research and participant observation. In doing this I argued that the idea of trying to see the world through the eyes of others (the emic perspective) is the dominant philosophical motivation for contemporary ethnography, and as such virtual humans and virtual social worlds pose no real problem to an ethnography dedicated to understanding people who inhabit these domains. This form of ethnography is no less real than that conducted in the concrete world.

However, our exploration of the utility of approaches of the world of human/animal relations provided a corrective to the idea of a limitless ethnographic field. The intersubjective experience and the attempt to attain an emic perspective are the very things that are challenged by that other sort of virtual human, the companion animal. It would be a human conceit to suggest we can know the mind of the animal, even though we acknowledge that they are intertwined in human's lives, exercising myriads forms of agency and dependency as they form relationships with humans. Nevertheless the human/animal relationship should be taken more seriously as an ethnographic subject, animals have always been 'good to think', but they are more than symbols of the human condition; they actively shape social relations and as such demand our attention.

LAST WORD

Being ethnographic, I have argued, is still as relevant a way to understand the human condition as it ever was. Over 100 years of research and associated theorising have seen some contradictory outcomes; as sociological and anthropological theories have risen and fallen, the basic methodology of systematically observing, conversing with and being with other people, be they familiar or unfamiliar, has persisted as a useful form of knowledge creation. The new frontiers of cyber sociality do not pose a fundamental threat or challenge for the ethnographic approach. As long as we understand the virtual/real dichotomy as not constitutive of radically differing socialites, then the ethnographer's work remains one of participating in order to create knowledge, regardless if it is face-to-face or in an online community. The evolving nature of the human/animals relationship, especially with regard to companion animals, throws up some interesting opportunities and some challenges for ethnography. The more humans and animals socially co-constitute each other, the more ethnography can be used to understand this relationship. The limits of human/animal intersubjectivity continue to test the boundaries of ethnography, but ethnography is in a position to articulate with other ways of knowledge creation to produce a valid social portrait of the posthuman condition. Ethnography is in this position, is still relevant, because it is *endlessly tested and retested* by active anthropologists, sociologists and other social science and humanities disciples, out there in the world being ethnographic.

QUESTIONS

After taking this journey through ethnographic thought and practice, what do you see as the key defining characteristics of ethnography? What is there in past ethnographic practice that contemporary ethnography cannot do without?

How do you understand the ultimate aim of ethnographic research? Does it exist only to produce an endless stream of ethnographic representations?

Is cyber ethnography impoverished by the loss of face-to-face contact? How can it call itself 'proper' ethnography if it doesn't involve the coming together of real people in real worlds?

What about companion species makes them appropriate subjects for ethnographic research? Discuss with reference to an ethnographic methodology.

Animals are not humans, and the closeness of companion animals to humans in no way makes them virtual humans. As such, ethnography is not suitable to study the humans/animal relationship. Discuss.

SUGGESTED READINGS

Hammersley's *What's Wrong with Ethnography?: Methodological Explorations* (1992) provides a more sceptical view on ethnographic practice than that which is presented in this text. In order to explore cyber ethnography, in particular participant observation in cyber space, see Marshall's *Living on Cybermind* (2007) and Boellstorff's *Coming of Age in Second Life* (2008). Also, see Dicks et al.'s *Qualitative Research and Hypermedia: Ethnography in the Digital Age* (2005) and Pink et al.'s *Digital Ethnography: Principles and Practice* (2015). '"Piling on layers of understanding": The use of connective ethnography for the study of (online) work practices' (Dirksen et al., 2010) provides an interesting account of how online practices might inform offline connectivity. For some ethnography that deals with the human/animal relationship see Cassidy's *The Sport of Kings* (2002), and for a more general theoretical perspective on human/animal relations see Franklin's *Animals and Modern Cultures* (1999). See also Weil's article on 'A report on the animal turn' (2010). For more information on multispecies ethnography, see a special issue from *Cultural Anthropology* at https://culanth.org/fieldsights/277-the-emergence-of-multispecies-ethnography.

BEING ETHNOGRAPHIC

Ethnography is a wonderful way to appreciate social situations, but be constructively critical, and appreciate not all situations lend themselves to being ethnographic.

REFERENCES

Abbott, A. (2008) 'Chicago School: Social change', in G. Ritzer (ed.), *Blackwell Encyclopedia of Sociology Online*. Available at: www.sociologyencyclopedia.com (accessed 30 September 2008).

Abu-Lughod, L. (1999) 'The interpretation of culture(s) after television', in S. Ortner (ed.), *The Fate of 'Culture'*. Berkeley: University of California Press.

Adams, V. (2013) *Markets of Sorrow, Labors of Faith: New Orleans in the Wake of Katrina*. Durham: Duke University Press.

Adriansen, H.K. (2012) 'Timeline interviews: A tool for conducting life history research', *Qualitative Studies*, 3(1): 40–55.

Agar, M. (1996) *The Professional Stranger: An Informal Introduction to Ethnography*. San Diego: Academic Press.

Ahmady, K. (2009) Available at: www.kameelahmady.com/ (accessed 16 March 2009).

Alexeyeff, K. (2009) *Dancing from the Heart: Movement, Gender and Cook Islands Globalization*. Honolulu: Hawai'i University Press.

Alger, J. and Alger, S. (1997) 'Beyond Mead: Symbolic interaction between humans and felines', *Society and Animals*, 5(1): 65–81.

Alger, J. and Alger, S. (1999) 'Cat culture, human culture: An ethnographic study of a cat shelter', *Society and Animals*, 7(3): 199–218.

Alger, J. and Alger, S. (2003) *Cat Culture: The Social World of a Cat Shelter*. Philadelphia: Temple University Press.

Anderson, B. (1983) *Imagined Communities: Reflections on the Origin and Spread of Nationalism*. London: Verso.

Angrosino, M. (2007) *Doing Ethnographic and Observational Research*. London: Sage.

Arluke, A. (2006) *Just a Dog: Understanding Animal Cruelty and Ourselves*. Philadelphia: Temple University Press.

Asad, T. (1994) 'Ethnographic representation, statistics and modern power', *Social Research*, 61(1): 55–89.

Atkinson, P., Coffey, A., Delamont, S., Lofland, J. and Lofland, L. (eds) (2007) *Handbook of Ethnography*. London: Sage.

Babcock, B. (1980) 'Reflexivity: Definitions and discriminations', *Semiotica*, 30(1–2): 1–14.

Bekoff, M. (2007) *Animals Matter*. Boston & London: Shambhala.

Bekoff, M. (2009) 'Animal emotions, wild justice and why they matter: Grieving magpies, a pissy baboon, and emphatic elephants', *Emotion, Space and Society*, 2: 82–5.

Bekoff, M. and Jamieson, D. (eds) (1996) *Readings in Animal Cognition*. Massachusetts: MIT Press.

Bekoff, M. and Pierce, J. (2009) *Wild Justice: The Moral Lives of Animals*. Chicago: The University of Chicago Press.

Bekoff, M., Allan, C. and Burghardt, G. (eds) (2002) *The Cognitive Animal: Empirical and Theoretical Perspectives on Animal Cognition*. Massachusetts: MIT Press.

Berger, J. (1972) *Ways of Seeing: A Book Made*. Harmondsworth: Penguin.

Bernard, H. (2002) *Research Methods in Anthropology: Qualitative and Quantitative Methods*. Newbury Park: Sage.

Boellstorff, T. (2008) *Coming of Age in Second Life*. New Jersey: Princeton University Press.

Boon, J. (1982) *Other Tribes, Other Scribes: Symbolic Anthropology in the Comparative Study of Cultures, Histories, Religions, and Texts*. Cambridge: Cambridge University Press.

Bourdieu, P. (1977) *Outline of a Theory of Practice*. Cambridge: Cambridge University Press.

Bourdieu, P. (1990) *The Logic of Practice*. Cambridge: Polity Press.

Bourdieu, P. and Wacquant, L. (1992) *An Invitation to Reflexive Sociology*. Chicago: University of Chicago Press.

Branigan, C. (2004) *The Reign of the Greyhound*. New Jersey: Wiley Publishing.

Brewer, J. (2000) *Ethnography*. Buckingham: Open University Press.

Broom, A. (2005a) 'Virtually He@lthy: A study into the impact of internet use on disease experience and the doctor/patient relationship', *Qualitative Health Research*, 15(3): 325–45.

Broom, A. (2005b) 'The eMale: Prostate cancer, masculinity and online support as a challenge to medical expertise', *Journal of Sociology*, 41(1): 87–104.

Bryman, A. (2001) *Ethnography*. London: Sage.

Calvey, D. (2017) *Covert Research: The Art, Politics and Ethics of Undercover Fieldwork*. London: Sage.

Cassidy, R. (2002) *The Sport of Kings*. Cambridge: Cambridge University Press.

Chagnon, N. (1977) *Yanomamo: The Fierce People*. New York: Holt, Rinehart and Winston.

Chandler, D. (1998) *Notes on 'The Gaze'*. Available at: www.aber.ac.uk/media/ Documents/gaze/gaze.html (accessed 17 October 2008).

Clifford, J. and Marcus, G. (eds) (1986) *Writing Culture: The Poetics and Politics of Ethnography*. Berkeley: University of California Press.

Coffey, A. (1999) *The Ethnographic Self*. London: Sage.

Cook, J., Laidlaw, J. and Mair, J. (2009) 'What if there is no elephant? Towards a conception of an un-sited field', in M. Falzon (ed.), *Multi-sited Ethnography: Theory, Praxis and Locality in Contemporary Research*. Burlington: Ashgate.

Crang, M. and Cook, I. (2007) *Doing Ethnographies*. London: Sage.

Crapanzano, V. (1992) *Hermes' Dilemma & Hamlet's Desire: On the Epistemology of Interpretation*. Massachusetts: Harvard University Press.

Cressey, P. (1932) *The Taxi-Dance Hall: A Sociological Study in Commercialized Recreation and City Life*. New York: Greenwood Press.

de Mille, R. (2000) *Castaneda's Journey: The Power and the Allegory*. Lincoln: iuniverse. com Inc.

de Mille, R. (2001) *The Don Juan Papers: Further Castaneda Controversies*. Lincoln: iuniverse.com Inc.

Derrida, J. (2008) *The Animal That Therefore I Am*. New York: Fordham University Press.

Dicks, B., Mason, B., Coffey, A. and Atkinson, P. (2005) *Qualitative Research and Hypermedia: Ethnography for the Digital Age*. London: Sage.

Dirksen, V., Huizing, A. and Smit, B. (2010) '"Piling on layers of understanding": The use of connective ethnography for the study of (online) work practices', *New Media & Society*, 12(7):1045–1063.

Eades, D. (1991) 'They don't speak an Aboriginal language, or do they?', in I. Keen (ed.), *Being Black: Aboriginal Cultures in 'Settled' Australia*. Canberra: Aboriginal Studies Press.

Eipper, C. (1996) 'Ethnographic Testimony, Trust and Authority', *Canberra Anthropology*, 19(1): 15–30.

Elias, N. (1986) 'An essay on sport and violence', in N. Elias and E. Dunning (eds), *Quest for Excitement*. Oxford: Blackwell.

Elias, N. (1994) *The Civilising Process*. Oxford: Blackwell.

Emerson, R., Fretz, R. and Shaw, L. (1995) *Writing Ethnographic Fieldnotes*. Chicago: University of Chicago Press.

Evans-Pritchard, E.E. (1969[1940]) *The Nuer: A Description of the Modes of Livelihood and Political Institutions of a Nilotic People*. Oxford: Oxford University Press.

Fabian, J. (1983) *Time and the Other: How Anthropology Makes its Object*. New York: Columbia University Press.

Falzon, M. (ed.) (2009) *Multi-sited Ethnography: Theory, Praxis and Locality in Contemporary Research*. Burlington: Ashgate.

Fetterman, D. (1989) *Ethnography: Step by Step* (2nd edn). Thousand Oaks: Sage.

Fine, G. (2004) 'Review essay: Rats and cats', *Journal of Contemporary Ethnography*, 33(5): 638–44.

Firth, R. (1963[1936]) *We, the Tikopia*. Boston: Beacon Press.

Flick, U. (2014). The *SAGE Handbook of Qualitative Data Analysis*. London: Sage.

Foucault, M. (1979) *Discipline and Punish: The Birth of the Prison*. Harmondsworth: Penguin.

Foxen, S. (2015) 'What they don't tell you about ethnographic fieldwork'. Available at https://blogs.exeter.ac.uk/exeterblog/blog/2015/11/30/what-they-dont-tell-you-about-ethnographic-fieldwork/ (accessed 23 March 2017).

Franklin, A. (1999) *Animals and Modern Cultures: A Sociology of Human–Animal Relations in Modernity*. London: Sage.

Franklin, A. (2002) *Nature and Social Theory*. London: Sage.

Franklin, A. (2006) *Animal Nation: The True Story of Animals and Australia*. Sydney: University of New South Wales Press.

Frazier, E. (1932) *The Negro Family in Chicago*. Chicago: University of Chicago Press.

Friedman, J. (1994) *Cultural Identity and Global Process*. London: Sage.

Fuller (1999) 'Part of the action, or "going native"? Learning to Cope with the Politics of Integration', *Area*, 31(3): 221–227.

Glaser, B. and Strauss, A. (1967) *The Discovery of Grounded Theory: Strategies for Qualitative Research*. Chicago: Aldine de Gruyter.

Glesne, C. and Peshkin, A. (1992) *Becoming Qualitative Researchers: An Introduction*. White Plains: Longman.

Goldstein, D. (2003) *Laugher out of Place: Race Class, Violence and Sexuality in a Rio Shantytown*. Berkeley: University of California Press.

Hammersley, M. (1992) *What's Wrong with Ethnography? Methodological Explorations*. London: Routledge.

Hammersley, M. and Atkinson, P. (2007) *Ethnography: Principles in Practice*. New York: Routledge.

Haraway, D. (2003) *The Companion Species Manifesto: Dogs, People and Significant Otherness*. Chicago: Prickly Paradigm Press.

Hastrup, K. (1987) 'Fieldwork among friends: Ethnographic exchange within the northern civilisation', in A. Jackson (ed.), *Anthropology at Home: ASA Monographs 25*. London: Tavistock. pp. 94–108.

Hayward, E. (2010) 'Fingereyes: Impressions of cup corals', *Cultural Anthropology*, 25(4): 577–99.

Heyl, B. (2007) 'Ethnographic interviewing', in P. Atkinson, A. Coffey, S. Delamont, J. Lofland and L. Lofland (eds), *Handbook of Ethnography*. London: Sage. pp. 369–83.

Hobbs, D. and Wright, R. (eds) (2006) *The Sage Handbook of Fieldwork*. London: Sage.

Hutchison, R. (2007) 'Chicago School', in G. Ritzer (ed.), *Blackwell Encyclopedia of Sociology Online*. Available at: www.sociologyencyclopedia.com (accessed 29 September 2008).

Ingold, T. (1998) 'The animal in the study of humanity', in T. Ingold (ed.), *What is an Animal?* London: Routledge. pp. 84–99.

Irvine, L. (2004a) 'A model of animal selfhood: Expanding interactionalist possibilities', *Symbolic Interaction*, 27(1): 3–21.

Irvine, L. (2004b) *If You Tame Me: Understanding Our Connection with Animals.* Philadelphia: Temple University Press.

Irvine, L. (2007) 'The question of animal selves: Implications for sociological knowledge and practice', *Qualitative Sociological Review*, 3(1): 5–22.

Jackson, A. (ed.) (1987) *Anthropology at Home: ASA Monographs 25.* London: Tavistock.

Jackson, M. (1995) *At Home in the World.* Sydney: Harper Perennial.

Jackson, M. (1998) *Minima Ethnographica: Intersubjectivity and the Anthropological Project.* Chicago: The University of Chicago Press.

Jacobs, B. (2006) 'The case for dangerous fieldwork', in D. Hobbs and R. Wright (eds), *The Sage Handbook of Fieldwork.* London: Sage. pp. 157–68.

Jensen, E. and Laurie, C. (2016) *Doing Real Research: A Practical Guide to Social Research.* Thousand Oaks: Sage.

Kahn, J. (1989) 'Culture: Demise or resurrection?', *Critique of Anthropology*, 9(2): 5–25.

Kahn, J. (1991) 'The "culture" in multiculturalism: A view from anthropology', *Meanjin*, 50(1): 48–52.

Kosek, J. (2010) 'Ecologies of empire: On the new uses of the honeybee', *Cultural Anthropology*, 25(4): 650–78.

Kouritzin, S. (2002) 'The "half-baked" concept of "raw" data in ethnographic observation', *Canadian Journal of Education*, 27(1): 119–39.

Kürti, L., Nas, P., Dean, B. and Fardon, R. (2005) 'The ethics of spying: Responses to F. Moos, R. Fardon and H. Gusterson', *Anthropology Today*, 21(4): 19–20.

Landzelius, K. (ed.) (2006) *Native on the Net: Indigenous and Diasporic Peoples in the Virtual Age.* Abingdon: Routledge.

Latour, B. (1993) *We Have Never Been Modern.* Cambridge: Harvard University Press.

LeCompte, M. and Schensul, J. (1999a) *Designing and Conducting Ethnographic Research.* Walnut Creek: AltaMira Press.

LeCompte, M. and Schensul, J. (1999b) *Analyzing and Interpreting Ethnographic Data.* Walnut Creek: AltaMira Press.

LeCompte, M, Schensul, J. and Schensul, S. (1999) *Essential Ethnographic Methods: Observations, Interviews, and Questionnaires.* Walnut Creek: AltaMira Press.

Lee, H. (2006) 'Debating language and identity online: Tongans on the net', in K. Landzelius (ed.), *Native on the Net: Indigenous and Diasporic Peoples in the Virtual Age.* Abingdon: Routledge. pp. 152–68.

Lowe, R. (2002) *The Mish.* Brisbane: Queensland University Press.

MacDougall, D. (1995) 'The subjective voice in ethnographic film', in L. Devereaux and R. Hillman (eds), *Fields of Vision: Essays in Film Studies, Visual Anthropology, and Photography.* Berkeley: University of California Press.

MacDougall, D. (1998) *Transcultural Cinema*. Princeton: Princeton University Press.

MacDougall, D. (2006) *The Corporeal Image: Film, Ethnography, and the Senses*. Princeton: Princeton University Press.

Madden, R. (1999) 'Home town anthropology', *TAJA*, 10(3): 259–70.

Madden, R. (2003) *Aborigines, Anthropology and Culture: A Home-town Perspective*, unpublished PhD Thesis, La Trobe University.

Madden, R. (2010) 'Imagining the greyhound: Racing and rescue narratives in a human and dog relationship', *Continuum*, 24(4): 503–15.

Madden, R. (2014) 'Animals and the limits of ethnography', *Anthrozoos*, 27(2): 279–93.

Magolda, P. (2010) 'Accessing, waiting, plunging in, wondering, and writing: Retrospective sense-making of Fieldwork', in P. Atkinson and S. Delamont (eds), *SAGE Qualitative Research Methods*. London: Sage. pp. 169–193.

Malinowski, B. (1961[1922]) *Argonauts of the Western Pacific: An Account of Native Enterprise and Adventure in the Archipelagos of Melanesian New Guinea*. New York: Dutton.

Malinowski, B. (1967) *A Diary in the Strict Sense of the Term*. London: Routledge and Kegan Paul.

Manganaro, M. (ed.) (1990) *Modernist Anthropology: From Fieldwork to Text*. Princeton: Princeton University Press.

Marcus, G. (1998) *Ethnography Through Thick and Thin*. Princeton: Princeton University Press.

Marshall, J. (2007) *Living on Cybermind: Categories, Communication and Control*. New York: Peter Lang.

Mead, M. (1961) *Coming of Age in Samoa: A Psychological Study of Primitive Youth for Western Civilization*. New York: W. Morrow.

Messerschmidt, D. (ed.) (1981) *Anthropology at Home in North America: Methods and Issues in the Study of One's Own Society*. Cambridge: Cambridge University Press.

Miller, P. and Strang J. (eds) (2010) *Addiction Research Methods*. Chichester: Wiley Blackwell.

Monaghan, L. (2006) 'Fieldwork and the body: Reflections on an embodied ethnography', in D. Hobbs and R. Wright (eds), *The Sage Handbook of Fieldwork*. London: Sage. pp. 225–41.

Narayan, K. (2012) *Alive in the Writing: Crafting Ethnography in the Company of Chekhov*. Chicago: University of Chicago Press.

Okely, J. (1987) 'Fieldwork up the M1: Policy and political aspects', in A. Jackson (ed.), *Anthropology at Home: ASA Monographs 25*. London: Tavistock. pp. 55–73.

Oldrup, H.H. and Cartensen, T.A. (2012) 'Producing geographical knowledge through visual methods', Geografiska Annaler: Series B, *Human Geography*, 94(3): 223–37.

O'Reilly, K. (2005) *Ethnographic Methods*. London: Routledge.

O'Reilly, K. (2009) *Key Concepts in Ethnography*. London: Sage.

Orwell, G. (1951) *Animal Farm: A Fairy Story*. Harmondsworth: Penguin Books.

Ottenberg, S. (1990) 'Thirty years of fieldnotes: Changing relationships to the text', in R. Sanjek (ed.), *Fieldnotes: The Making of Anthropology*. Ithaca: Cornell University Press. pp. 139–60.

Pink, S. (2009) *Visual Interventions: Applied Visual Anthropology*. Oxford: Berghahn Books.

Pink, S. (2014) *Doing Visual Ethnography: Images, Media and Representation in Research* (3rd edn). London: Sage.

Pink, S. (2015) *Doing Sensory Ethnography* (2nd edn). London: Sage.

Pink, S., Horst, H., Postill, J., Tacchi, J., Hjorth, L. and Lewis, T. (2015) *Digital Ethnography: Principles and Practice*. London: Sage.

Price, D. (2000) 'Anthropologists as spies', *The Nation* [Online], 20 November. Available at: www.thenation.com/doc/20001120/price (accessed 17 March 2009).

Robben, A. and Sluka J. (eds) (2012) *Ethnographic Fieldwork: An Anthropological Reader*. Chichester: Wiley Blackwell.

Rutherford, D. (2012) 'Commentary: What affect produces', *American Ethnologist*, 39(4): 688–91.

Sahlins, M. (1999) 'Two or three things I know about culture', *Journal of the Royal Anthropological Institute*, 5(3): 399–421.

Saldaña, J. (2016) *The Coding Manual for Qualitative Researchers*. London: Sage.

Sanders, C. (1999) *Understanding Dogs: Living and Working with Canine Companions*. Philadelphia: Temple University Press.

Sanders, C. (2007) 'Mind, self and human–animal joint action', *Sociological Focus* 40(3): 320–36.

Sanjek, R. (ed.) (1990) *Fieldnotes: The Making of Anthropology*. Ithaca: Cornell University Press.

Scheper-Hughes, N. (1992) *Death without Weeping: The Violence of Everyday Life in Northeast Brazil*. Berkeley: University of California Press.

Shapiro, K. (1990) 'Understanding dogs through kinesthetic empathy, social construction, and history', *Anthrozoos*, 3(3): 184–95.

Shapiro, K. (2002) 'The state of human–animal studies: Solid at the margin!', *Society and Animals*, 10(4): 331–7.

Sperber, D. (1985) *On Anthropological Knowledge: Three Essays*. Cambridge: Cambridge University Press.

Spradley, J. (1979) *The Ethnographic Interview*. New York: Holt, Rinehart and Winston.

Spradley, J. and Mann, B. (1975) *The Cocktail Waitress: Woman's Work in a Man's World*. New York: John Wiley.

Stein, M. (2006) 'Your place or mine: The geography of social research', in D. Hobbs and R. Wright (eds), *The Sage Handbook of Fieldwork*. London: Sage. pp.59–75.

Stocking, G. (1968) *Race, Culture, and Evolution: Essays in the History of Anthropology*. New York: The Free Press.

Stocking, G. (ed.) (1974) *The Shaping of American Anthropology 1883–1911: A Franz Boas Reader*. New York: Basic Books.

Taylor, C. (2007) *A Secular Age*. Cambridge: Bellknap.

Taylor, N. (2007) '"Never an It": Intersubjectivity and the creation of animal personhood in animal shelters', *Qualitative Sociology Review*, 3(1): 59–73.

Tester, K. (1989) 'The pleasure of the rich and the labour of the poor', *Journal of Historical Sociology*, 2(2): 161–72.

Tester, K. (1992) *Animal and Society: The Humanity of Animal Rights*. London: Routledge.

Thomas, R. (1983) *The Politics of Hunting*. Aldershot: Gower.

Thrasher, F. (1927) *The Gang*. Chicago: University of Chicago Press.

Tuan, Y.F. (1977) *Space and Place: The Perspective of Experience*. Minneapolis: University of Minnesota Press.

Van Maanen, J. (1988) *Tales of the Field: On Writing Ethnography*. Chicago: University of Chicago Press.

Wacquant, L. (2004) *Body & Soul: Notebooks of an Apprentice Boxer*. New York: Oxford University Press.

Watson, G. (1987) 'Make me reflexive – but not yet: Strategies for managing reflexivity in ethnographic discourse', *Journal of Anthropological Research*, 43(1): 29–41.

Weil, K. (2010) 'A report on the animal turn', *Differences: A Journal of Feminist and Cultural Studies*, 21(2): 1–23.

Weil, S. (1987) 'Anthropology becomes home; Home becomes anthropology', in A. Jackson (ed.), *Anthropology at Home: ASA Monographs 25*. London: Tavistock. pp. 196–212.

Werner, O and G. Schoepfle. (1987) *Systematic Fieldwork*. Newbury Park: Sage.

Williams, R. (1988) *Keywords: A Vocabulary of Culture and Society*. London: Fontana Press.

Whyte, W.F. (1993) *Street Corner Society: The Social Structure of an Italian Slum* (4th edn). Chicago: University of Chicago Press.

Wirth, L. (1928) *The Ghetto*. Chicago: University of Chicago Press.

Wolcott, H.F. (2008) *Ethnography: A Way of Seeing*. Plymouth: AltaMira Press.

Zorbaugh, H. (1929) *Gold Coast and Slum: A Sociological Study of Chicago's Near North Side*. Chicago: University of Chicago Press.

INDEX